GLENN LIGON

OCTOBER Files

Rosalind Krauss (founding editor), Annette Michelson (founding editor, 1922–2018), George Baker, Yve-Alain Bois, Benjamin H. D. Buchloh, Huey Copeland, Leah Dickerman, Devin Fore, Hal Foster, Denis Hollier, David Joselit, Carrie Lambert-Beatty, Pamela M. Lee, Mignon Nixon, and Malcolm Turvey, editors

Richard Serra, edited by Hal Foster with Gordon Hughes
Andy Warhol, edited by Annette Michelson
Eva Hesse, edited by Mignon Nixon
Robert Rauschenberg, edited by Branden W. Joseph
James Coleman, edited by George Baker
Cindy Sherman, edited by Johanna Burton
Roy Lichtenstein, edited by Graham Bader
Gabriel Orozco, edited by Yve-Alain Bois
Gerhard Richter, edited by Benjamin H. D. Buchloh
Richard Hamilton, edited by Hal Foster with Alex Bacon
Dan Graham, edited by Alex Kitnick
John Cage, edited by Julia Robinson
Claes Oldenburg, edited by Nadja Rottner
Louise Lawler, edited by Helen Molesworth with Taylor Walsh
Robert Morris, edited by Julia Bryan-Wilson
John Knight, edited by André Rottmann
Isa Genzken, edited by Lisa Lee
Hans Haacke, edited by Rachel Churner
Michael Asher, edited by Jennifer King
Mary Kelly, edited by Mignon Nixon
William Kentridge, edited by Rosalind Krauss
Bruce Nauman, edited by Taylor Walsh
Sherrie Levine, edited by Howard Singerman
Michael Snow, edited by Annette Michelson and Kenneth White
Carrie Mae Weems, edited by Sarah Elizabeth Lewis with Christine Garnier
Donald Judd, edited by Annie Ochmanek and Alex Kitnick
Hollis Frampton, edited by Michael Zryd
Kara Walker, edited by Vanina Géré
David Hammons, edited by Kellie Jones
Tacita Dean, edited by George Baker and Annie Rana
Pierre Huyghe, edited by André Rottmann
Glenn Ligon, edited by Huey Copeland

GLENN LIGON

EDITED BY HUEY COPELAND

Essays by Richard Meyer, Wayne Koestenbaum, Mignon Nixon, Huey Copeland, Hilton Als, Lauren DeLand, Krista Thompson, Janet Kraynak, Helen Molesworth, Hamed Yousefi, Rizvana Bradley, and Thomas Lax

OCTOBER Files 32

The MIT Press
Cambridge, Massachusetts
London, England

The MIT Press
Massachusetts Institute of Technology
77 Massachusetts Avenue
Cambridge, MA 02139
mitpress.mit.edu

The MIT Press would like to thank the anonymous peer reviewers who provided comments on drafts of this book. The generous work of academic experts is essential for establishing the authority and quality of our publications. We acknowledge with gratitude the contributions of these otherwise uncredited readers.

This book was set in Bembo MT Pro and Bebas Neue Pro by New Best-set Typesetters Ltd. Printed and bound in the United States of America.

Library of Congress Cataloging-in-Publication Data is available.

ISBN: 978-0-262-05262-7

10 9 8 7 6 5 4 3 2 1

EU Authorised Representative: Easy Access System Europe, Mustamäe tee 50, 10621 Tallinn, Estonia | Email: gpsr.requests@easproject.com

Contents

Series Preface

OCTOBER Files addresses individual bodies of work of the postwar period that meet two criteria: they have altered our understanding of art in significant ways, and they have prompted a critical literature that is serious, sophisticated, and sustained. Each book thus traces not only the development of an important oeuvre but also the construction of the critical discourse inspired by it. This discourse is theoretical by its very nature, which is not to say that it imposes theory abstractly or arbitrarily. Rather, it draws out the specific ways in which significant art is theoretical in its own right, on its own terms and with its own implications. To this end we feature essays, many first published in OCTOBER magazine, that elaborate different methods of criticism in order to elucidate different aspects of the art in question. The essays are often in dialogue with one another as they do so, but they are also as sensitive as the art to political context and historical change. These "files," then, are intended as primers in signal practices of art and criticism alike, and they are offered in resistance to the amnesiac and antitheoretical tendencies of our time.

The Editors of *OCTOBER*

Acknowledgments

This volume, the first to compile the critical literature on one of the most significant artists to emerge in postmodern America, would be unimaginable without the profound generosity of its eponymous subject. My first thanks go, then, to Glenn Ligon: in indulging my questions, keeping up with my passions, and supporting my scholarship, you have opened me to the limitless possibilities of black being from our earliest conversations. As for so many African/Diasporic critics, curators, and cultural historians then and since, that introduction was facilitated by the largesse of Thelma Golden; I am forever grateful for her transformative vision and brass-tacks realness.

I am also pleased to thank my comrades at the journal *October*—George Baker, Yve-Alain Bois, Benjamin Buchloh, Leah Dickerman, Devin Fore, Hal Foster, David Joselit, Rosalind Krauss, Carrie Lambert-Beatty, Pamela Lee, Mignon Nixon, and Malcolm Turvey—for their enthusiastic support of this project from the get-go and their continuing engagement with the art historical reorientation toward black studies to which it contributes. The production of this volume is especially indebted to the care and rigor of senior editor Matthew Abbate at the MIT Press; to the grace and guidance of the journal's executive editor, Adam Lehner; to the oversight of Lisa Kohli, the archival assistance of Emily Knapp, and the logistical support of Michael Quintanilla, all at Glenn Ligon Studio; and, most of all, to the meticulous organization and cheerful professionalism of Janina López, my research assistant at the University of Pittsburgh, without whom neither the text nor the image program would have come together, let alone in such good time. Unless otherwise noted, all works reproduced here are featured courtesy of the artist.

As goes without saying, I am deeply appreciative for all of the contributors to this project and their willingness to reprint previous work here: Hilton Als, Rizvana Bradley, Lauren DeLand, Wayne Koestenbaum, Janet Kraynak, Thomas Lax, Richard Meyer, Helen Molesworth, Mignon Nixon, Krista Thompson, and Hamed Yousefi; you all *make* this book. I treasure each of your texts, not only as touchstones of the Ligon discourse, but also as interventions that have reshaped our sense of what ethically attuned art criticism, history, and writing might be and might enable today. Each essay has been lightly corrected, updated, or amended to function as a stand-alone text in accordance with the author's wishes and MIT style guidelines. Thanks, finally, to the agencies, galleries, journals, museums, and presses who granted their permissions to reproduce their Ligons as well as the authors' works, which originally appeared as follows.

Richard Meyer, "Borrowed Voices," in *Glenn Ligon: Unbecoming*, ed. Judith Tannenbaum (Philadelphia: Institute of Contemporary Art, University of Pennsylvania, 1997), 13–35; © Richard Meyer; reprinted with permission of the Institute of Contemporary Art, University of Pennsylvania. Wayne Koestenbaum, "Color Me Glenn," in *Coloring: New Work by Glenn Ligon*, ed. Kathleen McLean (Minneapolis: Walker Art Center, 2001), 9–25; © Wayne Koestenbaum; reprinted with permission of the Walker Art Center. Mignon Nixon, from "On the Couch," *October* 113 (Summer 2005): 39–76 [excerpt, 64–70]; © Mignon Nixon; reprinted with the permission of the MIT Press. Huey Copeland, "Glenn Ligon and Other Runaway Subjects," *Representations* 113 (Winter 2011): 73–110; © Huey Copeland; reprinted with the permission of University of California Press. Hilton Als, "Strangers," in *Glenn Ligon: America*, ed. Scott Rothkopf (New York: Whitney Museum of American Art, 2011), 208–218; Copyright © 2011 by Hilton Als, used by permission of The Wylie Agency LLC; © 2011 Whitney Museum of American Art. Lauren DeLand, "Black Skin, Black Masks: The Citational Self in the Work of Glenn Ligon," *Criticism* 54, no. 4 (Fall 2012): 507–537; © Lauren DeLand; © 2012 by Wayne State University Press, Detroit, Michigan. Krista Thompson, "'Negro Sunshine': Figuring Blackness in the Neon Art of Glenn Ligon," in *Black Is, Black Ain't*, ed. Hamza Walker and Karen Reimer (Chicago: Renaissance Society, 2013), 17–25; © Krista Thompson; © The Renaissance Society at the University of Chicago. Janet Kraynak, "How to Hear What Is Not

Heard: Glenn Ligon, Steve Reich, and the Audible Past," *Grey Room* 70 (Winter 2018): 54–79; © Janet Kraynak; © 2018 by Grey Room, Inc. and the Massachusetts Institute of Technology. Helen Molesworth, "What's Black and White and Red All Over?," in *Glenn Ligon: Untitled (America)/ Debris Field/Synecdoche/Notes for a Poem on the Third World* (Los Angeles: Regen Projects, 2019), 44–49; © Helen Molesworth; Courtesy of Regen Projects, Los Angeles. Hamed Yousefi, "The Race for Appropriation: Blackness, Authorship, and Ligon on Mapplethorpe," *October* 183 (Winter 2023): 50–74; © Hamed Yousefi, © 2023 October Magazine, Ltd. and the Massachusetts Institute of Technology. Rizvana Bradley, from "The Black Residuum, or That Which Remains," in *Anteaesthetics: Black Aesthesis and the Critique of Form* (Stanford, CA: Stanford University Press, 2023), 221–279 [excerpt, 257–279]; © 2023 Rizvana Bradley; reprinted with permission of the publisher, Stanford University Press. Thomas Lax, "Our Glenn," in *Distinguishing Piss from Rain: Writings and Interviews by Glenn Ligon*, ed. James Hoff (New York: Hauser & Wirth Publishers, 2024), 11–22; © Thomas Lax; © Hauser & Wirth Publishers, 2024.

Contributors

Hilton Als is an award-winning journalist, critic, and curator. He has been a staff writer at the *New Yorker* since 1994. Prior to the *New Yorker*, Als was a staff writer for the *Village Voice* and an editor-at-large at *Vibe*. He has received numerous awards for his work, including the Pulitzer Prize for Criticism (2017), Yale's Windham-Campbell Literature Prize (2016), the George Jean Nathan Award for Dramatic Criticism (2002-03), and a Guggenheim Fellowship (2000). His first book, *The Women*, was published in 1996. His next book, *White Girls*, was a finalist for the National Book Critics Circle Award and the winner of the Lambda Literary Award in 2014. *My Pinup: A Paean to Prince*, based on a 2012 *Harper's* essay, was published in 2022. In 2024 he edited *God Made My Face: A Collective Portrait of James Baldwin* for the centenary of Baldwin's birth. He is currently a teaching professor at the University of California, Berkeley, and has also taught at Columbia University's School of the Arts, Princeton University, Wesleyan University, and the Yale School of Drama.

Rizvana Bradley is Associate Professor of Film and Media and Affiliated Faculty in the History of Art at the University of California, Berkeley. Bradley is the author of *Anteaesthetics: Black Aesthesis and the Critique of Form*, shortlisted for the 2024 MLA Prize for a first book and named one of the top books of 2023 by *Frieze*. She has published articles in *Diacritics*, *TDR*, *Discourse*, *Rhizomes*, *Black Camera*, *Film Quarterly*, and *Women and Performance*. Her art criticism appears in the *Yale Review*, *Artforum*, *e-flux*, *Art in America*, and *Parkett*. Bradley serves on the Advisory Boards of *October* and *Camera Obscura*.

Huey Copeland is Andrew W. Mellon Professor of Modern Art and Black Study at the University of Pittsburgh. His research focuses on modern and contemporary art with an emphasis on articulations of blackness in the "Western" visual field, as exemplified by his book *Bound to Appear: Art, Slavery, and the Site of Blackness in Multicultural American* (2013). His work has been published in numerous journals, exhibition catalogs, and essay collections. Copeland's essay collection *Touched by the Mother: Black Men, American Art, Feminist Horizons* is forthcoming in 2026 from University of Chicago Press.

Lauren DeLand is a scholar of contemporary art whose work intersects with feminist and queer theory and considers strategically the politics of vision and visibility. She is a contributing author to *Contemporary Transnational Feminist Visual Activism and Gender-Based Violence* (Routledge, 2025). Her essays and criticism have appeared in *Performance Research*, *TDR: The Drama Review*, *Criticism*, *Frieze*, and *Art in America*. Her curatorial activities include the exhibitions *Embodying Anew: Simone Leigh, Magdalene Odundo & Thaddeus Mosley* (Maximillian William Gallery, London, 2021) and *Queer Forms* (Katherine E. Nash Gallery, the University of Minnesota, 2019). She lives and works in Atlanta.

Wayne Koestenbaum—poet, critic, fiction writer, artist, filmmaker—has published over twenty books, including *Stubble Archipelago*, *Ultramarine*, *The Cheerful Scapegoat*, *Figure It Out*, *Camp Marmalade*, *My 1980s & Other Essays*, *Humiliation*, *Hotel Theory*, *Circus*, *Andy Warhol*, *Jackie Under My Skin*, and *The Queen's Throat* (nominated for a National Book Critics Circle Award). Recipient of a Guggenheim Fellowship in Poetry, an American Academy of Arts and Letters Award in Literature, and a Whiting Award, he is a Distinguished Professor of English, French, and Comparative Literature at the CUNY Graduate Center.

Janet Kraynak is a professor in the Department of Art History and Archaeology at Columbia University, where she is also Director of the MA in Modern and Contemporary Art: Critical and Curatorial Studies. A widely published author and critic, she is the author of *Contemporary Art and the Digitization of Everyday Life* (University of California Press, 2020). Her most recent book, *The Rise of the Therapeutic Museum: Decolonization and the Crisis of Knowledge*, is forthcoming from Routledge (2025).

Thomas Lax is a curator at New York's Museum of Modern Art, where he has co-organized *Judson Dance Theater: The Work Is Never Done* (2018), *Just Above Midtown: Changing Spaces* (2022), and *Ceremonies Out of the Air: Ralph Lemon* (2024), among others. He began his career at the Studio Museum in Harlem, where he contributed to the landmark "f show" contemporary art series in 2012 and put together *When the Stars Begin to Fall: Imagination and the American South* in 2014.

Richard Meyer is the Robert and Ruth Halperin Professor in Art History at Stanford. His most recent book, *Master of the Two Left Feet: Morris Hirshfield Rediscovered* (MIT Press, 2022), received the 2023 Dedalus Foundation Award for "an outstanding exhibition catalogue that makes a significant contribution to the scholarship of modern art or modernism." He is also the author of *Outlaw Representation: Censorship and Homosexuality in Twentieth-Century American Art* (Beacon Press, 2002) and *What Was Contemporary Art?* (MIT Press, 2013), the former of which was awarded the Charles C. Eldredge Prize for Outstanding Scholarship from the Smithsonian American Art Museum. He is coeditor, with Catherine Lord, of *Art and Queer Culture*, and coauthor, with Peggy Phelan, of *Contact Warhol: Photography without End*.

Helen Molesworth is a writer, podcaster, and curator based in Los Angeles and Provincetown. In 2023 Phaidon published *Open Questions: Thirty Years of Writing about Art*, an anthology of her essays. Her podcasts include *Death of an Artist*, a six-part podcast about the intertwined fates of Carl Andre and Ana Mendieta, and the inaugural season of *Recording Artists* with the Getty. She is also the host of *Dialogues*, a podcast that features interviews with artists and thinkers, hosted by the David Zwirner Gallery. She is the author of numerous catalog essays, and her writing has appeared in *Artforum*, *Art Journal*, *Documents*, and *October*. The recipient of the 2011 Bard Center for Curatorial Studies Award for Curatorial Excellence, Molesworth received a Guggenheim Fellowship in 2021, and in 2022 she was awarded the Clark Art Writing Prize.

Mignon Nixon is Professor of History of Modern and Contemporary Art at University College London and a coeditor of *October*. Mignon's publications include *Fantastic Reality: Louise Bourgeois and a Story of Modern Art* and October Files volumes on Mary Kelly and Eva Hesse.

Krista Thompson is the Mary Jane Crowe Professor of Art History at Northwestern University, where she teaches art and visual culture of the African diaspora and the Caribbean. She is the author of *An Eye for the Tropics* (Duke University Press, 2006), *Developing Blackness* (The National Art Gallery of the Bahamas, 2008), and *Shine: The Visual Economy of Light in African Diasporic Aesthetic Practice* (Duke University Press, 2015). Thompson has two books forthcoming: *The Evidence of Things Not Captured: Photographic Fugitivity in Jamaica* (Duke University Press) and *Refracting Light: Tom Lloyd and the Effect of Art Historical Disregard* (University of Chicago Press).

Hamed Yousefi is a historian of modern art, focusing on artistic and critical practices that challenge European formations of art history. His in-progress book manuscript, entitled *How Modern Art Became Islamic*, explores the consequences that emerge in art-making from the invention of the category of "Islamic art" in modern scholarship. Questioning the formative assumption in art history that modern art is secular, this work argues that in the period between 1880 and 1980, Iranian artists appropriated "Islamic art," turning this art historical category into a future-oriented project in which the Islamic notion of imagination (*khayal*) was refashioned as a response to modernity's regimes of representation.

1 Borrowed Voices: Glenn Ligon and the Force of Language

Richard Meyer

The work of Glenn Ligon mines the history of African American culture, from slave narratives to the Million Man March, from the icons of the abolitionist movement to the raunchy jokes of Richard Pryor. In the series of paintings that remain his best known, Ligon stencils black text across the surface of white, door-size canvases. The words presented are not the artist's own but have been borrowed from such writers as Zora Neale Hurston (figure 1.1), Ralph Ellison, and James Baldwin. Typically, Ligon will repeat an especially charged sentence ("How it feels to be colored me," "I am an invisible man," "I feel most colored when I am thrown against a sharp white background") until it verges, through the force of excess paint, on illegibility. The resulting pictures set up a series of dialogues between visibility and erasure, between the naming of color and its painterly absence on the canvas, and between the "black space" of the stenciled letters and the "white space" into which they increasingly bleed. For all the seeming dispassion of Ligon's formal method (monochrome palette, stenciled letters, repeated words), his text paintings are supercharged with affect. They speak a first-person voice of black subjectivity while registering the denial and relentless silencing of that same voice.

An artist who is always reading, Ligon has said that he "wants to make language into a physical thing, something that has real weight and force to it."[1] He listens hard to specific forms of both spoken and written language, to the inflections of vernacular and period use, and to the subtleties of syntax and style. Equally as important, Ligon looks hard at the material forms and mechanical reproduction of language, at printing methods,

Figure 1.1 Glenn Ligon, *Untitled (I Feel Most Colored When I Am Thrown Against a Sharp White Background)*, 1990. Oil stick, gesso, and graphite on wood, 80 × 30 inches. © Glenn Ligon; Courtesy of the artist, Hauser & Wirth, and Thomas Dane Gallery.

paper formats, and typefaces. In a 1993 series of prints entitled *Narratives*, for instance, Ligon mimicked the rhetoric and typography of nineteenth-century slave narratives while replacing the details of the text with information drawn from his own biography:

> THE LIFE AND ADVENTURES OF GLENN LIGON, a Negro who was sent to be educated amongst white people in the year 1966 when only about six years of age and has continued to fraternize with them to the present time.

Ligon historicizes the language of self-description to draw out the trauma, but also the ironies, of modern black experience. Rather than situating the slave narrative securely in the past, the artist insists on the continuing relevance of that narrative to contemporary black life, including, and especially, his own. The power of *Narratives* lies largely in the way it *studies* (rather than simply appropriates) its source material, in the way it updates such texts as *Incidents in the Life of a Slave Girl* and *Narrative of the Life of Frederick Douglass* while carefully retaining the period format of their frontispieces.[2]

By routing slave narratives into a series of late twentieth-century self-portraits, Ligon complicates the status of those narratives as documents of authentic black experience. As we are reminded throughout *Narratives*, antebellum accounts of the slave's life were prepared, edited, and often fictionalized to conform to the perceived desires of a white audience. Because it was illegal for slaves to learn to read or write, and because the veracity of the slave's word was so frequently questioned, slave narratives were almost always prefaced by extended testimonials as to their authenticity. In many cases, these testimonials were penned by white abolitionists who had transcribed the narrative or otherwise helped to secure its publication.[3] *Narratives* draws out the tension between the first-person voice of the slave and the white reader for and by whom that voice was recorded. In a print entitled "Black Like Me, or The Authentic Narrative of Glenn Ligon, A Black Man," the artist appends a long—and hilariously long-winded—testimonial, which is signed, "Yours, very truly, A WHITE PERSON" (figure 1.2). By framing the white person as a generic category, an undifferentiated type, Ligon satirizes the white authentication of black experience while suggesting that it was the very category of whiteness, rather than the testimonial of any one abolitionist, that carried the power of legitimation.[4]

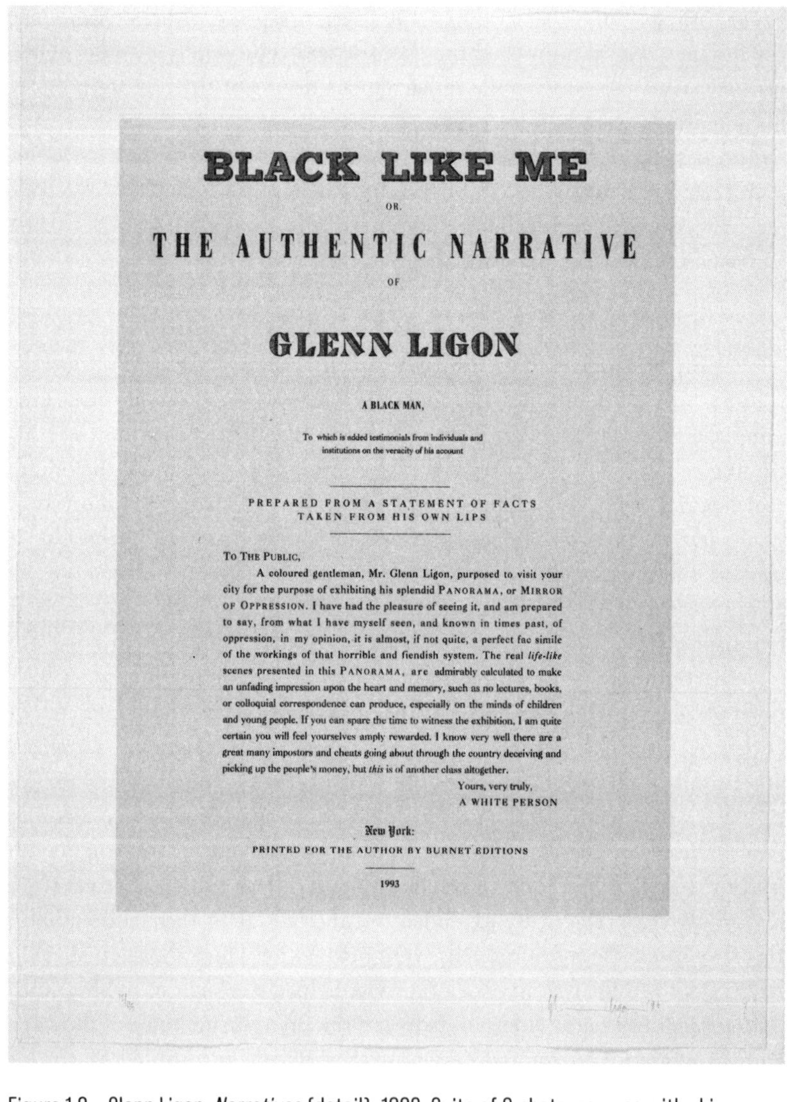

BLACK LIKE ME

OR,

THE AUTHENTIC NARRATIVE

OF

GLENN LIGON

A BLACK MAN,

To which is added testimonials from individuals and institutions on the veracity of his account

PREPARED FROM A STATEMENT OF FACTS TAKEN FROM HIS OWN LIPS

TO THE PUBLIC,

A coloured gentleman, Mr. Glenn Ligon, purposed to visit your city for the purpose of exhibiting his splendid PANORAMA, or MIRROR OF OPPRESSION. I have had the pleasure of seeing it, and am prepared to say, from what I have myself seen, and known in times past, of oppression, in my opinion, it is almost, if not quite, a perfect fac simile of the workings of that horrible and fiendish system. The real *life-like* scenes presented in this PANORAMA, are admirably calculated to make an unfading impression upon the heart and memory, such as no lectures, books, or colloquial correspondence can produce, especially on the minds of children and young people. If you can spare the time to witness the exhibition, I am quite certain you will feel yourselves amply rewarded. I know very well there are a great many impostors and cheats going about through the country deceiving and picking up the people's money, but *this* is of another class altogether.

Yours, very truly,
A WHITE PERSON

New York:

PRINTED FOR THE AUTHOR BY BURNET EDITIONS

1993

Figure 1.2 Glenn Ligon, *Narratives* (detail), 1993. Suite of 9 photogravures with chine collé, 28 × 21⅜ inches, edition of 45 and 10 artist's proofs. © Glenn Ligon; Courtesy of the artist, Hauser & Wirth, and Thomas Dane Gallery. Photography credit: Sheldan Collins.

In *Runaways* (1993), a series of prints created in conjunction with *Narratives* (figure 1.3), Ligon revises fugitive slave posters of the mid-nineteenth century by inserting various descriptions of himself in place of the runaway slave. The descriptions were drawn from ten friends of the artist, each of whom was asked to provide a verbal account of Ligon as though reporting his disappearance to the police. The texts that emerged from this process combine the casual language of physical appearance with the brute force of slavery (figure 3.2):

> RAN AWAY, Glenn Ligon. He's a shortish broad-shouldered black man, pretty dark-skinned, with glasses. Kind of stocky, tends to look down and turn in when he walks. Real short hair, almost none. Clothes nondescript, something button-down and plaid, maybe, and shorts and sandals. Wide lower face and narrow upper face. Nice teeth.

That last phrase, "Nice teeth," set off as its own sentence, resonates with the blunt language of the slave auction block. The entire print, in fact, closely mimics the format of its source material, down to the crowning visual icon of a white man in hat and topcoat restraining a shackled, half-naked black slave. In *Runaways*, as in *Narratives*, Ligon insinuates the historical legacy and language of slavery into a set of otherwise current descriptions of himself. In so doing, he situates slavery as a symbolic force that continues to reverberate within contemporary black life.

In both *Narratives* and *Runaways*, Ligon locates his art at the intersection of oral and written language, at the meeting place of verbal description, textual transcription, and historical source material. Tensions between the written and spoken word inflect a great deal of Ligon's art, including several projects that take up far more recent examples of black representation than the slave narrative. In *Cocaine (Pimps)* and *Mudbone (Liar)* (1993; figures 1.4 and 1.5), Ligon appropriates two jokes popularized by Richard Pryor in his stand-up routines of the 1970s and early 1980s. These jokes, which play on the image of the black man as well-endowed and obsessed with his own sexual power, blithely speak in the vernacular language of the street. As presented by Ligon, the improper grammar, syntax, and spelling of these jokes constitute merely one aspect of their larger "impropriety." For one thing, Pryor's jokes are meant to be heard rather than read, listened to rather than looked at. In their original context, the jokes depend on Pryor's vocal performance for their success, on the rhythms and intonations of his particular

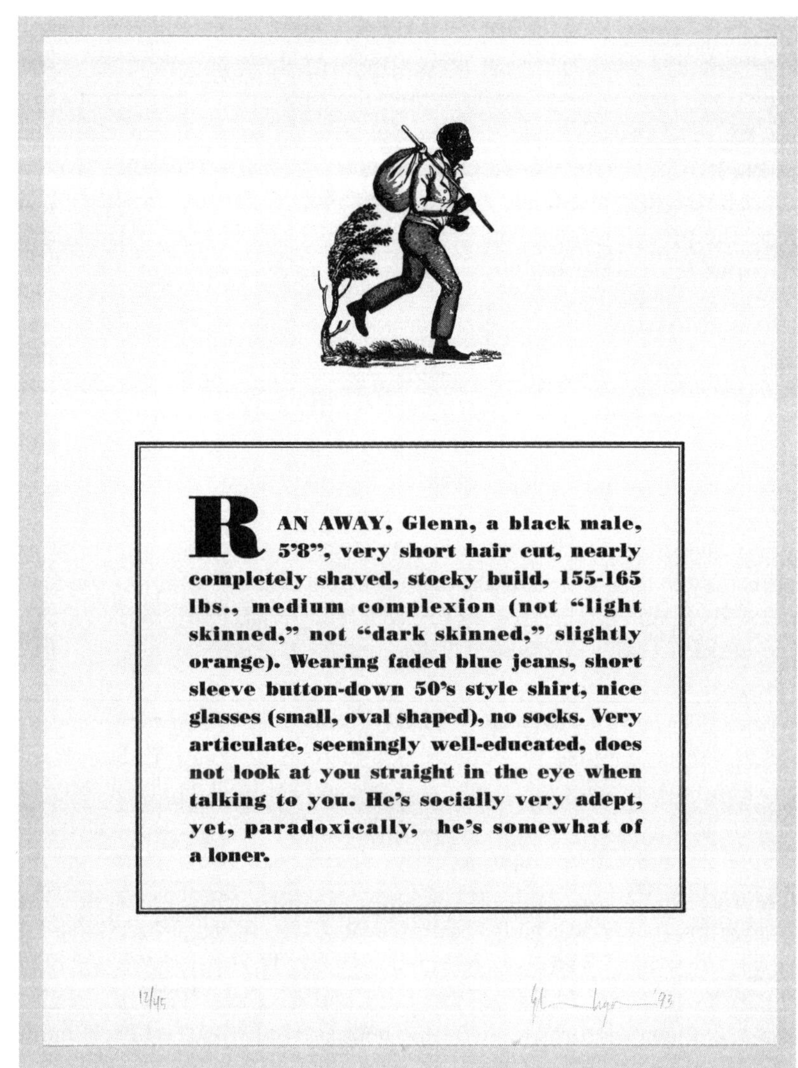

Figure 1.3 Glenn Ligon, *Runaways* (detail), 1993. Suite of 10 lithographs, 16 × 12 inches, edition of 45 and 10 artist's proofs. © Glenn Ligon; Courtesy of the artist, Hauser & Wirth, and Thomas Dane Gallery. Photography credit: Jeff McLane.

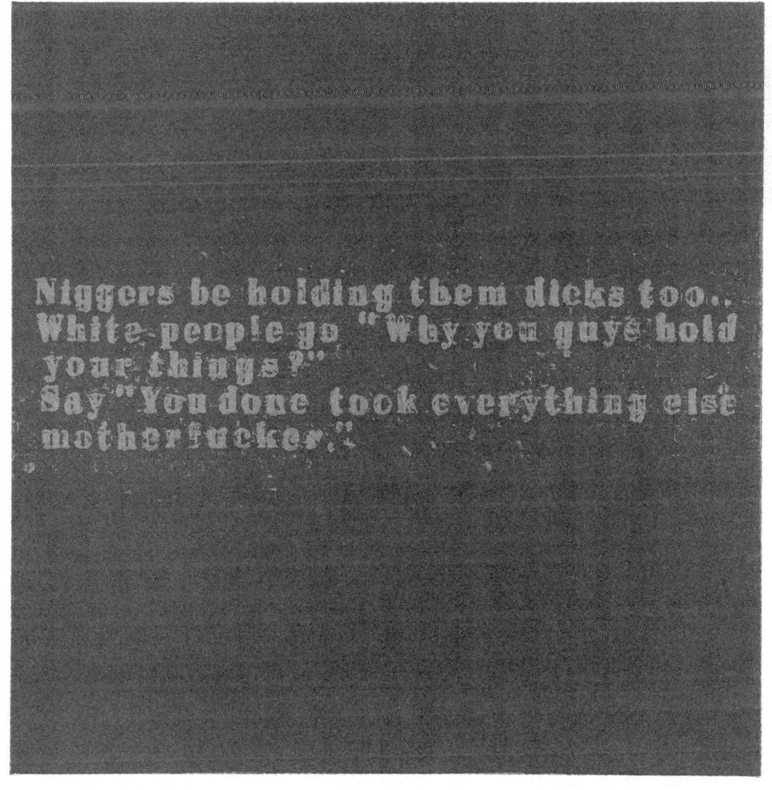

Figure 1.4 Glenn Ligon, *Cocaine (Pimps)*, 1993. Oil stick, synthetic polymer, and graphite on linen, 32 × 32 inches. Collection of the Whitney Museum of American Art, New York. © Glenn Ligon; Courtesy of the artist, Hauser & Wirth, and Thomas Dane Gallery.

delivery.[5] Resituated as text paintings, the jokes become dissociated from Pryor's voice and linked instead to the viewer's. It is the viewer who must now read this script, who must mouth, however silently, these words. In rewriting Pryor's jokes as text paintings, Ligon forces us to consider the vehemence of their stereotypes, the rage barely veiled beneath their humor, and the power of their obscenity in the face of a dominant (white) culture that simultaneously desires and dehumanizes black manhood.

In a review of the 1993 Whitney Biennial, the *Village Voice* described Glenn Ligon as "a closet aesthete."[6] The description was used to contrast the visual elegance of Ligon's work with the self-conscious crudeness of

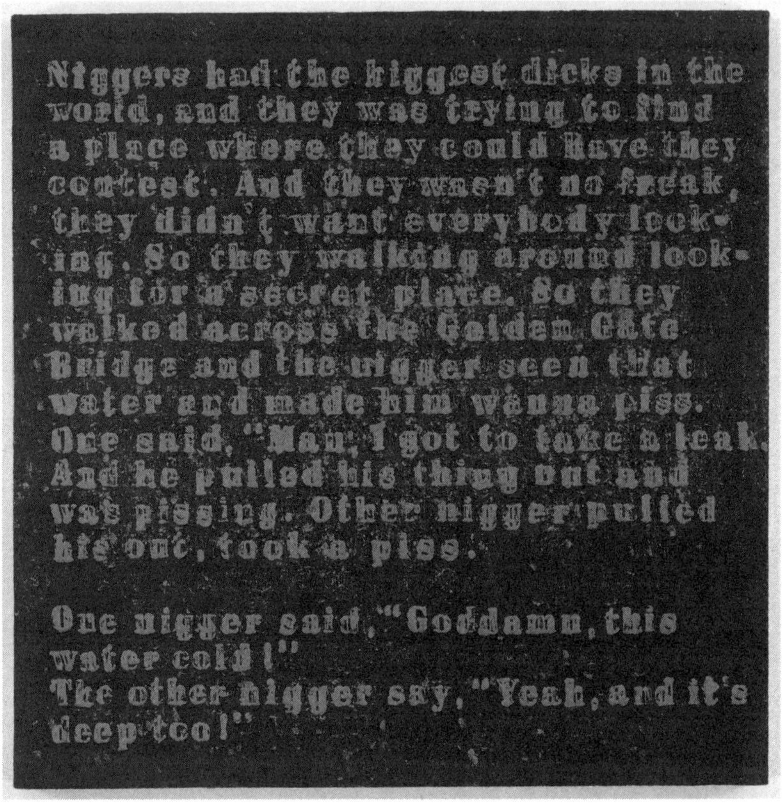

Figure 1.5 Glenn Ligon, *Mudbone (Liar)*, 1993. Oil stick, synthetic polymer, and graphite on canvas, 32 × 32 inches. © Glenn Ligon; Courtesy of the artist, Hauser & Wirth, and Thomas Dane Gallery.

several other artists in the show. Yet the comment also implied another layer of meaning. Ligon's contribution to the 1993 Biennial, *Notes on the Margin of the Black Book*, was his first work to deal with an explicitly gay theme. In it, Ligon juxtaposes Robert Mapplethorpe's photographs of nude black men with a wide range of textual commentaries, including those of artists, politicians, Christian commentators, queer theorists, and drag queens (figure 1.6). Ligon multiplies voices within *Notes*, not in order to create a happy plurality of diverse perspectives but to reveal how Mapplethorpe's black male nudes function as a cultural screen onto which both fears and fantasies are projected. Rather than situating Mapplethorpe's work as either a positive image or a negative stereotype of black sexuality, Ligon directs our attention to the ways the *Black Book* functions as a symbolic battleground on which conflicting claims—about race, desire, disease, art, and freedom—are registered.

Notes on the Margin of the Black Book inaugurated a moment in Ligon's career in which the artist increasingly came to focus on the relationship between race and sexuality, including, but not limited to, his own. "In a sense, my work 'outed' me," says Ligon. "I had already been out [to friends and family] but not in the public, professional world in that way."[7] As this remark suggests, the process of coming out is not a simple declaration of sexual identity—made once, duly noted, and then left behind—but an ongoing series of negotiations between the gay subject and the multiple social worlds (e.g., private and public, familial and professional) in which he or she circulates. These negotiations are further shaped by the varying degrees of recognition and refusal, of silence and (half-) spoken acknowledgment that the gay subject encounters in response to "coming out." Notice, for example, how the *Voice*'s description of Ligon as a "closet aesthete" suggests, without specifying, a gay aspect to the artist's work, how it displaces the homoerotic content of *Notes on the Margin of the Black Book* onto the plane of formalism.

Yet such a displacement is not an entirely erroneous or regrettable one. Throughout his career, Ligon has suffused his work with a high degree of formal resolution and pictorial presence. The symmetry and elegance of *Notes*, for instance, is central to its critical mission, not least because Mapplethorpe's photographs are themselves so painstakingly composed. Ligon began *Notes on the Margin of the Black Book* by jotting down his responses to the nudes on the pages of a personal copy of the book. The piece was born, then, from Ligon's direct criticism/defacement of Mapplethorpe's work. Yet, rather than present his own "notes" in the finished project, Ligon turned to a wider, and more volatile, chorus of commentators. Instead of superimposing the language of these commentators directly onto Mapplethorpe's photographs, Ligon centered two rows of framed and printed texts between two tiers of black male nudes. Ligon's wraparound grid of word and image respects, rather than violates, the formal logic of Mapplethorpe's work. *Notes on the Margin of the Black Book* opens a space, at once critical and visual, between Mapplethorpe's nudes and the voices that respond to them.

It is not coincidental that *Notes*, Ligon's first explicitly homoerotic work of art, was also his first photo-text installation. "I think it is easier,"

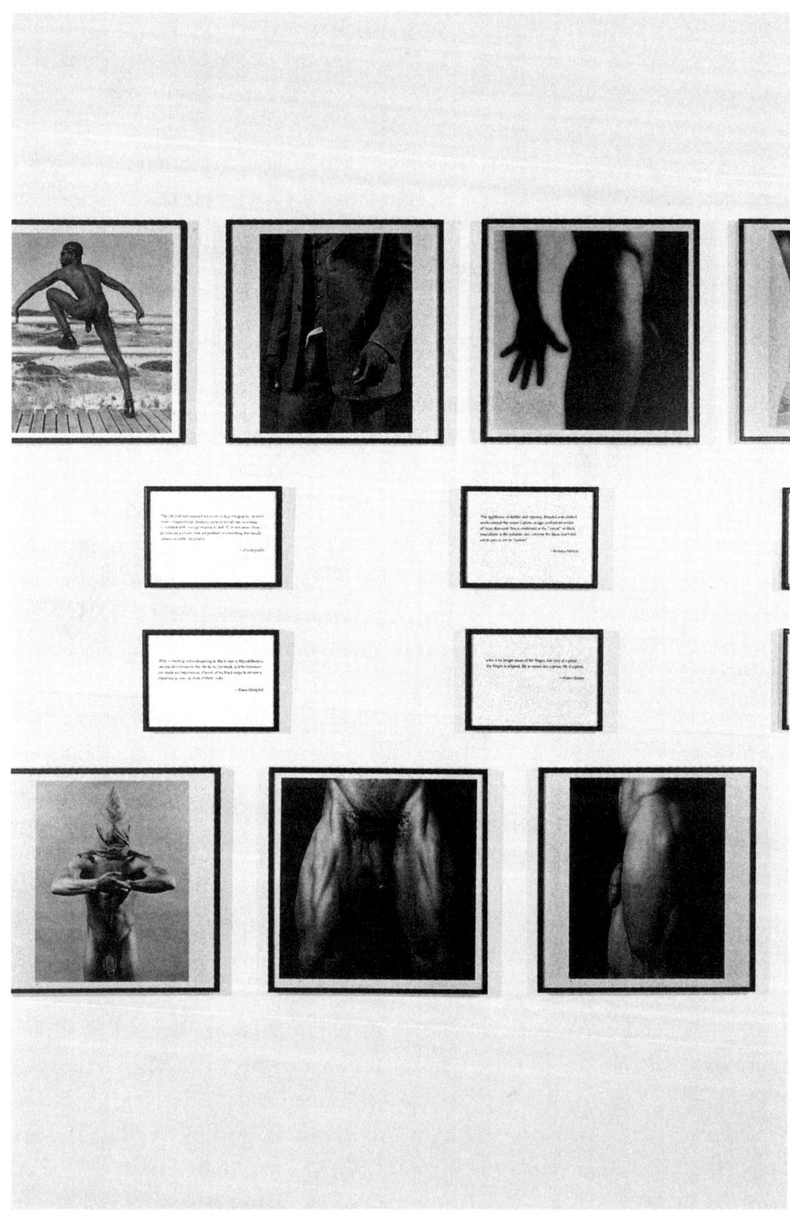

Figure 1.6 Glenn Ligon, *Notes on the Margin of the Black Book* (detail), 1991–1993. 91 offset prints, 78 text pages; each framed: prints 11½ × 11½ inches; text pages 5¼ × 7¼ inches. Collection of the Solomon R. Guggenheim Museum, New York. © Glenn Ligon; Courtesy of the artist, Hauser & Wirth, and Thomas Dane Gallery. Photography credit: Ronald Amstutz.

Ligon observes, "to speak about sexuality through specific photographic representations [than through painting or text]."[8] While he continues to produce paintings with oil stick, stencils, and canvas, Ligon now works with a wide range of other materials, including vintage gay porn, family snapshots, old issues of *Jet* magazine, thrift-shop furniture, and photographic portraits taken at Sears. In *A Feast of Scraps* (1994–1998; figures 1.7, 1.8), Ligon inserted pornographic photographs of black men, complete with self-invented captions ("Mother knew"; "I fell out"; "It's a process"), into photo albums of family snapshots, some of which depict Ligon's own family. In these albums, unbidden erotic fantasies and sexual stereotypes of black men suddenly, and altogether spectacularly, take their place beside vacation snapshots, graduation photographs, wedding showers, birthday celebrations, and church baptisms. *A Feast of Scraps* renders visible that which must be kept hidden, left unspoken, or otherwise repressed within traditional records of domestic and familial life.

Throughout his career, Ligon has investigated those moments when identity seems to slip or give way to its own erasure. For a recent installation entitled *Day of Absence* (1996), the artist combined larger-than-lifesize self-portraits resembling mug shots (figures 1.10, 1.11) with four monumental silkscreens of news photographs of the 1995 Million Man March in Washington, DC (figure 1.13). *Day of Absence* simultaneously registered Ligon's awe in the face of the march and his disappointment that the collective visibility of black men was purchased at the price of other absences: namely, those of black women and (many) black gay men, including the artist himself. The full title of the 1995 event, "The Million Man March / Day of Absence," referred to the fact that black women wishing to support the march were asked to absent themselves from work on that day. By borrowing the second half of that title for his installation, Ligon emphasizes the ways in which (male) presence was tied to (female) absence, both at the march itself and in the newspaper photographs documenting it.

In *Hands* (1996; figure 1.9), one of the silkscreen murals in *Day of Absence*, a sea of black hands reaches upward as though grasping or waving at something beyond the bounds of the visual field. The specific context for this photograph was a collective pledge in which march participants were asked to rededicate themselves to the cause of the family. In Ligon's mural, however, this context gives way to larger series of symbolic tensions between presence and absence (the hands vs. the men to whom they belong), between abstraction and figuration (the streaky expanse above

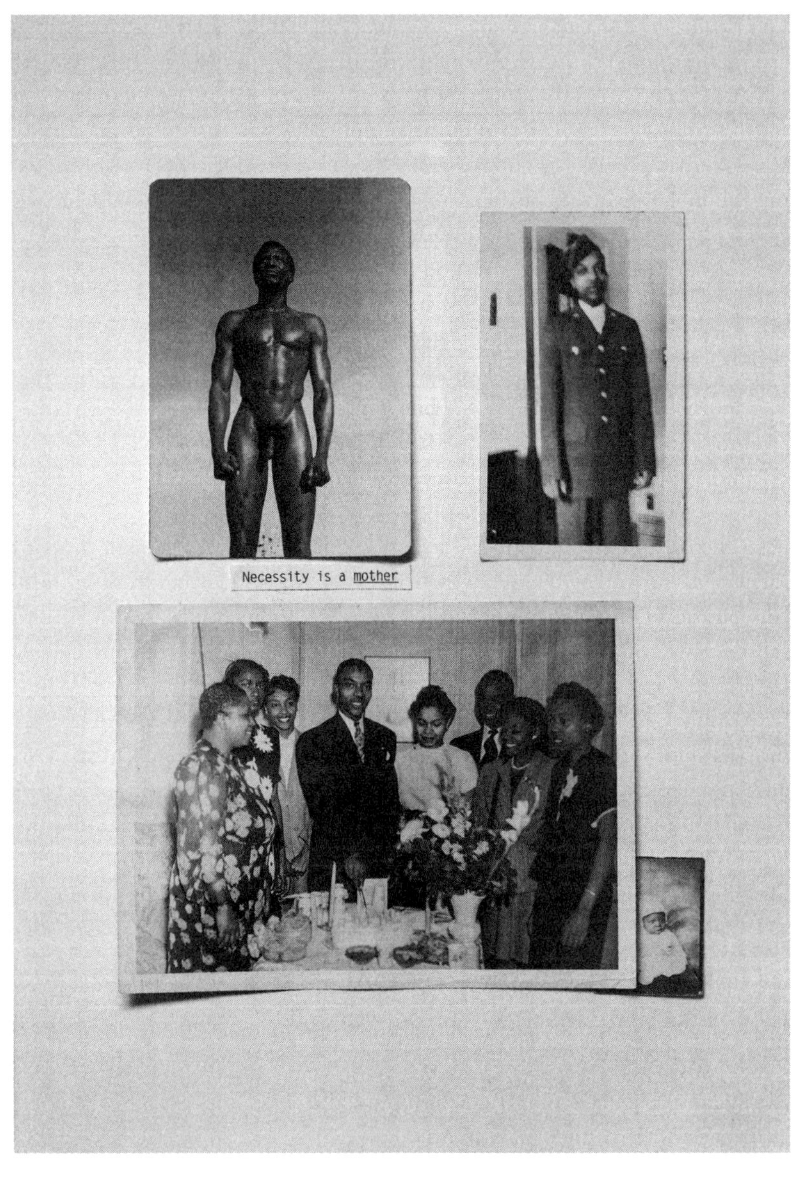

Figure 1.7 Glenn Ligon, *A Feast of Scraps* (detail), 1994–1998. Photographs and text, 20½ × 11½ inches. © Glenn Ligon; Courtesy of the artist, Hauser & Wirth, and Thomas Dane Gallery.

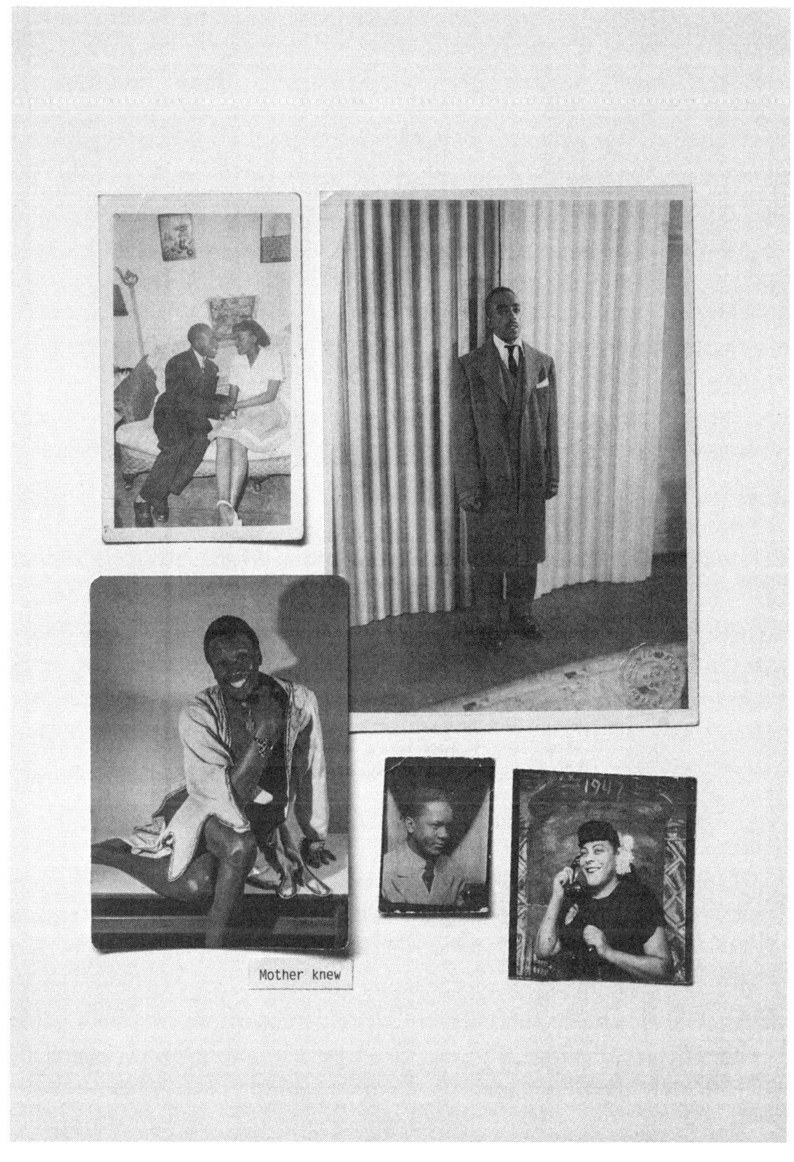

Figure 1.8 Glenn Ligon, *A Feast of Scraps* (detail), 1994–1998. Photographs and text, 20½ × 11½ inches. © Glenn Ligon; Courtesy of the artist, Hauser & Wirth, and Thomas Dane Gallery.

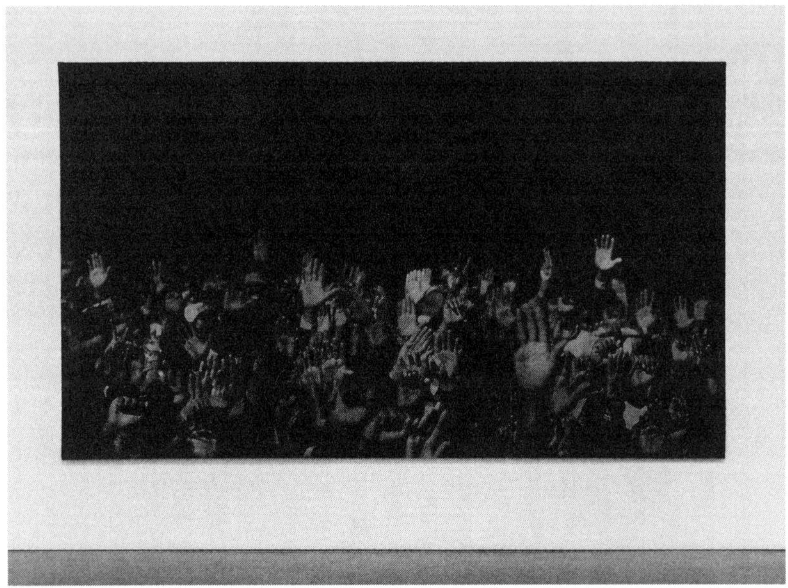

Figure 1.9 Glenn Ligon, *Hands*, 1996. Silkscreen ink and gesso on canvas, 82 × 144 inches. Collection of the Glenstone Museum, Potomac, Travilah, MD. © Glenn Ligon; Courtesy of the artist, Hauser & Wirth, and Thomas Dane Gallery. Photography credit: Brian Forrest.

vs. the outstretched fingers below), between the terms of political identity and those of invisibility (the mass of black men vs. their fragmentation and disappearance).

In another of the *Day of Absence* murals, a huge banner is hoisted above a mass of silhouetted heads and upraised fists (figure 1.12). Apart from the wind holes that have been punched through its surface, the banner is entirely blank, an expanse of seeming emptiness. To create this mural, Ligon not only cropped and dramatically enlarged his source photograph, he digitally removed the slogan, "We're Black and Strong," imprinted on the banner. By eliminating these words from the image, Ligon inserts absence at the core of the collective spectacle of the Million Man March. "Who," the empty banner now seems to ask, "is rendered invisible by this public moment of black male solidarity?" Having removed "We're Black and Strong" from the banner, Ligon retrieved the slogan to serve as the title of the mural. The slogan is absented from the visual field only to resurface, like the return of the repressed, on a wall label or catalog checklist.

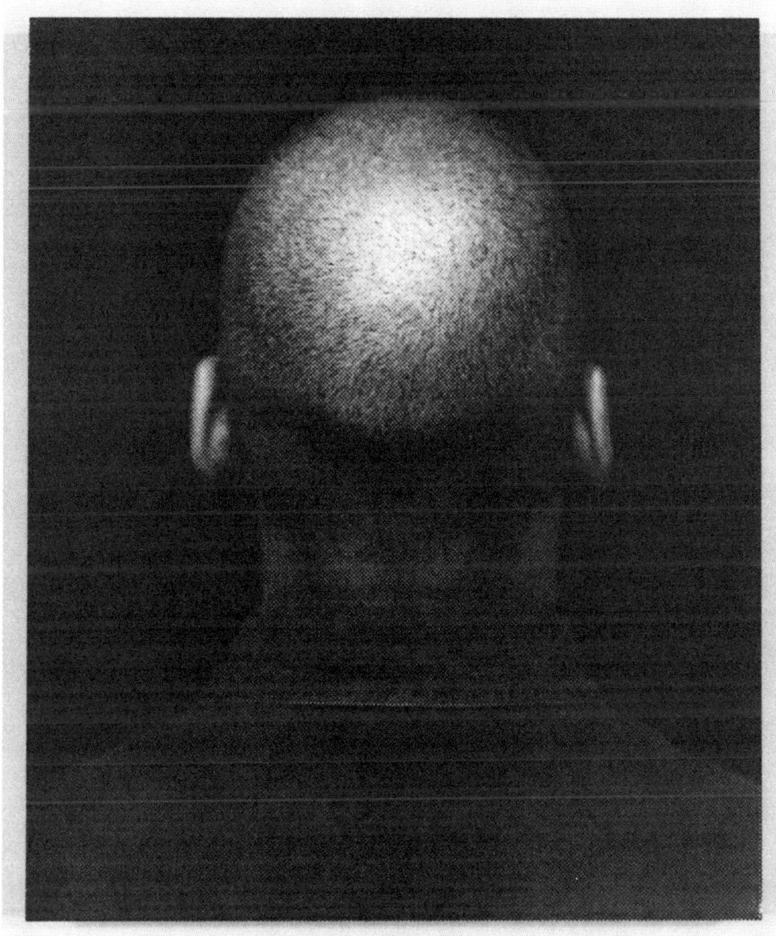

Figure 1.10 Glenn Ligon, *Self-Portrait #7*, 1996. Silkscreen ink and gesso on canvas, 48 × 40 inches. Collection of the Whitney Museum of American Art, New York. © Glenn Ligon. Digital image © Whitney Museum of American Art / Licensed by Scala / Art Resource, NY.

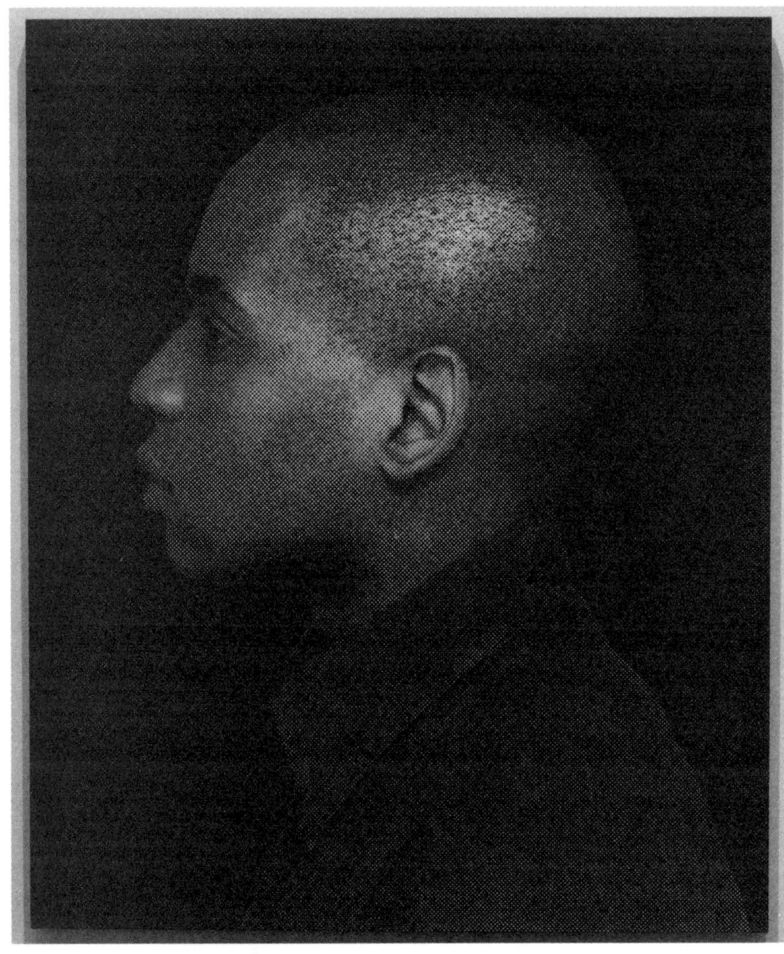

Figure 1.11 Glenn Ligon, *Self-Portrait (VIII)*, 1996. Silkscreen ink on canvas, 48 × 40 inches. Collection of the National Gallery of Art, Washington, DC. © Glenn Ligon.

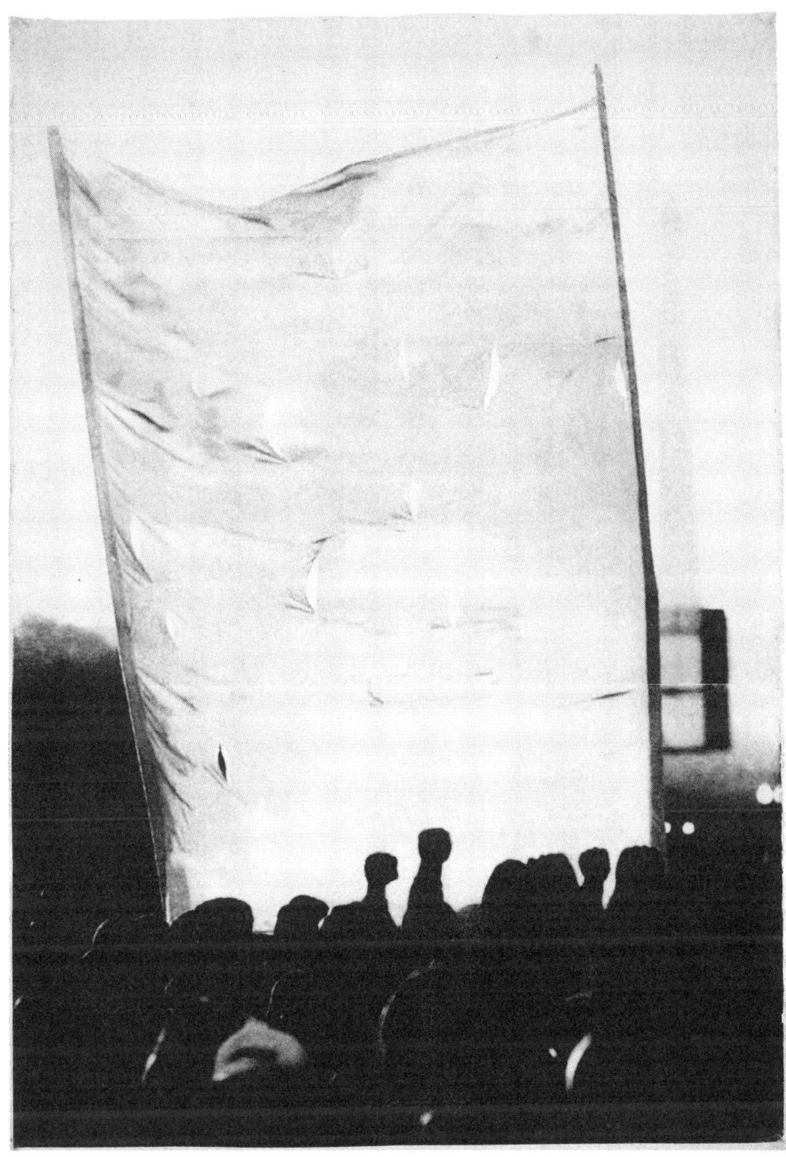

Figure 1.12 Glenn Ligon, *We're Black and Strong (I)*, 1996. Silkscreen ink and gesso on unstretched canvas, 120 × 84 inches. Collection of the San Francisco Museum of Modern Art. © Glenn Ligon; Courtesy of the artist, Hauser & Wirth, and Thomas Dane Gallery.

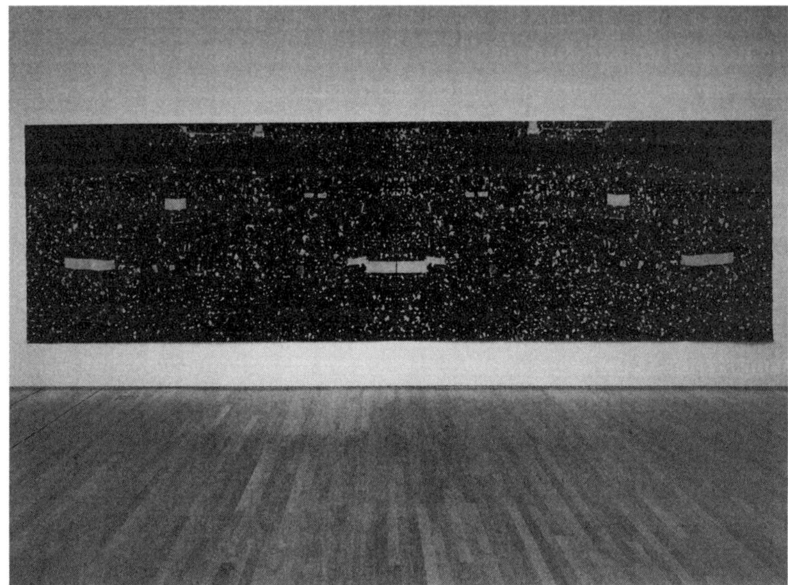

Figure 1.13 Glenn Ligon, *Gulliver*, 1996. Silkscreen ink on unstretched canvas, diptych, 84 × 288 inches. © Glenn Ligon; Courtesy of the artist, Hauser & Wirth, and Thomas Dane Gallery. Photography credit: Ben Blackwell.

From his earliest text paintings to his most recent installations, Ligon has challenged the apparent transparency of language by changing the intended conditions of its display and reproduction. These changes have resulted in language that is difficult, and sometimes impossible, to see. As Ligon himself observes, "I've always taken text to the point of disappearance in my work."[9] The artist uses disappearance to figure the limits and absences that lie at the heart of identity and to suggest that individual subjects never align neatly with the overarching terms of race or sexuality. Glenn Ligon teaches us that the material force of language, the legacy of the borrowed voice, may register most strongly at the very moment of its own vanishing.

Notes

1. Cited in Roberta Smith, "Lack of Location Is My Location," *New York Times*, June 16, 1991, H27.

2. Ligon consulted an archive of typography on the southern tip of Manhattan in order to match the period style of antebellum slave narratives. According to the artist, he used about twenty-five different typefaces for *Narratives*, some of which were common only in the nineteenth century (e.g., Orlans, Egyptian) and some of which continue to appear in printed materials today (e.g., Palatino, Century Schoolbook). For Ligon, "The idea was the mix. The typefaces don't match any one, original narrative exactly; they are a mix of typographical conventions from the period." Glenn Ligon, personal correspondence with the author, September 29, 1996.

3. On the literary form of the nineteenth-century slave narrative, including the issue of authentication, see Charles T. Davis and Henry Louis Gates Jr., eds., *The Slave's Narrative* (Oxford: Oxford University Press, 1985).

4. *Black Like Me* is the title of a 1961 nonfiction bestseller by John Howard Griffin, a white writer, who, with the help of skin-darkening steroids and sunlamp treatments, traveled throughout the South as a black man and then published his experiences as an exposé of racism. In using that same title within *Narratives*, Ligon suggests how the experience of an "authentic blackness" is continually claimed by, and framed for, white subjects.

5. The primacy of the jokes as spoken language is further suggested by the fact that Ligon transcribed them from an LP recording of Pryor's live stand-up routines rather than from a written source.

6. Peter Schjeldahl, "Missing: The Pleasure Principle," *Village Voice*, March 16, 1993, 34.

7. Glenn Ligon, personal correspondence with the author, July 22, 1996.

8. Glenn Ligon, personal correspondence with the author, July 22, 1996.

9. Cited in "An Interview with Glenn Ligon and Gary Garrels, March 15, 1996," in *Glenn Ligon: New Work*, exhibition brochure (San Francisco Museum of Modern Art, 1996), n.p.

2 Color Me Glenn

Wayne Koestenbaum

It is impossible to make a noncomedic reference to *Color Me Barbra*, the Streisand album on which, I recall, she sang the forgettable tune "My Coloring Book." A similar, intentional mirth suffuses Glenn Ligon's new paintings, which revisit a moment of historical optimism, an "uplift" he regards with pained, sympathetic levity. These paintings notice an epoch when African Americans were deliberately circulating images of blackness and of black identity: Malcolm X, Harriet Tubman, Isaac Hayes, George Washington Carver (figure 2.1). New heroes for a new age, these figures, placed in the crayon-wielding hands of children, incited pride, groundedness. However, Ligon's reliance on techniques of appropriation (silkscreening found images in new combinations, and circulating them in an art market) interrupts the cheerful, progressive momentum of the originals.

The most egregious—and artistically brilliant—interruption that Ligon performs is placing rouge on Malcolm X's cheeks (figure 2.2). (My guess is that this Malcolm painting will become one of the iconic images of the artist's career, much as Marilyn and then Mao served that purpose for Warhol.) The rouge was the brainchild of one of the coloring schoolchildren to whom Ligon gave these offset images, in order that he might learn from them the freedom of prelapsarian artistry. Adorning Malcolm with face paint is a profoundly irreverent gesture, but it also pays respect to him (or to everyone whom he has inspired) by proving that iconicity is a form of makeover, a color scheme laid over a neutral surface.

Clearly, Ligon enjoys performing these superimpositions. After a brief period of exile from the pleasures and exactions of paint, he wanted,

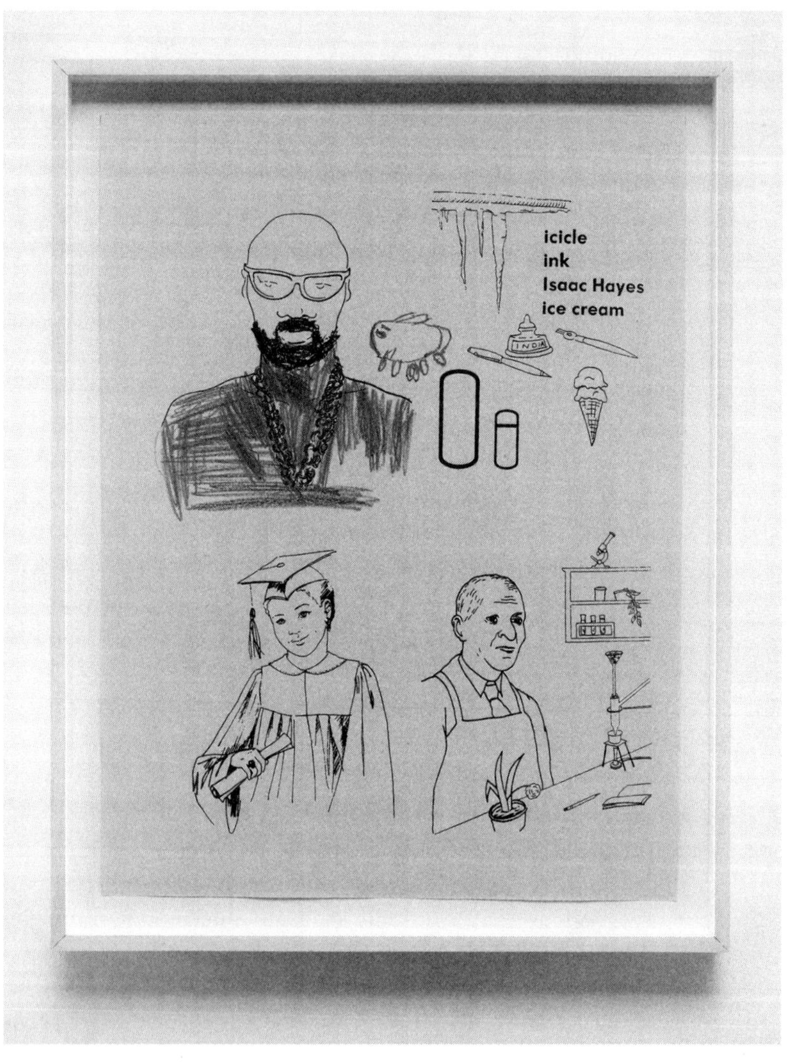

Figure 2.1 Glenn Ligon, *Isaac Hayes, Icicle, George Washington Carver, Graduating Girl (version 2) #3*, 2001. Silkscreen and oil crayon on paper, 23 × 16½ inches. © Glenn Ligon; Courtesy of the artist, Hauser & Wirth, and Thomas Dane Gallery. Photography credit: Ronald Amstutz.

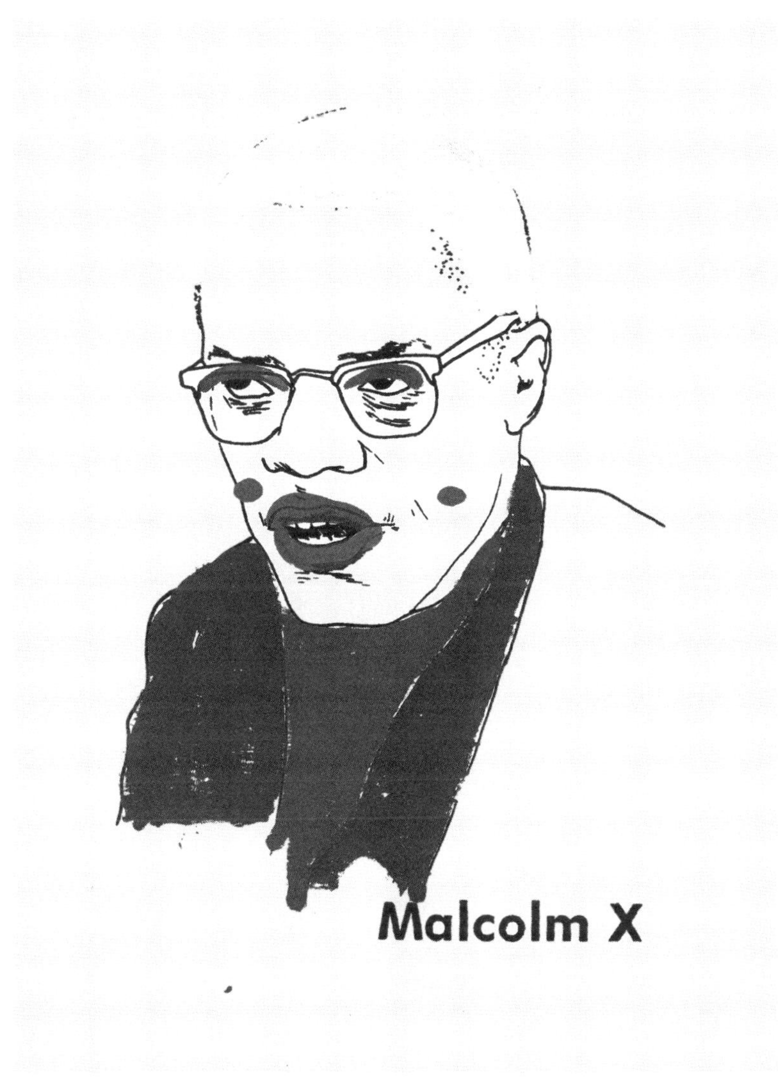

Figure 2.2 Glenn Ligon, *Malcolm X (Version 1) #1*, 2000. Vinyl-based paint, silkscreen ink, and gesso on canvas, 96 × 72 inches. © Glenn Ligon; Courtesy of the artist, Hauser & Wirth, and Thomas Dane Gallery.

again, to use his gifted hand, to "express" a surface, to mar an ideologically cramped canvas with the signs of his urgent and nearly calligraphic facture. One of the beauties of his paintings has always been the obsessive, repetitive, accretive use of brushstroke to signify the intensity of his modifications of received wisdom, which critic Roland Barthes called *doxa*. It has always been up for grabs, in a Ligon painting, whether he is crossing out—obliterating—the givens, or underscoring their importance. Is he highlighting the text with a reverent Magic Marker, or is he brutally and iconoclastically erasing it, as Rauschenberg erased the de Kooning drawing, or as hegemonic whiteness extinguishes blackness?

There comes a time in an artist's career when the story of "development" or artistic maturation must be told, or invented, in however slant and sly a fashion, if only to lay to rest the critical misconceptions that gather around the work; in these paintings, Ligon unfolds that necessary fiction of origins. From the beginning, he has been a resolutely "mature" artist—sober, serious, historical. His work with found photography (*A Feast of Scraps*, for example) called a momentary hiatus to the seriousness: family snapshots and porn pix brought the field of "kitsch" and its surrounding discourses into play, and reminded viewers that Ligon had a raging sense of humor. And yet his text paintings—in their reliance on shadow meanings, with each found phrase sending forth contradictory connotations—also were structured like jokes, though the audience was not encouraged to laugh. Now, with the deliberate use of children's artistic techniques, he is performing a regression; remarkably, these "regressive" paintings may be his most "mature" work yet. The coincidence of the gaze backward to childhood pleasures and the movement forward into artistic achievement sets spinning a welcome irony: Ligon is behaving like a child, and yet, by showing his paintings in the same space as the fauvist children's, he proves his triumphant, newfound adultness.

Though he disturbs the dichotomy between master and naif, the effect of his large paintings—masterpieces—next to the quirky, inevitably "cute" paintings of the children is paternal, or, more provocatively, avuncular. Indeed, Ligon's paintings stand as uncles to the kids' drawings, and his custodial, protective relation to them has the ambiguous characteristics of (gay) avuncularity. In the installation at the Walker Art Center, Uncle's paintings occupy a safely separate room; no chance that the kids will get in the way of the adult, or that the adult will interfere with the corporeal pleasures of the child. For an image of Ligon's relation to the children, or of his imagined paternal relation to his own past self, see the painting of "Dad," his face filled in with brown, the kid's face painted pink (figure 2.3). Is that man really the child's father? When the obvious is loudly reiterated (*Dad!*), trouble stirs.

The contiguity of childwork and adultwork—the nearness of the adult hand's pleasure and the child hand's pleasure—brings up sexuality, even if the images broach the subject only indirectly. (Is a topless woman indirect?) His use of color raises the subject more explicitly—if metaphor, too, is a type of explicitness. Ligon has cited the word "colored" before, in his painting *Untitled (I Feel Most Colored When I Am Thrown Against a Sharp White Background)* (1990). (He borrowed the phrase from Zora Neale Hurston. In Ligon's reinscription, one feels the lethal violence of the verb "thrown" and the adjective "sharp," and yet one also hears the noun "background" as salutary—the white people relegated, finally, to their proper place as backdrop to Hurston's "colored" and scene-stealing centrality.) Ligon has also used various reds in his paintings: recall his *Cocaine (Pimps)* and the color photographs included in his *Calling Card* series (1997) and *Feast of Scraps* family albums. However, when I think of classic Ligon works (such as his 1991–1993 *Notes on the Margin of the Black Book*, an exegesis/critique of Mapplethorpe photographs), I picture black and white, not only because of their thematic engagement with race, but because of their intellectual rigor, their print-based devotion to high principle, to ratiocination. Ligon's most sternly all-over black paintings are the *Stranger in the Village* series, overlays of coal dust adding an ironic glimmer. That many chestnuts of American abstract art (by white artists) have used the "color" black—Robert Motherwell, Franz Kline, Clyfford Still, Ad Reinhardt—is part of Ligon's point, though the pleasure we take in all-black paintings, or in black-and-white paintings, is visceral as well as ideological. We genuinely like the appearance, not merely the argument. Now Ligon has put aside his black-and-white work, though its forms remain, silkscreened outlines in which he and the children embed colorful marks.

Color short-circuits the signifying function of the outlined black-and-white images, and enacts a deviation within Ligon's career; thus, color suggests the taboo. This disguised reentrance of the obscene into his work has the medical brilliance of an awakening, the excitement of a CinemaScope biopic's world premiere (*A Star Is Born*). Color is the star, and s/he arrives with tiara-and-boa hoopla, a giddy sense of the unfettered and the disallowed (figure 2.4). Color brings with it the charge—the imputation—of

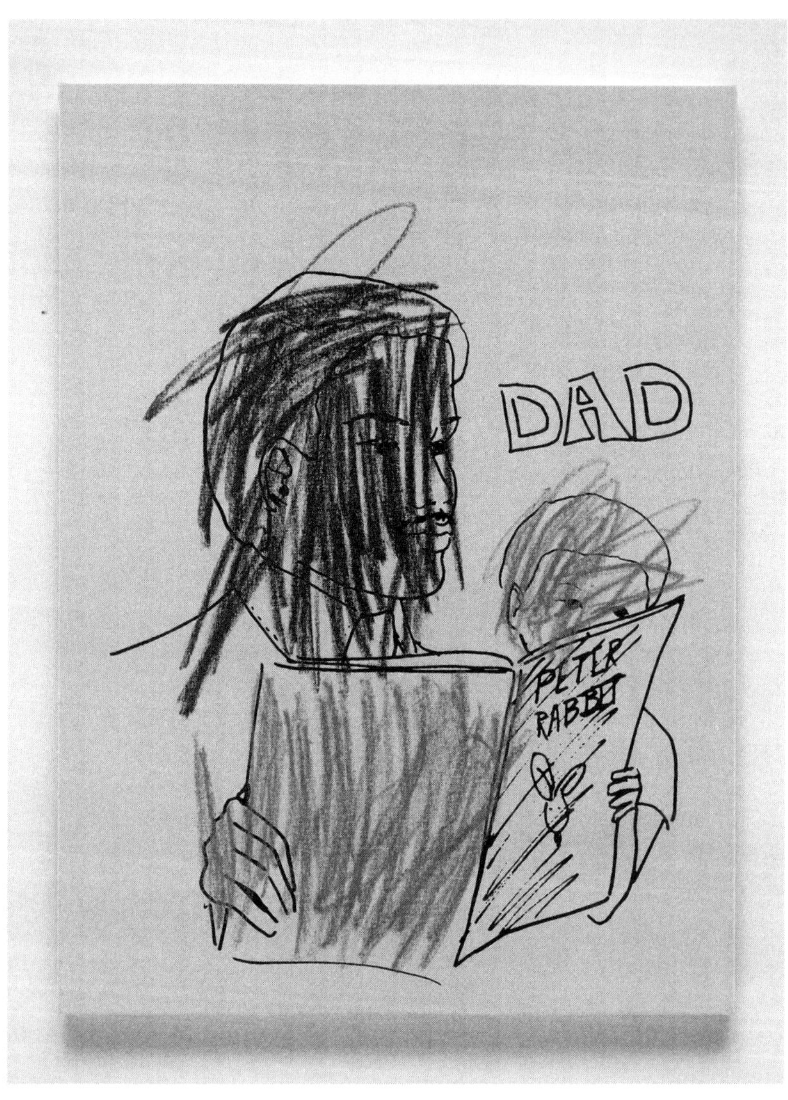

Figure 2.3 Glenn Ligon, *Dad (version 1) #1*, 2000. Silkscreen and oil crayon on canvas, 48 × 36 inches. © Glenn Ligon; Courtesy of the artist, Hauser & Wirth, and Thomas Dane Gallery. Photography credit: Ronald Amstutz

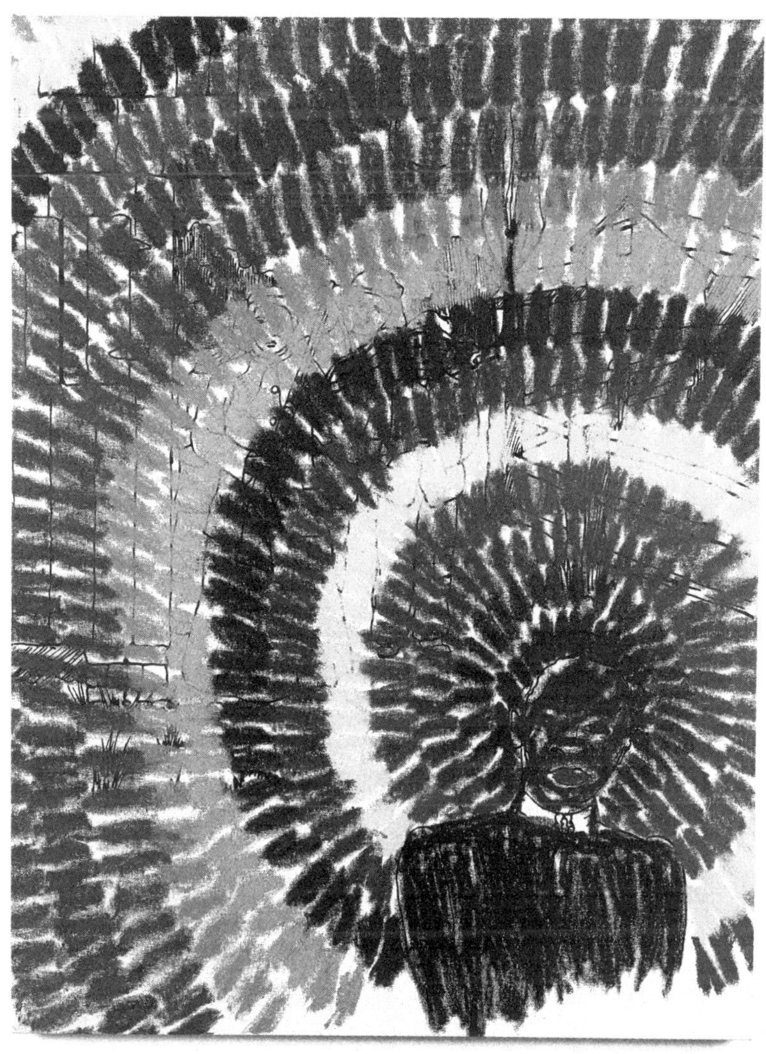

Figure 2.4 Glenn Ligon, *Harriet Tubman (Version 2) #1*, 2001. Silkscreen ink, oil stick, and gesso on canvas, 48 × 36 inches. © Glenn Ligon; Courtesy of the artist, Hauser & Wirth, and Thomas Dane Gallery.

happiness, of gaiety, and of vulgarity. Certainly Warhol's portraits from the 1970s and 1980s were considered vulgar not merely because they were commissioned, but because they were in brash and novel colors, the hues that interior decorators proposed for penthouse walls or that industrial designers chose for institutional Formica.

Ligon's colors (or the children's, which he copied) are not motel colors, but they are certainly pedagogic, and they are saturated with pleasure and upfrontness—candor about being simple, easy, and symbolic. There is no clear scheme to his color code; we are not in the country of deep meanings. But the use of brown on the faces of Harriet Tubman and her fugitives, or of yellow on the face of the graduating student, indicates "race," though not in a literal sense; it does not indicate that bizarre word "pigmentation." Brown, yellow, red, pink, and blue—the whole crowd—describe a series of wishes and projections, and, more than they signal a specific content, they offer a frenzy of inscription, the repeated, heated, effortful movement of the child's or adult's artistic hand letting the crayon travel over the inherited image. With pleasure, Ligon's paintings unveil the earnest and diligent movement of wish, of hypothesis: the coloring hand tries again and again, with lubricious emphasis, to represent the world as a fit, habitable place. There is no way that this dream can be made sufficiently actual, at least not now, not in this decade; and so the painting communicates pathos—futile, yet laudable, the hand's active striving for a something-else. That the striving must assume an obscene form—the pornography of scrawl, of color, of unsupervised superimposition—only proves that, for Ligon, the Good may be approached only through the sacrilegious vocabulary of the out-of-bounds.

3 Glenn Ligon: On the Couch

Mignon Nixon

A modest plaque at the entrance: “Dr. Freud, 2–4”; a not very attractive servant girl; a waiting room whose walls are decorated with four mildly allegorical engravings—Water, Fire, Earth, and Air—and with a photograph depicting the master among his collaborators; a dozen or so patients of the most pedestrian sort; and once, after the sound of a bell, several shouts in succession—not enough here to fill even the slimmest of reports. This until the famous padded door cracks open for me. I find myself in the presence of a little old man with no style who receives clients in a shabby office worthy of the neighborhood G.P.

—André Breton

Glenn Ligon’s *The Orange and Blue Feelings* (2003; figure 3.1) is an edited video recording of three meetings with his therapist. Its total length, about an hour, is that of a single session. Through the technique of dual-channel projection, therapist and patient are relegated to discrete frames, their respective scenes playing slightly out of sync. The therapist, a middle-aged woman partial to flowered prints and bangle bracelets, twirls in her swivel chair. Her foot in its kitten-heeled shoe rests delicately on a cushion. Stroking her bare arm rhythmically, she stirs the bangles. Her face is never seen. A pillow tucked into the chair cradles her body to this “habitual seat, a sort of nest padded with accustomed objects,” as Janet Malcolm has described the analyst’s armchair, comparing it to “a chronic invalid’s chair.”[1]

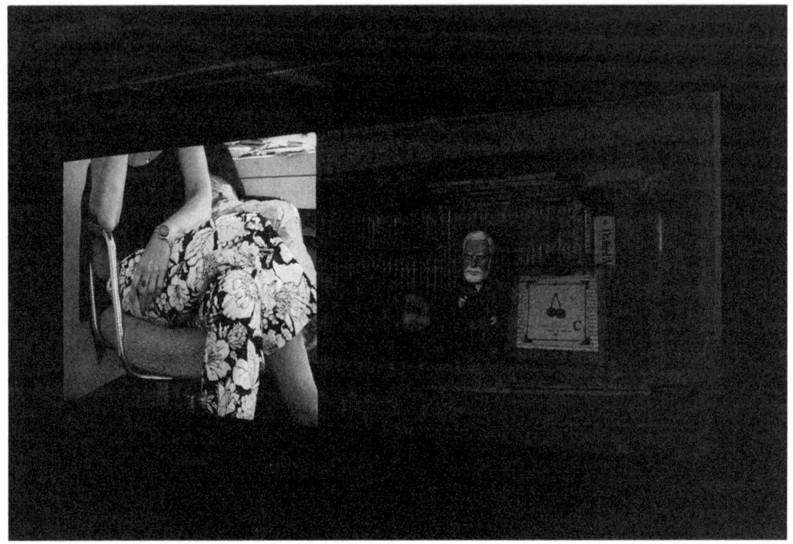

Figure 3.1 Glenn Ligon, installation view of *The Orange and Blue Feelings* (2003), The Fabric Workshop and Museum, Philadelphia, 2003. Double-channel video, 57 minutes, edition of 5. © Glenn Ligon; Courtesy of the artist, Hauser & Wirth, and Thomas Dane Gallery. Photography credit: Aaron Igler.

The patient, Ligon himself, remains offscreen, his frame filled by the unoccupied end of a couch. Camera movements are small and desultory, mimicking the glassy gaze of a patient undergoing the talking cure, eyes sliding aimlessly over a prosaic assortment of props. The camera lingers on a box of tissues in front of an open window. Catching the breeze, the paper ruffles. An untidy pile of bags sunk on the floor, a houseplant, a shelf lined with books, bric-a-brac, a Freud doll, a corner of patterned carpet, a vase of flowers, a row of framed photographs, a diploma, and a desk piled with papers provide the camera with other vignettes. Once, it jerks unexpectedly toward the window, briefly training its lens on the street below. For almost an hour we listen in as the invisible patient and his Gena Rowlands-esque therapist explore Ligon's anxieties about some recent work.

Transference, writes Laplanche, is "the very milieu of analysis, in the sense of its surrounding environment."[2] The milieu of the transference, he observes, is most perceptible when change is in the air, for "one notices a milieu less when one is plunged in it; more so when it is rather briskly altered or when one leaves it."[3] Ligon's video portrays an analysis in media res. The figure of the analyst, with her husky voice, coquettish wriggling, and flamboyant dress, is recorded with detachment. If the camera's gaze falls on the foot resting on the pillow, this seems to be as much because, in face-to-face therapy such as this, the patient cannot always be staring back at the therapist and must find relief from the other's gaze somewhere, as because the shoe seems flirtatious. The setting, too, is presented with scant curiosity, like the accustomed environment of a neighbor's living room in which a vase or a picture is occasionally moved but without altering the overall effect. And if the camera wanders around the room from time to time, poking into corners and grazing objects, its investigation is perfunctory. The long, static shots do not probe, highlight, or inventory the room's appointments so much as confirm their familiar presence. Bad taste and comfortable clutter have become the institutional furniture of the frame.

What returns attention to the milieu of psychoanalysis, according to Laplanche, is change. When the milieu is altered, it attracts fresh notice. This occurs especially when the analysand "acts out" by committing "an infidelity to the analytic relation."[4] The patient actualizes desire, goes outside the relationship, acts on an impulse (to have an affair, in the classic scenario) rather than bringing this wish to analysis. Freud called this lateral transference, an action that sidesteps the analyst. In *The Orange and Blue Feelings*, Ligon agonizes over the possibility that therapy will vitiate his art, that "a more balanced life makes for banal work." Preferring to keep his art separate from his therapy (for reasons that become evident as the recorded session's crash tutorial in postmodernism falters), he recognizes the threat to the analytic relation this withholding represents. His solution is to make his therapy the subject of his art, to turn the consulting room into a set, actually to move in. This gesture, however, goes beyond infidelity to the analytic situation and dissolves it.

The acting out that is the real drama of *The Orange and Blue Feelings* is Ligon's shattering of the frame. He nullifies the analytic contract by taking over the role of the analyst as "the director of the method."[5] The video begins with Ligon informing the analyst that overnight he had listened to the recording of a previous session. ("I thought my voice sounded really faggy," he tells her. "That's another thing I have to deal with in therapy, why I hate my voice"—to which the therapist weakly replies, "Oh dear.") Presently, in response to Ligon's account of a childhood memory that he holds in his mind as a photograph, uncertain when or even if the event ever occurred, the therapist, recovering her authority, announces, "It's called a screen memory, in fact." By this time, however, the analyst has become the star of the show, the body on the screen, and it is the patient who is directing the analysis.[6]

The analyst must be "director of the method," contends Laplanche. Failing this, "there is no analysis."[7] In Ligon's video, analysis dissolves. Yet the situation suggests another possibility. According to Laplanche, the patient's acting out does not lead inevitably to rupture. An act of infidelity, he proposes, "may be drawn back into that relation, interpreted, in sum, as a *transference of transference*: 'What you could not, did not wish to tell me, you have signified, enacted, outside.'"[8]

The Orange and Blue Feelings extends over three sessions and concerns the mysterious disappearance of a painting. A portrait of Malcolm X (figure 2.2), based on an image copied from a children's coloring book and intended for an exhibition at the Walker Art Center in Minneapolis—"the most interesting painting in the show"—turned out to be missing from the shipment, stirring anxieties of loss and longing that Ligon associates in therapy with early childhood experience. The portrait was actually produced with the help of a child, he explains to the therapist. As an artist-in-residence at the Walker, he was asked to take part in the museum's educational programming, an obligation he discharged by inviting local schoolchildren to "color in" motifs from his archival source material: vintage coloring books featuring black heroes of American history—figures such as Harriet Tubman, George Washington Carver, and Malcolm X. When one child responded with a vision of Malcolm resplendent with rouged cheeks and pink lipstick, Ligon, captivated by the fearlessness of "the little queer child who puts lipstick on the image of the father," translated the motif into a large-scale painting that was to be the centerpiece of the Walker exhibition.

"A little boy did that?" the therapist asks. "I'm assuming it was a he," Ligon answers uncertainly, sounding suddenly curious about what the therapist is saying, "unless I'm just projecting myself backward." Up to then, the therapist has been hung up on the fact that Ligon copies. Even as a child, he acknowledges, he "never drew from imagination," preferring to copy from source material. "Maybe it's time," she urges, adding, "Maybe it's long past time." "Throw your stencils onto the fire, so to speak?" he demands. "Mmm, I don't know." "I have a lot of anxiety about talking about art work in therapy." He tells her instead about making art in school as a small child, about being ridiculed by a teacher for painting a papier-mâché ocean liner orange and blue. "You'd think art class would be the one class where anything would be fine, where there wouldn't be rules," she replies. "Everybody has an agenda," he reminds her. "I ended up painting the boat black." "'You don't like my colors. Fuck you!'" she cheers. "I was just thinking about people in the gallery listening to this," he remarks. "It's embarrassing."

Ligon showed *The Orange and Blue Feelings* alongside the original portrait of Malcolm X. He recovered the rolled canvas from the trash after inadvertently—unconsciously, to say the word—discarding it in a studio sweep-up. "I found it between the first session we recorded and the second," he announces to the therapist toward the end of the tape, adding, "I was thinking about the fact that I didn't tell you." Ligon's infidelity, his lateral move—what he "could not, did not wish to tell" his therapist and has instead "signified, enacted outside"—cycles back into the analysis as the ending of the story. His disclosure is timed to conclude the work, the video-analysis he is directing. Ligon broke off therapy shortly after the work was first shown.[9] But if the video records the dissolution of the analysis, it also enacts what Laplanche calls "a transference of transference" from one locus to another: "In other places—during analysis, outside analysis—other possibilities of 'transference' are available to the analysand, other poles for the elaboration of an individual destiny."[10]

> Video's real medium is a psychological situation, the very terms of which are to withdraw attention from an external object—an Other—and invest it in the Self.
>
> —Rosalind Krauss

Critics reviewing *Going There*, the 2003 New York gallery exhibition in which Ligon first presented *The Orange and Blue Feelings*, expressed surprise and disappointment at its apparently confessional mode. In contrast to Ligon's previous work, including stenciled word paintings, in which passages of text are applied to white canvases—works that, as one critic observed, "managed to address subjectivity and its politics by way of elegantly conceived formal frameworks"[11]—*The Orange and Blue Feelings* instead seemed self-centered, seemed to summon Rosalind Krauss's early critique of video as producing "an aesthetics of narcissism."

By connecting the medium of video and the condition of narcissism, Krauss observed, "one can recast the opposition between the reflective and the reflexive into the terms of the psychoanalytic project. Because it is there, too, in the drama of the couched subject, that the narcissistic reprojection of a frozen self is pitted against the analytic (or reflexive) mode."[12] The reflexive mode of analysis facilitates alienation from a self-image that encapsulates the subject. "The process of analysis is one of breaking the hold of this fascination with the mirror."[13] Or, as Laplanche expresses it, there is a primordial split at the heart of transference, "which means quite simply that the other is the other . . . he is other than me because he is other than himself. External alterity refers back to internal alterity."[14]

As Laplanche observes, there is an "essential dissymmetry" in the analytic situation, a distance, or difference, that is preserved especially by the silence of the analyst. In Ligon's video, dissymmetry is the organizing principle. Therapist and patient are relegated to separate screens. One is visible, the other is not. One is a woman, the other a man. One is white and the other, as we know, is black. For Ligon's work has often referred, indirectly, to the identity and subjectivity of the artist. His early paintings quote from literary texts. In one particularly well-known work, *Untitled (I Feel Most Colored When I Am Thrown Against a Sharp White Background)* (1990; figure 1.1), this sentence written by Zora Neale Hurston is stenciled in black oil stick on a door-sized white panel. The writing is crisply legible at the top but, like a newspaper passed from hand to hand, becomes smudged and murky from overuse toward the bottom. Gummed and clotted, the stencils transfer the inky oil from one application to the next down the panel so that each line is less distinct than the one above. Toward the bottom end, the text fades out into illegibility.

Continuing to investigate the medium of printing in *Runaways* (1993), Ligon solicited physical descriptions of himself from ten friends and typeset the texts in the format and graphic style of his archival source, mid-nineteenth-century posters designed to track down fugitive slaves. One read: "Ran away, Glenn Ligon. He's a shortish broad-shouldered black man, pretty dark-skinned, with glasses" (figure 3.2). Throughout his work, Ligon mines text to represent the historical and cultural construction of identity, using the figure Glenn Ligon as a frequent, but not exclusive, point of reference. He returns to this strategy in *The Orange and Blue Feelings*, at one point handing over to the therapist a school evaluation report in which the child, Glenn Ligon, is described as a moody boy who sometimes

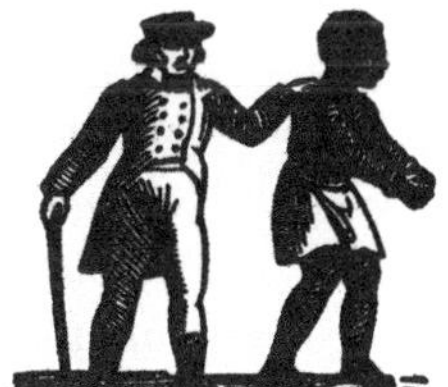

Figure 3.2 Glenn Ligon, *Runaways* (detail), 1993. Suite of 10 lithographs, 16 × 12 inches, edition of 45 and 10 artist's proofs. © Glenn Ligon; Courtesy of the artist, Hauser & Wirth, and Thomas Dane Gallery. Photography credit: Jeff McLane.

withdraws. When he brought the report home, he recounts, "My mother did a dramatic reading of that," warning him, "This will go on your record"—meaning, he elaborates, "my record with a capital *R*." As she saw it, "That's how black kids get labeled."

Text, Krauss observes, is what is missing from performance-based video. Its absence is what renders the medium narcissistic. For performance, she notes, conventionally relies on some form of text, "whether that is a fixed choreography, a written script, a musical score, or a sketchy set of notes around which to improvise."[15] By contrast, video performance, centered on the body of the performer before the camera, produces the effect of a "collapsed present" equivalent to the space-time of mirror reflection, or the patient on the couch—the very task of analysis being to convert the "fascination with the mirror," or reflective mode, into a reflexive one. "The analytic project," Krauss observes, is one in which "the patient disengages from . . . his reflected self, and through a method of reflexiveness, rediscovers the real time of his own history. He exchanges the atemporality of repetition for the temporality of change."[16] In short, psychoanalysis is not a confessional mode, in which self-image is nurtured, but a gradual process of alienation from the sovereign self.

Ligon has consistently relied on thick citation to represent the historical construction of identity through transference. "Making a painting, for me," he explains, "is akin to making a film adaptation of a text: it's just one possible way out of many of responding to a given text."[17] His experiment with video-analysis appears to be a departure from this practice of citation because the text it adapts, or interprets, is an autobiographical narrative. But if we understand psychoanalysis as a reflexive mode, opening onto the dimension of alterity, then its task is to render the subject, to borrow a term favored by Ligon, "opaque."[18] "Yes, you can take me for an other, because I am not what I think I am; because I respect and maintain the other in me."[19] This, writes Laplanche, is the statement the analyst addresses to the analysand. It also offers a possible description of how the work of Glenn Ligon attempts to address its audience.

Notes

1. Janet Malcolm, *Psychoanalysis: The Impossible Profession* (London: Granta Books, 1983), 47.

2. Jean Laplanche, "Transference: Its Provocation by the Analyst," in *Essays on Otherness* (London: Routledge, 1999), 216.

3. Laplanche, "Transference," 217.

4. Laplanche, "Transference," 217.

5. Laplanche, "Transference," 227.

6. Ligon reports that he paid the therapist a location fee for the use of the consulting room for filming, including footage of the empty office shot after hours. Glenn Ligon, conversation with the author, March 9, 2005.

7. Laplanche, "Transference," 227.

8. Laplanche, "Transference," 217.

9. Glenn Ligon, conversation with the author, March 7, 2004.

10. Laplanche, "Transference," 231.

11. Johanna Burton, "Glenn Ligon, D'Amelio Terras," *Artforum* (March 2004), 184.

12. Rosalind Krauss, "Video: The Aesthetics of Narcissism," *October* 1 (Spring 1976): 57.

13. Krauss, "Video," 58.

14. Laplanche, "Transference," 221.

15. Krauss, "Video," 53.

16. Krauss, "Video," 58.

17. Byron Kim, "Interview with Glenn Ligon," in *Glenn Ligon: Unbecoming*, exh. cat., ed. Judith Tannenbaum (Philadelphia: Institute of Contemporary Art, 1997), 53.

18. As Lacan puts it, "In this labor, which he undertakes to reconstruct this construct *for another*, he finds again the fundamental alienation which made him construct it *like another one*, and which has always destined it to be stripped from him *by another*." Lacan, *The Language of the Self*, trans. Anthony Wilden (New York: Delta, 1968), 11; cited in Krauss, "Video," 58.

19. Laplanche, "Transference," 228.

4 Glenn Ligon and Other Runaway Subjects

Huey Copeland

> My subject, then, fellow-citizens, is AMERICAN SLAVERY. I shall see this day and its popular characteristics from the slave's point of view. Standing there, identified with the American bondman, making his wrongs mine, I do not hesitate to declare, with all my soul, that the character and conduct of this nation never looked blacker to me than on this Fourth of July. Whether we turn to the declarations of the past, or to the professions of the present, the conduct of the nation seems equally hideous and revolting. America is false to the past, false to the present, and solemnly binds herself to be false to the future.[1]
>
> —Frederick Douglass, 1852

In 1991, the artist Glenn Ligon set out to draw a history of American freedom. He began by inscribing the year 1776 into the upper left-hand corner of a red ground before proceeding to record what came next: 1777, then 1778, 1779, 1780 (figure 4.1). Occasionally, splotches of paint undermine the numbers' rectitude; gradually, the dragging of black oil stick and plastic stencil decreases their clarity; and every other line or so, a year is cut in half by the paper's right framing edge. Such incidents of smear and shadow hardly count, because one year after another, the story and the drawing unfold, the digits dutifully plodding across the surface until they meet its margin, wrap around it, and continue onward. When their journey concludes, it does so abruptly, even anticlimactically, leaving a jagged red strip beneath the year 1865. "Liberty and justice for all" have somehow arrived, their uncertainty intact.

Figure 4.1 Glenn Ligon, *Untitled (1776–1865)*, 1991. Gouache, oil stick, and graphite on paper, 30 × 22¾ inches. © Glenn Ligon; Courtesy of the artist, Hauser & Wirth, and Thomas Dane Gallery.

In its movement from the declaration of independence to the abolition of slavery, *Untitled (1776–1865)* marks out the disparity between two moments of American emancipation so as to materialize the distance between the realities of black oppression and the myths of white freedom. In drawing them together like so many links in a chain, Ligon's work not only points to the lapses of memory that have been required for the republic to imagine itself but also suggests how the selective occlusion of the past continues to falsify our imagining of the present. Executed for the artist's first show at a commercial venue, which opened—perhaps not coincidentally—on July 2, 1991, at New York's Jack Tilton Gallery, *1776–1865* can hardly do otherwise. Ligon's understated indictment thus seems to echo Frederick Douglass's scathing assessment of the nation's hypocrisy and thereby to keep alive, nearly 140 years later, his still pressing question: "What to the slave is the Fourth of July?"

Both men, I would argue, implicitly answer "nothing," though the ways each goes about giving shape to that nothingness—to the lack of voice, autonomy, and personhood that characterizes the position of the black subject—are, of course, purposefully different. Unlike the former slave, whose oration unfolds with dizzying rhetorical brilliance, Ligon dispenses with words and settles for the unassailable march of numbers themselves. Yet like Douglass, who cannot rejoice—"*I*," he declares, "must mourn" on the Fourth of July, Ligon has made a somber drawing, a listing that runs together, collapsing dates and darkly compressing time.[2] Here it is not the clock but the hand that keeps on ticking, patiently inscribing each numeral in its place within a grid while physically registering the occasional errors that arise in the course of such an exercise: an errant "18" crops up between 1824 and 1825, the year 1855 is missing altogether, but the work's core proposal still holds.

As did Douglass, Ligon seems to understand the political disavowal with which assertions of black freedom are met, and, like so many modernists, he mourns for a loss that we still cannot get over, a difficulty brought straight into the present by the conceptual pendant to *1776–1865*.[3] Beginning where that drawing left off, *Untitled (1865–1991)*—as its unassuming moniker implies—makes even less of a claim for the epochal status of its featured dates, merely holding out another cascade of digits that halt at the year of the work's execution (figure 4.2). The accounting of American history in these pieces cleaves at the date of abolition, materially enacting the disjuncture between eras of black oppression. Yet the works' almost

Figure 4.2 Glenn Ligon, *Untitled (1865–1991)*, 1991. Gouache, oil stick, and graphite on paper, 30 × 22¾ inches. © Glenn Ligon; Courtesy of the artist, Hauser & Wirth, and Thomas Dane Gallery.

identical modes of rote execution also intimate how the effects of the "peculiar institution" continue to induct us into the future even as we ostensibly move ever further from the primal scenes of the antebellum past. Taken together, these untitled drawings begin to make manifest the grounds from which this essay departs: namely, that the attempt to figure slavery, its legacies, and the modes of resistance to them, were of formative importance for Ligon's conception of history as well as his aesthetic means in the late 1980s and early 1990s, a tendency most dramatically evidenced by his large-scale exhibition *To Disembark* (1993).

Little of this inheritance, however, was brought to bear in initial accounts of his art. Just a few weeks before his opening at Jack Tilton, the "up and coming" painter was the subject of a Sunday *New York Times* profile. In her write-up, critic Roberta Smith situated Ligon's work not within traditions of black radical critique, but in relation to his seemingly antithetical personal experiences, beginning with his daily childhood commute from a South Bronx housing project to a West Side private school, and ending with his shift from painterly abstraction to a multimedia practice pointedly engaged with social issues. Ligon's peripatetic life had, according to Smith, enabled his art to "negotiate an unusually effective course between the visual and the linguistic, the visceral and the cerebral, and the personal and the political."[4]

In the quotation that gave the profile its title, the artist confirms his status as a nomad ever marooned between antinomies: "Lack of location is my location. I'm always shifting positions and changing my mind."[5] More than just a clue about his personal disposition, Ligon's statement sums up an attitude toward identity quite befitting his moment. The late 1980s and early 1990s were, after all, the salad days of identitarian critique, perhaps epitomized by cultural theorist Stuart Hall's well-known declaration of "the end of the innocent notion of the essential black subject."[6] Such interventions aimed to trouble the fixity so often presumed whenever race rears its impossible head, though for all the talk of hybrid and performative selves, mainstream criticism, by and large, further trivialized the work of black artists even as it was brought forward to capitalize on the reigning taste for alterity.[7] Fully aware of the limitations imposed upon so many practitioners of color during what he would later call the age of "High Multiculturalism," at the time, Ligon acknowledged his investment in African American history but was careful to hedge his bets toward the ambiguous.[8] When Smith asked if he considered himself a political artist, he responded: "I don't have any problem with the term if it means you're doing art about real life and what's most important to you. But sometimes it's used as a pejorative to criticize work that pushes a specific agenda. I hope my work is more open-ended, more about questioning positions than establishing a single position."[9]

This assertion has established something like an interpretive baseline for the whole of Ligon's practice, which has modeled a topical diversity and aesthetic promiscuity shaped by his social positioning as a gay man of African descent, even as his work interrogates the bases of social positioning as such. In the last fifteen years, he has gone on to recruit household furniture items in fantasizing the image-world of black queer youth (*Twin*, 1995); to videotape a session with his therapist in order to deconstruct his anxieties about the trajectory of his practice (*The Orange and Blue Feelings*, 2003); and to create neon sculptures featuring the words "negro sunshine"—a phrase culled from Gertrude Stein's 1909 novella *Melanctha*—in glowing three-foot-high letters (*Warm Broad Glow*, 2005).[10]

It is the paintings, however, that initially garnered Ligon a place among the foremost artists of his generation. Consider the earliest work included in his retrospective *Unbecoming*, which opened at Philadelphia's Institute of Contemporary Art in 1998 (figure 4.3). This untitled painting reiterates, destabilizes, and subtly queers the declaration of manhood featured on placards held out by protesting Memphis sanitation workers in 1968 as guards against scopic and bodily harm. The most recent work in the exhibition cast the first lines of James Baldwin's 1953 essay "Stranger in the Village"—an account of the writer's self-imposed exile to Switzerland—as a dark monochromatic screen that visually materialized the writer's double negation as black and gay. These two pieces functioned almost as bookends for Ligon's work of the previous decade, underlining how his art has consistently looked back to earlier moments for its historical and formal articulations.[11]

Along with any number of practitioners in this moment who evoked the socially marked body through figural surrogates—Janine Antoni, Robert Gober, and Byron Kim spring quickly to mind—Ligon was influenced by conceptualism's linguistic turn, minimalism's phenomenological address, and feminist critiques of media imagery. His wide-ranging engagements with and reframing of these practices have since become exemplary of how contemporary artists might take up yet ultimately resist univocal assertions of identity.[12] In his groundbreaking 1997 essay for the *Unbecoming* catalog, for example, Richard Meyer argues that Ligon mobilizes

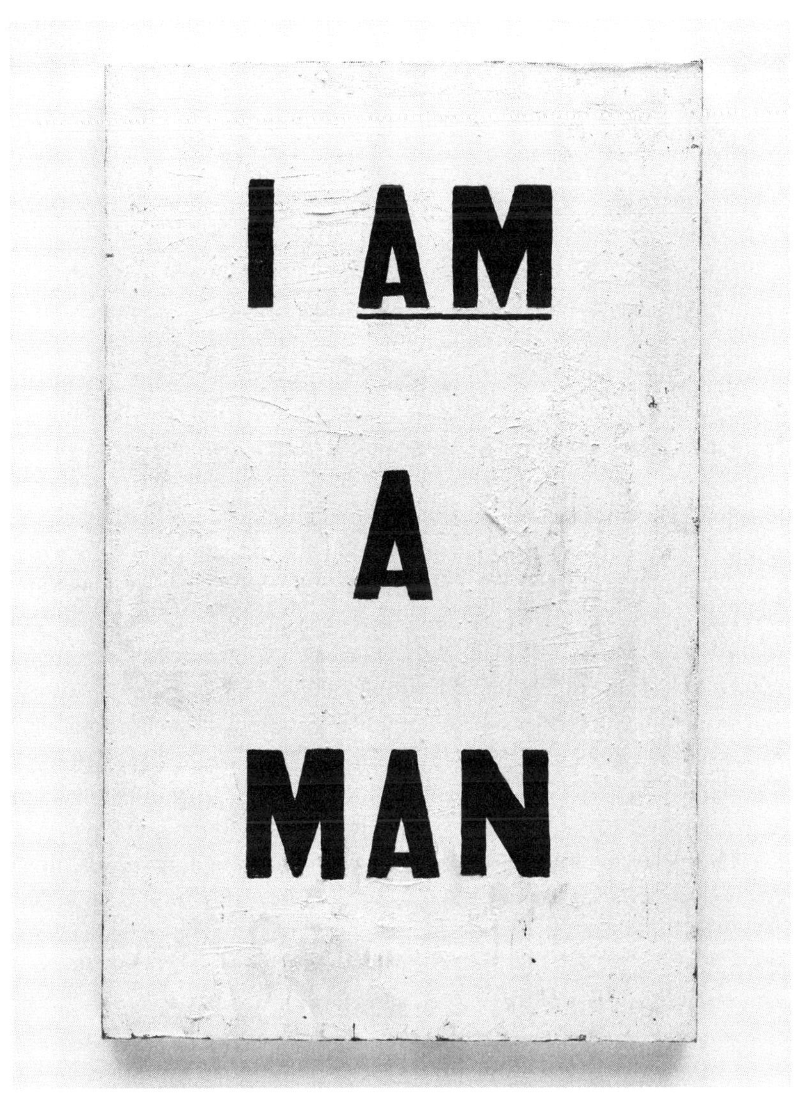

Figure 4.3 Glenn Ligon, *Untitled (I Am a Man)*, 1988. Oil and enamel on canvas, 40 × 25 inches. Collection of the National Gallery of Art, Washington, DC. © Glenn Ligon; Courtesy of the artist, Hauser & Wirth, and Thomas Dane Gallery. Photography credit: Ronald Amstutz.

language and its disappearance to demonstrate that particular subjects always necessarily exist in excess of the limits imposed by categories of racial or sexual difference.[13] Of late, Darby English has taken this line of thought to its logical conclusion in a series of rigorous meditations that explain how the artist dodges convenient dichotomies, sidestepping essentialist reductions of identity by rendering the "other" as an image always on the move.[14]

In their sustained attention to Ligon's practice, these art historians' readings help us to comprehend the relation between the artist's open-ended approach to language and his investment in revisiting specific figures and episodes. For Meyer, Ligon's work models a "dialectical engagement" with the past, while English suggests that history subtends the painter's "compositional method."[15] What I want to emphasize, however, is that in this artist's oeuvre history *matters*: his aesthetic means reflect an understanding of how modern discursive formations aimed at illuminating the contingency of the self are part and parcel of the epistemes of violence that continue to produce marked subjects. As Ligon would write of pioneering conceptual artist David Hammons and of equally innovative jazzman Sun Ra in his 2004 essay "Black Light," "not being from *here* is a movement toward placelessness, toward the utopic, *and* a deep critique of American society. Their genius was to employ a postmodern concern with the emptying of the self as a critical strategy, one that might have particular resonance with a people historically positioned at the margin of what was considered human."[16]

These comments are, I think, equally applicable to Ligon's own varied practice and contingent self-positioning, which root conceptions of the decentered subject in black peoples' storied tactics of survival and critique in the modern West. Indeed, over the course of his career, Ligon has consistently mined the archive, engaging the postures, fates, and visual technologies that produce African diasporic folk as runaways who define the limits of belonging and productively figure the aporias of representation. Whether he focuses on James Baldwin's eloquent prose or the protesting sanitation workers' blunt declaration, in bringing our attention to these men's words and demanding that we attempt to reread them, Ligon brings their fates to bear on the structuring of the self past and present, black and white, queer and otherwise. In so doing, he limns both their positions and his own, that sense of being continually unmoored, which Harold Cruse described more than forty years ago as the lot of the Negro intelligentsia as a whole, that "rootless class of displaced persons who are refugees from the social poverty of the black world."[17]

These facts of social fugitivity have engendered the artist's reflections on the homelessness of the black and the queer in the modern era. Just as important, his art reveals an attunement to and an understanding of the ways in which marginalized subject positions are anticipated by the placelessness of the enslaved, who long ago were forced to negotiate the "postmodern" problems attendant upon the dissolution of the self, the symbolic, and the social.[18] For, in addition to providing the linchpin of an emergent capitalist economy, captives served as prime objects for the regimes of knowledge, power, vision, and resistance that still differentially produce Western subjects.[19]

Another untitled work, this one from 1989, goes straight to the matter of these historical processes (figure 4.4). Here, the maroon ground of the paper has been reworked almost to the point of excoriation, though the stenciled text embedded within it can be made out readily enough: "Am I Not a Man and a Brother?" An inversion of the 1968 protesters' declaration and a rhetorical ploy much like Douglass's, this question was initially devised by eighteenth-century British abolitionists as a caption to accompany stock figures of half-dressed supplicating captives. Subsequently, the pairing of image and text was translated, revised, and reproduced throughout those nineteenth-century slave-holding societies in which abolitionist discourse had gained a foothold.[20] The scabrous surface of Ligon's drawing seems to memorialize the image's storied transmission while also recasting its ventriloquizing text. Instead of an inert motif that would again empty the enslaved of particularity, the work holds out a linguistic terrain whose very facture seems to crumble even as it freshly articulates an appeal to those ties of kinship and community that black subjects have historically been denied in their placement at the limit of, and as embodied loci for, modernity's modes of violence and visualization.

It is the legacy of these modes, either inaugurated within the peculiar institution or passionately posed against it, that haunts us in the present and that directly animates Ligon's exhibition *To Disembark*, first shown in 1993 at the Hirshhorn Museum and Sculpture Garden in Washington, DC. In this project, many of the concerns addressed in the artist's early work—the production of racial and sexual difference, the limits of American cultural politics, and the expansive capacities of placelessness—are historically moored, visually condensed, and so conceptually clarified through

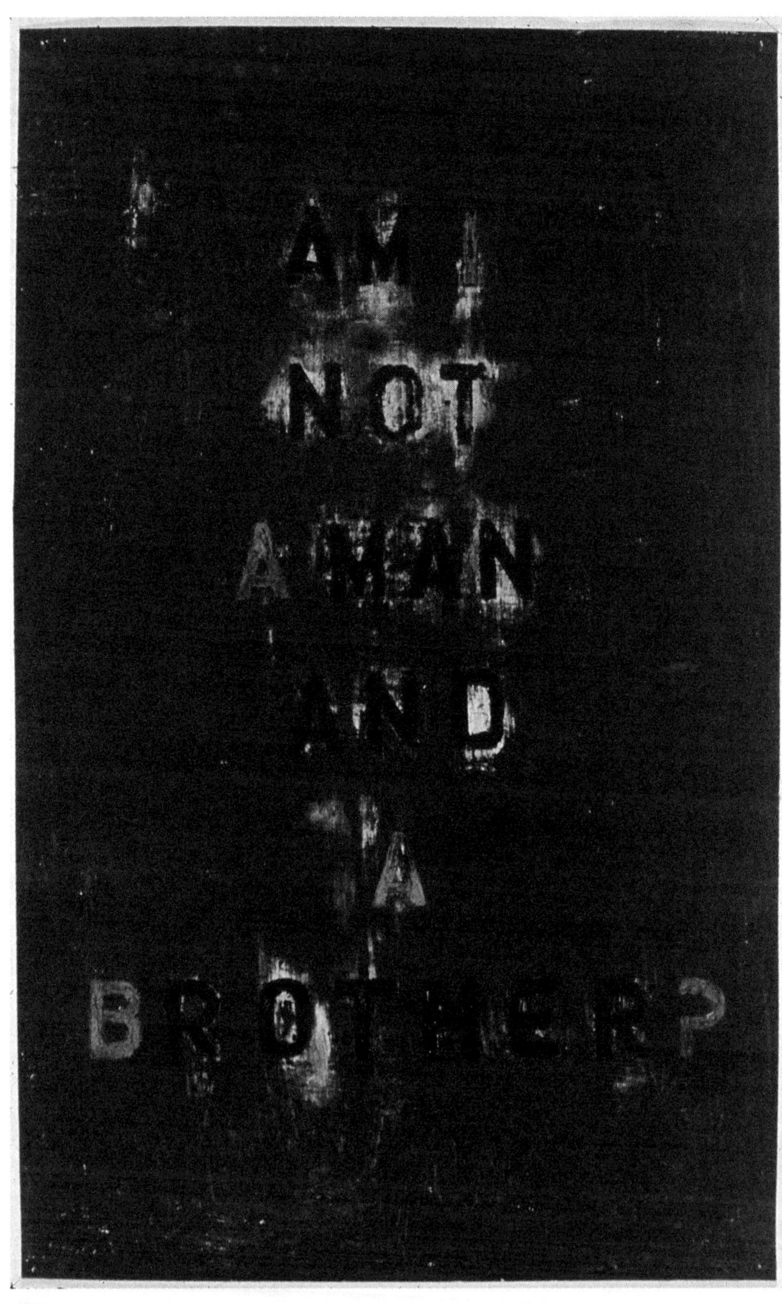

Figure 4.4 Glenn Ligon, *Untitled (Am I Not a Man And a Brother)*, 1989. Oil on paper, 48 × 30 inches. © Glenn Ligon; Courtesy of the artist, Hauser & Wirth, and Thomas Dane Gallery.

a multiplicity of forms that compulsively refer to the histories of slavery. What I want to argue is that in *To Disembark*, the peculiar institution and its various aftermaths are not simply agencies of oppression or marks of foreclosure but expansive openings through which we might begin to see the modern, the aesthetic, and ourselves differently both despite and because of the obstacles thrown up by representation and its remains in the archive.[21]

> You see, whites want black artists to mostly deliver something as if it were an official version of the black experience. But the vocabulary won't hold it, simply. No true account really of black life can be held, can be contained, in the American vocabulary. As it is, the only way that you can deal with it is by doing great violence to the assumptions on which the vocabulary is based. But they won't let you do that. And when you go along, you find yourself very quickly painted into a corner; you've written yourself into a corner.[22]
>
> —James Baldwin, 1987

In creating *To Disembark*, Ligon drew upon both generic framing conventions and highly specific historical episodes that he came upon while perusing various New York archives. In one gallery viewers confronted wooden shipping crates bearing international symbols for fragility. Collectively called *Untitled (To Disembark)*, the variously constructed containers in the exhibition were modeled after the 1849 conveyance in which Henry "Box" Brown shipped himself from captivity in Richmond to freedom in Philadelphia, where, upon arrival before his white benefactors, he broke into a hymn based on the Bible's fortieth Psalm, though his subsequent ballad would be sung to the tune of the popular air "Uncle Ned."[23] Ligon's boxes—scattered evenly about the room and all of roughly the same dimensions (30 by 36 by 24 inches)—pay appropriate homage to Brown's sonic celebration: each is outfitted with a tape recorder that emits barely audible sounds, from the songs of the McIntosh County Shouters to Billie Holiday's rendition of "Strange Fruit" to rapper KRS-One's "Sound of da Police."[24] Hung at regular intervals on the walls were ten offset lithographs (the work *Runaways*) that faithfully reproduce the format of nineteenth-century runaway handbills. In another gallery, viewers encountered *Narratives*, nine frontispieces to slave narratives that were never written, fictive texts loosely based in the artist's biography.[25] Drawn directly on these walls were four works in oil stick, each 80 by 30 inches and each deploying the title of and different sentences from Zora Neale Hurston's 1928 essay "How It Feels to Be Colored Me": "I remember the very day that I became colored," "I feel most colored when I am thrown against a sharp white background," and "I do not always feel colored."

As this description goes to show, every element of *To Disembark* pointed up the black body's absence from the representational frame, proffering indexes of its presence that betrayed nothing of the figure's actual location. Rather, in this project, the discursive materials of slavery were deployed to illuminate the structural coordinates of black being both past and present. Ligon might thus be said to comprehend, on a formal and a political level, the famous dictum from Walter Benjamin's "Theses on the Philosophy of History": "To articulate the past historically does not mean to recognize it 'the way it really was' (Ranke). It means to seize hold of a memory as it flashes up at a moment of danger. Historical materialism wishes to retain that image of the past which unexpectedly appears to man singled out by history at a moment of danger. The danger affects both the content of the tradition and its receivers."[26]

For the philosopher as for the artist, the memory of the past that volatilizes out of a moment of crisis cannot simply be held up as an example to be avoided, but must be held onto as revealing the exigencies that make our own moment possible in all of its ruinous tilt. In forging a link between the obstacles encountered by the fugitive slave and the dangers faced by the contemporary black subject, Ligon's work enacts a kind of repetition familiar to students of African American culture, so that history, text, and performance become circulating quantities always subject to reiteration and renewal.[27] In the process, the artist asks a question most eloquently posed in his own words: "Who are the other 'masters' from which we flee?"[28]

Historically, visuality itself has been construed as the mastering conceit from which black peoples have sought refuge. Indeed, the specular and panoptic modes of seeing that constituted the enslaved—on the one hand meant to display their abjection through an obscene violence, on the other to maintain their subjection through omnipresent surveillance—have been integral to the evolving production of the racialized body as a knowable site whose very being is not just revealed in the skin but rooted in the flesh.[29] Everywhere haunted by the gaze, African diasporic cultural practitioners have time and again turned to the word in posing alternative articulations of the self. Ligon was no exception.[30]

In the late 1980s, the artist came to realize that language could provide the basis for approaching what he called "a whole body of things," a whole body of blackness that could not otherwise be registered.[31] Words mattered because they expansively referred and they ably rerouted, bracketing the metonymic chain of associations—"tom-toms, cannibalism, intellectual deficiency"—which, as Frantz Fanon argued more than fifty years ago, are set off by the sight of dark skin and doggedly pursue black subjects whenever they appear.[32] In updating the theorist's laundry list of racial phantasms circa 1993, we might add the visage of "Willie" Horton, the "high-tech lynching" of Clarence Thomas, and of course the harrowing amateur videotape of motorist Rodney King being senselessly beaten.[33] Ligon and other contemporary African American artists, such as Gary Simmons, Lorna Simpson, and Danny Tisdale, felt compelled to address the demonization of black male subjectivity emblematized by such images; more than ever, the word was the faculty deemed most capable of doing so.[34] Language could take race out of the imaginary and make it a function of a larger symbolic system, revealing and short-circuiting the scenarios of violence and terror that have for centuries given blackness its objective weight within the psyche and throughout the mainstream media.[35]

At roughly the same time, black literary theory was rising in prominence within the academy, thanks to the efforts of scholars such as Henry Louis Gates Jr.; across the broader cultural landscape, there was growing acknowledgment of African American achievement in letters, from the approbation that greeted Toni Morrison's *Beloved* (1987) to the canonization of "lost" writers such as Zora Neale Hurston. Such developments were surely not lost on Ligon, whose work everywhere manifests a voracious appetite for the printed word. Yet he also well knew—as Baldwin's comments on the limits of the American vocabulary spell out—that language has never constituted a site of unfettered black expression, a fact best brought to light in *To Disembark* by the deployment of Hurston's text.[36]

Like the identically inscribed canvases that preceded them, these wall drawings transmute affective mantra into projective blur, figure into ground, word into image, white into black. This visual effect is a result of the artist's deductive procedure as he drags his stencil along the surface, one line after the next: "I feel most colored when I am thrown against a sharp white background. I feel most colored when I am thrown against a sharp white background. I feel most colored . . ." Regardless of the material on which the sentence is inscribed, we are eventually left in the dark, grasping at phrases that are a foregone conclusion. In these works, language in its corporeal and metaphorical dimensions casts blackness less as a fact of perception than as a frame of mind dependent upon the presence of whiteness for its meaning. The one is literally illegible without the other. Or, as Fanon stated about the making of men in modernity, "The Negro is not. Any more than the white man," both caught up in an antagonistic bind that disallows mutual recognition and therefore the attainment of the human on either side of the color line.[37]

In performing this impossibility and its perpetual recurrence within representation, Ligon's paintings stage the murkiness of racial thinking and run headlong into the dilemma thrown up by Fanon's negative ontology of race: black being cannot be accessed rationally, though its affective contours can be intimated in the gaps that structure hegemonic modes of speech. It is the plenitude, contingency, and symbolic import of black *feeling*, in other words, that open onto those fugitive states that the black image, in its liability for stereotypical reduction, would seem to preclude and that black letters can only obliquely manifest.[38] As the wall drawings intimate, every discourse can become a site of racial constraint, particularly given the dialectic of "I" and "we" that can at once bolster possibilities for African American collective action and stifle the particularity of individual lived experiences.[39]

This tension is exemplified by the life and work of Ligon's source. A prolific novelist, journalist, and ethnographer who came to prominence during the Harlem Renaissance, Hurston was nearly expunged from historical memory and roundly critiqued by her contemporaries for what they perceived as all manner of political incorrectness.[40] As if to drive this point home, Ligon has culled his lines from a text larded with stereotypes that fly in the face of its apparent insistence on the contextual character of racial identity; in fact, "How It Feels to Be Colored Me" has been cited as a prime example of Hurston's intransigence, even regression, by those who otherwise laud her writing as a model of black critical practice.[41] When cast as a darkening image, the author's words suggest how projective investments in racial filiation tend to cloud African American voices and ultimately to outstrip the command of language altogether.

The wall drawings thereby attest to Ligon's interest in the at once censoring and spectacularizing frameworks in which black being has been presented for public consumption, whether in the case of contemporary practitioners of color expected to speak compulsively of their identity,

Negro writers straining at the bonds of decorum, or ex-slaves attempting to prove their humanity through demonstrations of literacy. On this score, it is worth quoting the artist at length:

> I recently became interested in slave narratives because their modes of address and the conditions under which they were written had certain parallels to my questions about audiences and cultural authority. . . . I was interested in contemporary traces of the conditions under which former captives wrote their narratives. For example: what are the conditions under which works by black artists enter the museum? Do we enter only when our "visible difference" is evident? Why do many shows with works by colored people (and rarely whites) have titles that include "race" and "identity"? Who is my work for and what do different audiences demand of it?[42]

In asking such questions, Ligon does not posit an equal, direct, or analogical relation between himself and the slave. Instead, he looks for traces of those modes of subjection that have dispossessed black subjects and insistently conditioned their speaking, ever attentive to those threads that might be said to structure the possibilities of black expression and the figuration of the black "I."[43]

It is this imperative that also directs the titling of *To Disembark*'s frontispieces, the *Narratives*. Consider the page headed *Black Rage; or, How I Got Over*, which combines psychiatrists William H. Grier and Price M. Cobbs's fiery 1968 polemic with a gospel hymn made legendary by Mahalia Jackson. The titles introduce a text that promises "a full and faithful account of [Ligon's] commodification of the horrors of black life into art objects for the public's enjoyment." By roping book and song together, the text articulates the ways in which black aspiration is reproduced as spectacle, either anguished or transcendent. The third title of the narrative, "Sketches of the Life and Labors," refers back to accounts provided by nineteenth-century ministers of the gospel, situating the artist as a proselytizer for an autocritical engagement with his work and the production of blackness *tout court*.[44] Since slave narratives were often prefaced or concluded by the verifying testimony of white citizens, Ligon provides a quotation from African American cultural critic bell hooks that is meant to revise this tradition and license his own discourse: "When we talk about the commodification of blackness, we aren't just talking about how white people consume these images, but how black people and other people of color consume them, and how these become ways of knowing ourselves." The plays on convention in each *Narrative* thus construct historical continuities while also bringing forth constitutive disjunctures.

The page entitled *Incidents in the Life of a Snow Queen*, for example, riffs on Harriet Jacobs's 1861 narrative (figure 4.5), replacing the *Slave Girl* of her title with a present-day derogatory term for black gay men exclusively attracted to whites. Through this transcoding, it is possible to recover the queerness of Jacobs's text, from her attempted escape in sailor drag to her description of an enslaved male's sexualized humiliation at the hands of his young master.[45] Although the tactic of cross-gender impersonation is not unheard of in accounts provided by former runaways, references to homosexual practices on the plantation are exceedingly rare within the archive of slavery.[46] Such incongruities within the print are hyperbolized through the narration of the fictive author's "fall" toward homosexuality in nineteenth-century language rife with metaphors of whiteness as light, blindness, and snow, and by the simultaneous citation of contemporary black gay writer Hilton Als's account of drawing close to white men "in a climate so cold."

Ligon's engagements on this score reflect both his own concerns and an emergent cultural tendency. As evidenced by the work of Als, Essex Hemphill, Isaac Julien, and many others, the late 1980s and early 1990s were also a watershed moment for queer African diasporic practice.[47] Ligon's most well-known contribution to this discourse is his *Notes on the Margin of the Black Book* (1991–1993), a sprawling photo-text that interpolates Robert Mapplethorpe's images of nude black men with cultural commentaries indicative of the range of opinions generated by the white gay artist's work (figure 1.6). Seen in this light, the *Incidents in the Life* print offers a complementary take on the disruptive force of interracial homoerotic desire, holding out mannered text as opposed to vivid imagery in order to reveal the historical circumstances that continue to visually erase gays and lesbians of color from cultures that demand normative apparitions of blackness that are quickly categorized and easily devoured.

In their emphasis on the multiplicity of any given subject's possible affective identifications, the autobiographical fragments trotted out in the *Narratives* resist such totalizing racial and sexual scrims, just as *Runaways* stages the artist's successful escape from the very modes of epistemic violence to which he was never entirely available in the first place. Both bodies of work plunge into the well of figures and typefaces developed to

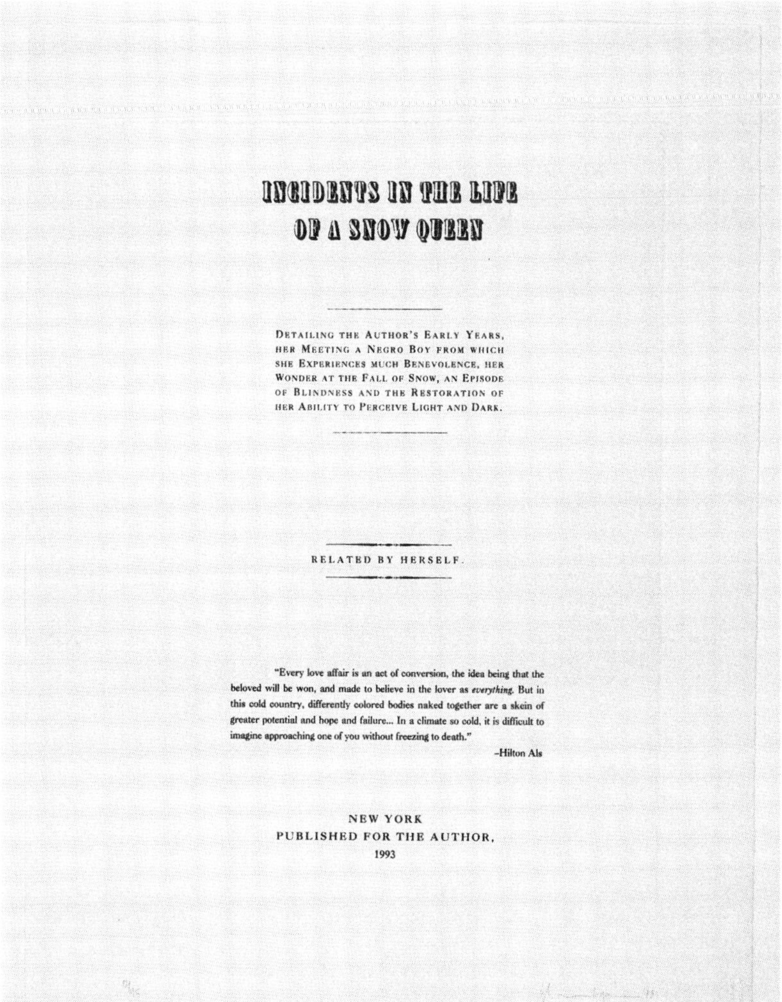

INCIDENTS IN THE LIFE
OF A SNOW QUEEN

DETAILING THE AUTHOR'S EARLY YEARS, HER MEETING A NEGRO BOY FROM WHICH SHE EXPERIENCES MUCH BENEVOLENCE, HER WONDER AT THE FALL OF SNOW, AN EPISODE OF BLINDNESS AND THE RESTORATION OF HER ABILITY TO PERCEIVE LIGHT AND DARK.

RELATED BY HERSELF.

"Every love affair is an act of conversion, the idea being that the beloved will be won, and made to believe in the lover as *everything*. But in this cold country, differently colored bodies naked together are a skein of greater potential and hope and failure... In a climate so cold, it is difficult to imagine approaching one of you without freezing to death."

–Hilton Als

NEW YORK
PUBLISHED FOR THE AUTHOR,
1993

Figure 4.5 Glenn Ligon, *Narratives* (detail), 1993. Suite of nine photogravures with chine collé, 28 × 21⅜ inches, edition of 45 and 10 artist's proofs. © Glenn Ligon; Courtesy of the artist, Hauser & Wirth, and Thomas Dane Gallery. Photography credit: Sheldan Collins.

frame the enslaved, assuring a formal affinity between the prints and their sources so that the latter might be better destabilized. Like the frontispieces of nineteenth-century slave narratives, Ligon's etchings are executed with chine collé, a process in which a fine sheet of paper is affixed to a cheaper backing material.[48]

However, his *Narratives* leave the scale of the book behind, assuming dimensions more fit to a portrait, and the *Runaways* lithographs—printed on creamy paper with rich brown inks—possess a sumptuous facture that is a far cry from the utilitarian look and feel of the original handbills that inspired them. Produced with the assistance of master printmaker Gregory Burnet and the backing of the artist's gallery, *To Disembark*'s printed matter is the result of techniques associated with nineteenth-century large-scale image manufacture, though they are intended for an art market that prizes limited runs and the artist's hand. Accordingly, each print is inscribed with an edition number and Ligon's signature, which index his engagement with the market for black authenticity even as his *Runaways*, in their production and referent, signify his removal from such networks of circulation.[49]

> Ran away, Glenn, a black male, 5'8", very short hair cut, nearly completely shaved, stocky build, 155–165 lbs., medium complexion (not "light-skinned," not "darkskinned," slightly orange). Wearing faded blue jeans, short sleeve button-down 50's style shirt, nice glasses (small, oval shaped), no socks. Very articulate, seemingly well-educated, does not look at you straight in the eye when talking to you. He's socially very adept, yet, paradoxically, he's somewhat of a loner.

This is one of the ten descriptions written by an unnamed friend of the artist (figure 1.3). Ligon instructed his accomplices to describe him, to render him in words as if he had gotten loose from language's grip, slipping out onto the streets of New York City to disappear into the crowd.[50] The writer in question has chosen first to concentrate on the formal qualities of the subject at hand, restlessly compiling an array of data that seem appropriate to a police report but are equally fitting as an update of a runaway advertisement. With its breathless clauses and elliptical closing assessment of the artist's interpersonal behavior, the paragraph seeks to characterize Ligon as a subject, to sketch a portrait in shorthand that gives some clue to what it might be like to bump into the artist on the street or at an art opening: the two final sentences bear the marks of time spent, of having acquaintance with Ligon's idiosyncrasies, the tics that constitute his presentation of self. What the description achieves, however, is not so much a lasting image as a set of rapidly thrown off impressions: Ligon refuses to cohere into a tangible picture, becoming a fantasized absence, though the outlines of a figure do emerge possessed of considerably greater specificity than that allowed by the fugitive icon.

In the pages that comprise *Runaways*, the descriptive text is paired with a visual header, generic male or female figures that operate in contradistinction to the specificity aimed at in the prints' language. These images have no pretensions to serving as representations, but work more along the lines of symbolic placeholders that mark out the runaway's structural location. Without the aid of language, the image can only serve to alert the reader that something is amiss, that some species of black flesh has gotten loose from its moorings within the social hierarchy and must be put back in its place. This, of course, was the function the runaway slave bulletin performed in its heyday, a function exemplified by the following advertisement printed in the 1850s in the New Orleans *Daily Picayune*:

> Twenty Dollars Reward—Ran away from the subscriber, the boy Tom. Said boy is black, 5 feet 7 or 8 inches high, has a piece cut out of one ear, is about 26 years old. The above reward will be paid if he is lodged in any jail in the State; if caught in a free State, I will pay $500 if he is brought to me in New Orleans.
>
> —John Ermon, corner of Camp and Race streets.[51]

To put it mildly, this description lacks all the insouciant charm, psychological probity, and queer sensibility displayed in Ligon's prints, instead focusing on the vagaries of the hunt and the restitution of property. "Twenty Dollars Reward" puts the cash on the table right up front, though this sum would have been a mere fraction of the exchange value of the slave, which might well have been in the vicinity of two thousand dollars.[52] The real money was to be made in recapturing escapees who had somehow managed to make it north, and advertisements like this one served to heighten the intensity of the gaze that fell on black bodies.

Every dark figure might be searched for telltale signs of fatigue, disorientation, or foreignness that might transform an unattended person back into a fungible asset. Most telling for the bounty hunter were the specific markers pointing to acts of physical violence inscribed upon the slave's body. As his former master recounts, Tom's ear has been cut or mutilated, a standard punishment for those who had attempted to escape from bondage only to be tracked down, re-enslaved, and confronted with the violent retribution of their masters.[53] For the large portion of runaways—like Tom, mostly males in their late teens and twenties—fleeing was a dangerous proposition with no guarantee of success, the possibility of recapture looming everywhere as owners attempted to reassert control over what they saw to be rightfully theirs.[54] But despite the prospect of whipping, further mutilation, and being separated from their kinfolk, the enslaved did run away: the penultimate act of defiance amidst a range of resistive tactics that included sabotage, willful incompetence, outright rebellion, and suicide. Captives seized upon whatever means were available to frustrate the repression of slavery, to refuse its way of life, and subsequently to upset the myth of the docile slave so prevalent in pro- and anti-abolitionist imagery.

In this respect fugitives no doubt succeeded. Although the advertisement run in the *Picayune* in aid of Tom's procurement does not dwell for any time on his psychological makeup, many masters felt it necessary to qualify their descriptions with a battery of behavioral as well as physical characteristics. Slave owners developed a complex lexicon of terms, both words on the page and inscriptions on the flesh, intended to telegraph the color, proportions, and persona of the runaway. Adjectives like proud, artful, plausible, cunning, amiable, polite, wily, and deceitful reappeared with astonishing frequency in the descriptions given by masters, registering the individuality of the slave, but also constituting a shifting portrait of the fugitive subject.[55]

Above all, slavery's status quo was endangered by the fugitive's ability to dissemble, to put on a false impression that allowed him to pass for what he was not, to make his disposition absent just as his body would subsequently become. The runaway slave signified the onus on the owner to recover his property and the threat that the peculiar institution had gone awry, its order undone and its objects restored to themselves, even if only momentarily. Consequently, the fugitive is a figure who muddies and disturbs fantasies of the idyllic antebellum South, leaving the confines of the plantation in order to inhabit a placeless horizon. Just as the runaway sought to move beyond his status as property, to duck the system of surveillance and representation meant to curtail, restrict, and ultimately cease his sojourn, his vivid absence remained a blight in the memory of his owner and a bastion of hope for those still enslaved.

The whole of *To Disembark* seeks to explore this liminal condition, mobilizing the trope of fugitivity in its limiting and liberatory capacities. Throughout the work, the repetition and deformation of that which persists within the archive becomes a substitute for the ability to access a storehouse of black collective memory that in point of fact was never available and that exists now only as a set of traces whose refiguring allows us to recollect the runaway subject.[56] "Glenn" and "Tom" are summoned through the force of word and image, which serve as surrogates for black bodies no longer available either as sight or as property, objects of speculation that have disappeared. Though they seem to occupy vastly divergent historical situations, there is a sense in which both men are fleeing from the same master: the white overlord has simply been replaced by the specter of the symbolic order for which he claimed to stand.

Another print, which includes a scene of a white gentleman clasping the shoulder of a half-dressed slave, helps illustrate this contention (figure 3.2). The text here is rather more laconic than in the first of the *Runaways* addressed, but for that reason even more striking in its foci:

> Ran away, Glenn Ligon. He's a shortish broad-shouldered black man, pretty dark-skinned, with glasses. Kind of stocky, tends to look down and turn in when he walks. Real short hair, almost none. Clothes nondescript, something button-down and plaid, maybe, and shorts and sandals. Wide lower face and narrow upper face. Nice teeth.

This writer has made no attempt to characterize the artist's persona but has stayed true to the facts as they presented themselves, an emphasis on the data of visual perception summarized in that final clinching phrase: "Nice teeth."

It is precisely this type of proscription imposed in representation and by institutional structures that Glenn, like Tom, is running away from. The stakes are different but the problematic remains, for it is in the disjunctions as much as in the continuities that the resonance of Ligon's work lies: "nice teeth" is not the same as saying "good teeth," the latter an index of health, a selling point for the slave master, the former a compliment of purely cosmetic nature paid to a friend. Both assessments speak to appearance, but the one serves to indicate value and the other to register its attainment, casting the artist within a particular socioeconomic milieu that goes along swimmingly with "something button-down and plaid, maybe, shorts and sandals." As ever, language places, makes evident some kind of real or imagined societal location.

Which is not to say that Ligon believes language itself to be suspect by virtue of its ability to prescribe or interpellate the subject, since it is those very qualities in which his work takes such pleasure. Despite the fact that several different writers with rather different voices have taken stabs at describing the artist, their words do end up resting on a set of shared terms, as evidenced by the following *Runaways* text, which seems to combine and reorder the other two (figure 4.6).

> Ran away, Glenn. Medium height, 5'8", male. Closely-cut hair, almost shaved. Mild looking, with oval shaped, black-rimmed glasses that are somewhat conservative. Thinly-striped black-and-white short-sleeved T-shirt, blue jeans. Silver watch and African-looking bracelet on arm. His face is somewhat wider on bottom near the jaw. Full-lipped. He's black. Very warm and sincere, mild-mannered and laughs often.

In this case, the artist's race appears very late in the passage, almost as an afterthought bracketed by "full-lipped" and "very warm and sincere, mild-mannered and laughs often." What becomes apparent here is the way the black male body in any description, however benign, bears some relation to a history of stereotype and racial prejudice.[57]

Ligon is well aware of these mechanisms, and every aspect of *To Disembark* points up the historical and ongoing conditions in which African Americans enter the cultural frame.[58] In fact, he has gone on to exhibit the various elements of the installation in a number of different combinations. The work is not, then, a site-specific project in the original sense of the term, which implied the physical inseparability of an object from the site in which it was executed, as in the case of, say, Robert Smithson's *Partially Buried Woodshed* (1970), whose moldering fragments can still be found on the campus of Kent State University. Rather, like the projects of his contemporary Renée Green, Ligon's installation represents a mode of site-sensitive practice, in which the peripatetic status of the work of art indexes that of the black body, thus referring us back to the racialized frameworks of institutional display regardless of locale.[59] As such, *To Disembark*, like Ligon's art as a whole, models tactics—in Michel de Certeau's sense of "calculated action[s] determined by the absence of a proper locus"—aimed at disrupting the logic of its own conditions of appearance.[60]

Just as the artist turned to installation to turn the genre out, his objects figure the self as a set of tactile surfaces and texts without a sure

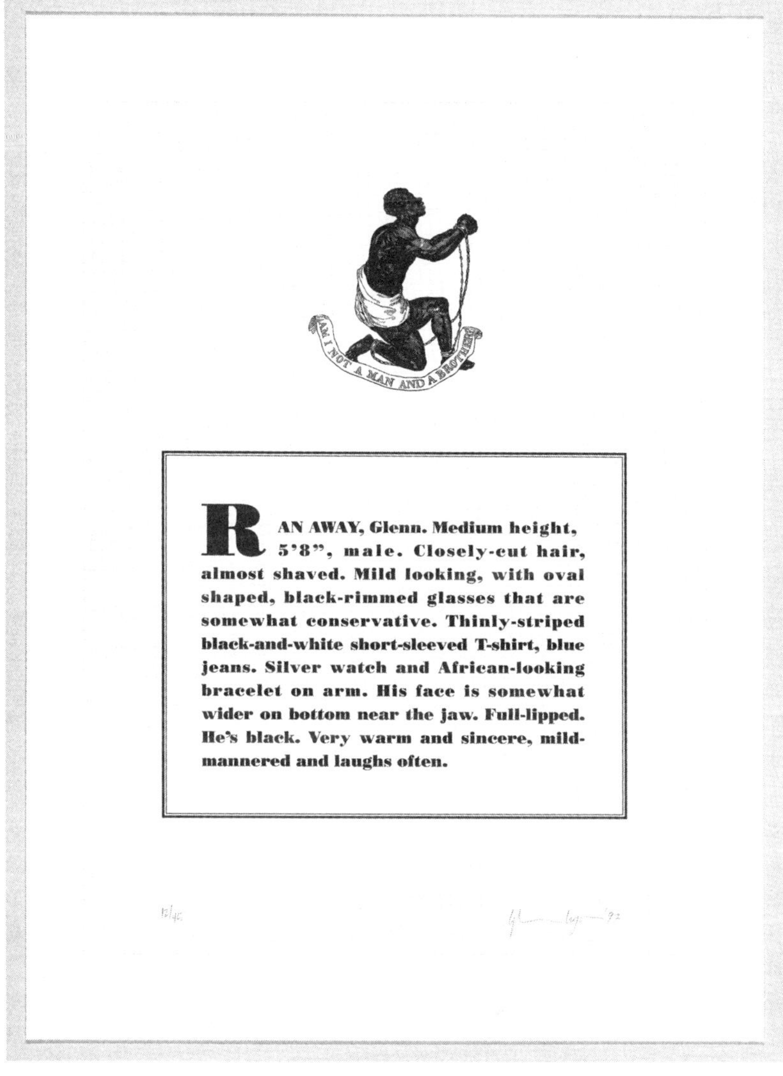

Figure 4.6 Glenn Ligon, *Runaways* (detail), 1993. Suite of ten lithographs, 16 × 12 inches, edition of 45 and 10 artist's proofs. © Glenn Ligon; Courtesy of the artist, Hauser & Wirth, and Thomas Dane Gallery. Photography credit: Jeff McLane.

autobiographical referent: the *Runaways* declare his absence, the wall drawings are haunted by the hand that executed them, and the frontispieces, despite their offerings of accompanying portraits and their assertions to have been written by the artist himself, are unstable and conflicting revisions of a life story that cannot be countenanced. Ligon comes to us as a fugitive from history who models the various modes of narration deployed by himself and others to contest it, producing incident rather than authenticity and questioning the viewer's demand for forms of blackness that ostensibly give life to the subject but often only manage to reiterate the slave's social death.[61]

> A number of persons soon collected round the box after it was taken in to the house, but as I did not know what was going on I kept myself quiet. I heard a man say "let us rap upon the box and see if he is alive"; and immediately a rap ensued and a voice said, tremblingly, "Is all right within?" to which I replied—"all right." The joy of friends was very great; when they heard that I was alive they soon managed to break open the box, and then came my resurrection from the grave of slavery.[62]
>
> —Henry "Box" Brown, 1851

The most striking aspect of the exhibition *To Disembark* is surely the presence of the crates that shape the viewer's movement through the space (figure 4.7). With them, Ligon moved fully into three dimensions for the first time, a shift prompted, I think, by the difficulty of bringing enslavement into view in purely imagistic or textual terms: in Brown's box, the artist recovered a form capable of marking the slave's conflicted status as person and property, of spatially charting the black subject's lack of location, and of figuring the body without requiring its appearance, avoiding the spectacular representation of suffering colored souls.[63]

For his part, Brown happily made himself a rather different sort of spectacle following his escape: for a while, he was the toast of the abolitionist lecture circuit, where he would arrive at each venue by box and burst forth with a Houdini-esque flourish in a reperformance of his miraculous "resurrection." However, he was not immediately free from the recriminations of his masters, and not merely because his flamboyant showmanship did not accord with prevailing notions of behavior appropriate for a grateful former slave.[64] The 1850 Fugitive Slave Act forced him to flee to England

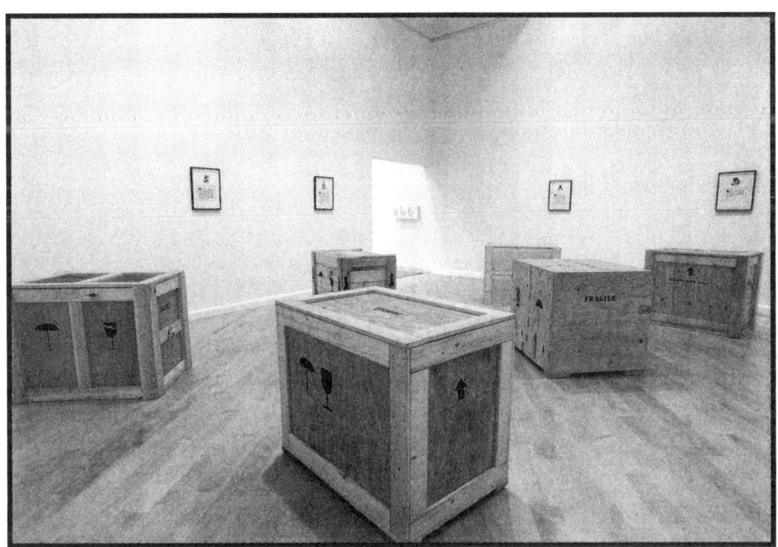

Figure 4.7 Glenn Ligon, installation view of *Untitled (To Disembark)* (1993), Smithsonian Hirshhorn Museum and Sculpture Garden, 1993. Nine wood crates with synthetic polymer, acrylic paint, and nine audio recordings, dimensions variable. © Glenn Ligon; Courtesy of the artist, Hauser & Wirth, and Thomas Dane Gallery. Photography credit: Lee Stalsworth.

and there to reconstitute his most useful public relations tool, a large multi-panel panorama entitled *Mirror of Slavery*. In contrast to his widely seen and much circulated narrative, song, and images, Brown's moving panorama—composed of scenes depicting the evils of the institution and once featured in town halls throughout the Northeast—is no longer extant. But in the surviving list of the work's some forty tableaux, we find evidence of Brown's awareness of the recursive turnings of subjection.[65] While the final image is said to have figured an immense jubilee in celebration of "Universal Emancipation," two previous scenes depict "Nubians Escaping by Night," followed somewhat later by "Nubian Slaves Retaken."[66]

Escape, it seems, is never definitive and freedom never absolute. Yet, in enduring a self-imposed thirty-hour imprisonment within its confines, Brown marked his unlikely transport as the focal point of a parodic tactic that made visible the pecuniary underpinnings of enslavement only to undo them: box as cell, slave, and talking commodity all at once. Perhaps the greatest irony that emerges from his adventure, then, is that this particular slave can only attain some semblance of worth through an elaborate act of masquerade in which he literalizes his status as a thing. In accomplishing this feat, a perverse rewriting of the Middle Passage, Brown pointed up the despotic relations between people that undergird capitalist production, while also describing the slave's aporetic position within them.[67] His box thus not only signifies on slavery's metaphorics of life, death, and rebirth, but also on its economics, the mechanics of monetary flow that still exert a tenacious grasp on the subject.[68]

I would argue that Brown's sojourn can be seen as a mode of black radical critique that disturbs and upends even the logic of Karl Marx's well-known disquisition in "The Fetishism of the Commodity and Its Secret." In this chapter of *Capital* (1867), Marx ventriloquizes the modes of speech conferred upon commodities by classical economists in order to lambaste the theory that objects have inherent value outside of exchange and the impossible notion that things might give voice to their desires.[69] Yet Brown's performance—like the testimony of so many ex-slaves—gives weight to the idea that the commodity does, indeed, speak: as Fred Moten has argued, "That speech . . . constitutes a kind of temporal warp that disrupts and augments not only Marx but the mode of subjectivity that the ultimate object of his critique, capital, both allows and disallows."[70]

This complex stew of capital, fetishism, and subjection is part and parcel of Ligon's turn to Brown's story as the structuring conceit of *Untitled (To Disembark)*. In so doing, he by no means reduces the slave to a void stuck in a box. Rather, the artist's maneuver short-circuits the logic of capital itself and forces us to realize the duplicity of its constructions, the arbitrariness of its object choices. Henry Brown's box is, after all, just a box; similarly, the commodity fetish is not so much the object itself, its material worth, or even its symbolic force, but its power to accrue meaning as value and to reproduce the network of exchange.[71] *Untitled (To Disembark)* points to these hyperbolic processes of systematization and disappears the literal enslaved body from their routes of commerce even as it conflates a whole set of fetishistic models with a single gesture—the commodity, the absent body, and the minimalist object.[72]

Ligon's boxes rewrite the gestalts of a Robert Morris with a twist, recalling the minimalist sculptor's *Untitled (Battered Cubes)* of 1965 as well as his 1974 audio installation *Voice*, which comprised an eight-channel stereo system and fourteen wooden boxes covered with felt.[73] The most salient referent, however, is Morris's *Box with the Sound of Its Own Making* of

1961, which consists of a tape recorder nestled within a wooden container that resounds with the noises of its construction and harks back to Marcel Duchamp's *With Hidden Noise* of 1916.[74] In each case, a thing is imbued with an ability to speak itself; in Ligon's works, which might be renamed *Boxes with the Sound of Self-Making*, such speech is recoded as that of a narrator describing his journey, taking viewers on an aural traipse through black musical history, only to suspend them on the perilous road where the benighted object becomes voiced subject. Just as important, the crates of *Untitled (To Disembark)* articulate the historical anteriority of resistive tactics employed by the enslaved that were aimed at simultaneously undoing and exploiting the conflation of persons and things that has shaped the contours of blackness and the direction of the aesthetic in the modern era.

To be sure, Ligon is not alone in his purposive recasting of Brown's conveyance as material object, a fact that attests to the resonance of the fugitive's journey as a metaphor for black experience that is at once uncanny, wondrous, demonstrative, and accusatory.[75] To wit, the section on the Underground Railroad at the National Great Blacks in Wax Museum in Baltimore, Maryland, has since 1988 featured an eerily animated effigy of Brown, who emerges from and disappears into a large crate marked "Adams Express," endlessly performing Brown's departure and arrival so as to vivify the experience of enslavement for the edification of the museum's audiences, particularly its youngest patrons.[76]

Most influential for Ligon, however, was the artist Pat Ward Williams's *32 Hours in a Box . . . And Still Counting* of 1987.[77] In this work, a rectangle of text written on the floor describes contemporary scenes of racial discrimination and encloses four white pillars mounted with images—a violin, a doll, a rose, and a skyscraper—which, in their turn, frame Williams's iteration of Brown's box. Her construction gives us two views of a black man doubled over in a container, revealing the contortions of his body beneath the latticework of its walls. Like panes of a window filled with photographs rather than glass, the sides of the structure function according to the conceit of transparency just as its title underlines the perpetuity of collective black incarceration and the text inscribed along its base—"HENRY BOX BROWN WHO ESCAPED SLAVERY ENCLOSED IN A BOX 3 FEET WIDE AND 2 LONG"—demands a cyclical movement around the sculpture.[78]

What enables *32 Hours*' feint of interpretive closure is a collapse of historical frames that constitutes slavery as a generative metaphor that asymptotically engages the present through recourse to an irrefutably tragic past. It is a canny maneuver, one that weaves Brown and his latter-day avatar into a seamless narrative in which fugitivity signifies only the promise of new forms of subjection. Because despite the images of civilized achievement depicted in the photographs on the pillar, if he were to escape his cell, the man depicted in Williams's work would surely not receive the same warm reception that greeted Mr. "Box" Brown: neither hearty applause from white liberal supporters nor a book contract, but the intractable reality of racialized aggression summed up so succinctly by the work's external ring of text and its loops of barbed wire.

Williams's and Ligon's projects are equally invested in the former slave's narrative and pay close attention to the dimensions of his incongruous carriage. Visually, the similarities seem to end there. Ligon shows no desire to offer us a freshly minted photograph of the black male body imprisoned. Nor does he construct an index of the real that eclipses the distance between now and then, making crystal clear the continuities between the two. Such divergences are ultimately symptomatic, I think, of Ligon's and Williams's differing understandings of how history ought to be conceived. For Williams, the past reads as a deferral of the present that must be vigilantly reimagined: representation becomes an aid to memory and history a refracting lens through which to judge the course of current events, which continue to reveal the inextricable link between barbarism and civilization.[79] Ligon, on the other hand, embarks on a path of re-presentation that interrogates the regimes of viewership that subtend the afterlife of slavery.[80] The boxes in *To Disembark* function as the opaque loci of a discursive field indicative of the visual forms that constructed the runaway and allowed him differing degrees of autonomy: the broadsheets' prescriptive account of personality, the narratives' confining conventions, and the word's inevitable fading from particular declaration to predictable if inscrutable blackness.

Viewed from this retrospect, Brown's own manic proliferation of autoexpressive media takes on a renewed poignancy. In addition to his performances, panorama, images, and hymn, the fugitive reconfigured his 1849 narrative two years later in order to get right what his white amanuenses could not see fit to print.[81] Not dissimilarly, the likeness of Brown that provided the frontispiece to his first narrative is itself a generic type, which served as the portrait for another ex-slave's narrative and which appears as the header for another of the *Runaways* (figure 4.8), as if to

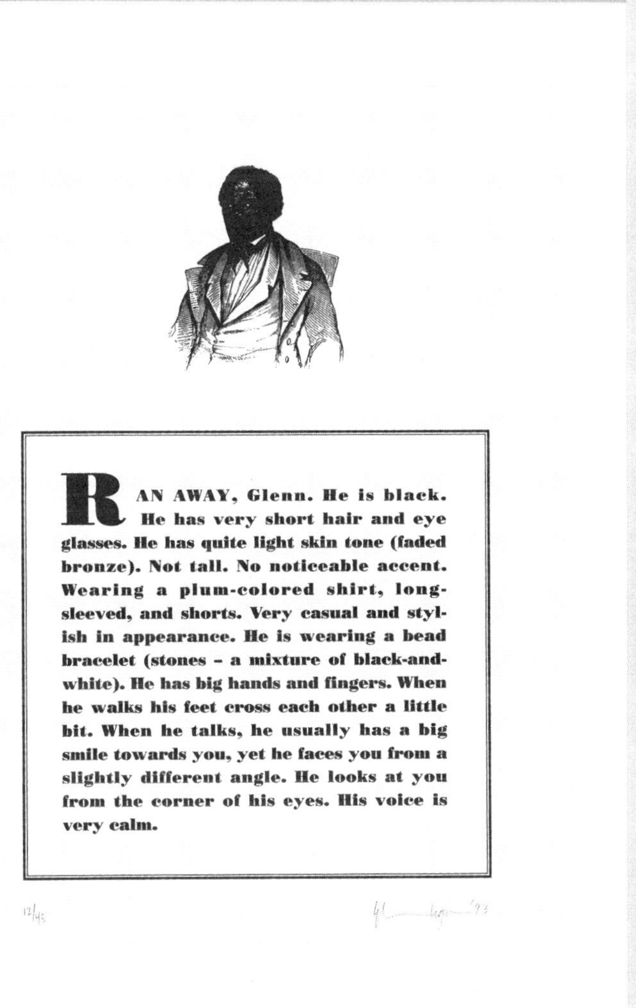

Figure 4.8 Glenn Ligon, *Runaways* (detail), 1993. Suite of ten lithographs, 16 × 12 inches, edition of 45 and 10 artist's proofs. © Glenn Ligon; Courtesy of the artist, Hauser & Wirth, and Thomas Dane Gallery. Photography credit: Jeff McLane.

intimate the black subject's constitutive exchangeability as object of slavery and subject of contemporary art.[82] Then as now, African American cultural practitioners have played numerous modes of representation off each other to secure space for the articulation of an autonomous self within verbal and visual regimes intent on their singular scripting.[83]

The various modes of figuration in the exhibition *To Disembark* reflect these aspects of slavery that continue to resonate for understandings of the self. In particular, nineteenth-century legal discourse on the runaway provided a model for intellectual property law's commodification of image, word, and voice, opening onto the analogical similarities between the fugitive subject and the fungible aspects of subjectivity, which map capitalist culture's ever-increasing subjugation of personhood to possession.[84] Ligon's ensemble casts the processes of theft and reification that shaped the production of the fugitive in the present tense, absconding with the properties of others to create a liminal space for the expression of black sounds and queer desires in excess of the representations that would constrain them. By pressing the verbal against the visual, the past against the present, the individual against the group, the black against the queer, *To Disembark* gestures to an exterior in order to carve out a space for being otherwise that takes its measure from the historical positioning of subjects cast as fugitives in life and in representation.[85]

With that said, we are now ready to disembark. As we have seen, Ligon is a master of felicitously chosen words that are capable of sampling multiple histories, traditions, and theoretical suppositions that find themselves evoked, only to be detained, as if to echo the complexity of the present and our positions within it, which emerges as a set of discourses that overlap and oppose one another. *To Disembark*, in other words, emblematizes both our relation to the archive and a tendency within Ligon's practice. Taken from this angle, the installation's titular phrase means not so much to reach the end of a journey as to endlessly retrace its course in search of openings always under threat of disappearance. This is what the work effectively demands of us. Moving through it means positioning oneself in relation to the history of slavery, unveiling the recursive logic of stereotype, and engaging with the artist's multiple "selves." "To disembark" is to assume responsibility for the production of meaning, to run away from the prison-house of language, and to reconstitute ourselves in the traces we leave in our wake.

The installation is a spatial text, and our movement within it becomes a bodily reading as we recode its utterances, turning them over in our hands, poaching them to arrive at our own meaning.[86] As viewers navigate the work, they become aware not only of their bodies in space but also of the circumstances that inducted them into the museum. Neither fully mooring us before the wall, nor entirely subjecting us to the sculptural demand, *To Disembark* relies upon a contingent relation to the visual that is not dependent on a point of mastery but that understands the placelessness from which the gaze itself originates.[87] The work proposes a kind of aporetic looking, a reading askance, a fugitive walking meant to refigure the self even as it is contained in the box of blackness. And it is from that location, the placeless place of the fugitive, where the present freshly comes into view, though the prospect that *To Disembark* offers is perhaps a damning one.

Are African American artists today unable to come to voice within mainstream artistic discourse despite their increasingly splashy landings on the shores of culture? Have black queer subjects just gotten off the boat, at times able to articulate themselves openly but still effectively denied a place within African American culture at large? Do these arrivals, such as they may be, signal not so much advancement as the beginning of a new, even more insidious stage in the exploitation of black difference and perversity? Who, finally, is arriving from where and when and with what avenues for redress? All of these queries fall somewhere close to the mark, though to privilege one more than the others would be to hamstring the discursive force of the work, if not to miss the point of its multiple voices altogether.

To get closer to the tenor and texture of those voices, it is helpful to turn to Gwendolyn Brooks's deceptively slim volume of poetry from which the exhibition takes its name. Published in 1981, her *To Disembark* looks to the recent past of black resistance movements in America and abroad in order to measure distance traveled, to take stock of the present political crisis, and to mourn the men and women lost in the arrival of a revolutionary black consciousness. This epoch-making moment in black culture often motivates the poet's descriptions, whether she is elegizing "young heroes," pointing out scenes of senseless black death, or condemning the petty slights and false self-importance of current black leaders.[88] Arguably, Ligon took up this volume because it evokes material circumstances on the ground so vividly and because it describes how blackness gets figured, felt, and lived at a moment when one journey seems to have ended and another to have begun. In this sense, Brooks's text sets out the ambitions for the artist's installation, which is also underwritten by the imperative to assess the current situation through the lens of history and to mourn its future.

For, in *To Disembark*, the subject darkened by the optics of race and sex arrives over and over again—from slavery, from segregation, from rebellion and persecution and catastrophe—though he never comes any closer to arriving at a destination that would emancipate him or entirely foreclose his individual possibilities. It is this sense of a missed encounter with the present that haunts the installation. Arising like a flash in the moment of danger, slavery serves as the meditative node where the contours of blackness now come into focus. In reaching back to the past, Ligon reaches out for what Saidiya Hartman has called the fugitive's dream, "a dream of autonomy rather than nationhood," "of an elsewhere, with all its promises and dangers, where the stateless might, at last, thrive."[89]

In their contingency and multivalence, the artist's visual means suggest the difficulty of keeping that dream alive and the wily disposition needed to do so, an ability to adapt and abandon and abscond, always alert to the losses such fugitivity entails and the liberation it promises. In the aftermath of the revolutionary upheavals of the 1960s, an agonistic engagement with the global order of things often feels impossible, especially given the economies that would constitute us and deliver the world as always already packaged, delimited, boxed. Under these conditions, there is little hope for escape, but there are perhaps no better tactics of evasion than those developed by fugitives who have long had to survive as material and phantasmatic grist for the machinery of capital and who have managed to do so by taking wing regardless of where they might land.

Notes

This article derives from my 2006 dissertation, completed at UC Berkeley under the inimitable direction of Anne M. Wagner, and is an excerpt from my book *Bound to Appear: Art, Slavery, and the Site of Blackness in Multicultural America* (Chicago: University of Chicago Press, 2013). In preparing this essay for publication, I have benefited from the comments and criticism of numerous scholars, but in particular, my thinking has been deepened by the comments of T. J. Clark and Saidiya Hartman—both members of my dissertation committee—as well as by the thoroughgoing engagements of Stephen Best, Nicholas Sammond, Krista Thompson, and the anonymous readers at the University of Chicago Press.

1. Frederick Douglass, "What to the Slave Is the Fourth of July?," extract from an oration at Rochester, New York, July 5, 1852, in Douglass, *My Bondage and My Freedom* (New York: Dover, 1969), 442.

2. Douglass, "What to the Slave," 441; emphasis in original.

3. On mourning and modernist painting, see Yve-Alain Bois, "Painting: The Task of Mourning," in *Painting as Model* (Cambridge, MA: MIT Press, 1990), 229–244.

4. Roberta Smith, "Lack of Location Is My Location," *New York Times*, June 16, 1991, H27.

5. Glenn Ligon, quoted in Smith, "Lack of Location," H27.

6. Stuart Hall, "New Ethnicities," in *Black Film, British Cinema, ICA Document* 7, ed. Kobena Mercer (London: Institute of Contemporary Arts, 1988), 28.

7. Charles Gaines, "The Theater of Refusal," in *The Theater of Refusal: Black Art and Mainstream Criticism*, ed. Catherine Lord and Charles Gaines (Irvine: University of California Fine Arts Gallery, 1993), 13–21. For more on this problem in relation to African American artistic practice of the late 1980s and early 1990s, see my "'Bye, Bye Black Girl': Lorna Simpson's Figurative Retreat," *Art Journal* 64, no. 2 (Summer 2005): 62–77.

8. The artist, as quoted in Huey Copeland, "Post/Black/Atlantic: A Conversation with Thelma Golden and Glenn Ligon," in *Afro Modern: Journeys through the Black Atlantic*, ed. Tanya Barson and Peter Gorschlüter (Liverpool: Tate Publishing, 2010), 79.

9. Smith, "Lack of Location," H27.

10. All of the Ligon works cited but not pictured in these pages are illustrated in *Glenn Ligon: Some Changes*, exh. cat., ed. Thelma Golden and Wayne Baerwaldt (Toronto: The Power Plant, 2005).

11. These lines redact a key thread of my argument in "Untitled (Jackpot!)," in *Glenn Ligon: Some Changes*, 119–132.

12. Richard Meyer, "Light It Up, or How Glenn Ligon Got Over," *Artforum* (May 2006), 241.

13. Richard Meyer, "Borrowed Voices: Glenn Ligon and the Force of Language," in *Glenn Ligon: Unbecoming*, exh. cat., ed. Judith Tannenbaum (Philadelphia: Institute of Contemporary Art, 1997), 34 (reprinted in this volume).

14. Darby English, *How to See a Work of Art in Total Darkness* (Cambridge, MA: MIT Press, 2007), 204; and English, "Glenn Ligon: Committed to Difficulty," in *Glenn Ligon: Some Changes*, 60.

15. See Meyer, "Light It Up," 245; and English, "Committed to Difficulty," 58.

16. Glenn Ligon, "Black Light: David Hammons and the Poetics of Emptiness," *Artforum* 43, no. 1 (September 2004): 249; emphasis in original.

17. Harold Cruse, *The Crisis of the Negro Intellectual* (New York: Morrow, 1967), 454.

18. On this score, see Toni Morrison's remarks in Paul Gilroy's "Living Memory: A Meeting with Toni Morrison," in Gilroy, *Small Acts: Thoughts on the Politics of Black Cultures* (London: Serpent's Tail, 1993), 178; as well as William Beverly's *On the Lam: Narratives of Flight in J. Edgar Hoover's America* (Jackson: University of Mississippi, 2003), which has shaped my sense of the ways slavery informs subsequent notions of fugitivity in an American context.

19. Robyn Wiegman, *American Anatomies: Theorizing Race and Gender* (Durham, NC: Duke University Press, 1995), 42.

20. Marcus Wood, *Blind Memory: Visual Representations of Slavery in England and America, 1780–1865* (New York: Routledge, 2000), 19–23.

21. The reading of *Untitled (To Disembark)* that follows rhymes with, yet ultimately departs from, the analysis of Kimberly Rae Connor, who emphasizes the work's belonging within African folk, slave narrative, black uplift, and sacred traditions. See her "Disembarking the

Past: Glenn Ligon," in *Imagining Grace: Liberating Theologies in the Slave Narrative Tradition* (Urbana: University of Illinois Press, 2000), 157–193. For a more recent engagement with the installation, see Peter Erickson, "Black Like Me: Reconfiguring Blackface in the Art of Glenn Ligon and Fred Wilson," *Nka* 25 (Winter 2009): 30–47.

22. As quoted in Quincy Troupe, "Last Testament: An Interview with James Baldwin," in *Conversations with James Baldwin*, ed. Fred L. Standley and Louis H. Pratt (Jackson: University Press of Mississippi, 1989), 285.

23. Marcus Wood, "'All Right!': *The Narrative of Henry Box Brown* as a Test Case for the Racial Prescription of Rhetoric and Semiotics," *Proceedings of the American Antiquarian Society* 107, no. 1 (1997): 80–83.

24. The other sonic materials included in *Untitled (To Disembark)* were a heartbeat, the artist's reading of Brown's narrative, and performances of the following songs: "Didn't My Lord Deliver Daniel" (Paul Robeson), "Traveling Light" (Billie Holiday), "Four Women" (Nina Simone), "Can You Party" (Royal House), "Redemption Song" (Bob Marley). Glenn Ligon, correspondence with the author, September 27, 2010.

25. Phyllis Rosenzweig, *Glenn Ligon: To Disembark* (Washington, DC: Hirshhorn Museum and Sculpture Garden, 1993).

26. Walter Benjamin, "Theses on the Philosophy of History," in *Illuminations*, ed. Hannah Arendt, trans. Harry Zohn (New York: Harcourt, Brace & World, 1968), 255.

27. See James A. Snead, "Repetition as a Figure of Black Culture," in *Out There: Marginalization and Contemporary Cultures*, ed. Russell Ferguson et al. (Cambridge, MA: MIT Press, 1990), 213–230.

28. Ligon quoted in Rosenzweig, *Glenn Ligon*, n.p.

29. Wiegman, *American Anatomies*, 35–42.

30. Key texts in this vein are Michele Wallace, "Modernism, Postmodernism, and the Problem of the Visual in Afro-American Culture," in Ferguson, *Out There*, 39–50; Henry Louis Gates Jr., "The Face and Voice of Blackness," in *Facing History: The Black Image in American Art, 1710–1940* (San Francisco: Bedford Arts, 1990), xxix–xliv; and, most saliently, Thelma Golden, *Glenn Ligon: Good Mirrors Are Not Cheap* (New York: Whitney Museum of American Art, 1992), which takes up and refigures Gates's and Wallace's terms in introducing Ligon's work. The four paragraphs that follow revisit and expand upon arguments first staged in my "Untitled (Jackpot!)," 124–125.

31. Ligon as quoted in the unsigned interview "Matrix" in the Wadsworth Atheneum newsletter, August 1992, 6.

32. Frantz Fanon, "The Fact of Blackness," in *Black Skin, White Masks*, trans. Charles Lam Markmann (New York: Grove Press, 1967), 112.

33. For an overview of this terrain in artistic and cultural terms, see *Black Male: Representations of Masculinity in Contemporary American Art*, exh. cat. (New York: Whitney Museum of American Art, 1994).

34. I examine Simpson and Danny Tisdale's responses to the Rodney King beating and subsequent riot in "Outtakes," *Art Journal* 67, no. 4 (Winter 2008): 28–29.

35. My thinking in these lines is inspired by Saidiya V. Hartman, *Scenes of Subjection: Terror, Slavery, and Self-Making in Nineteenth-Century America* (New York: Oxford University Press, 1997).

36. In fact, Ligon inscribed the Baldwin quotation that serves as the epigraph to this section directly into the corner of a gallery for his 1992 installation at the Wadsworth Atheneum.

See Andrea Miller-Keller, *Glenn Ligon/Matrix 120* (Hartford: Wadsworth Atheneum, 1992), as well as my "Untitled (Jackpot!)," 126–127.

37. Frantz Fanon, "By Way of Conclusion," in *Black Skin, White Masks*, 231.

38. My reading here draws upon Kara Keeling, "'In the Interval': Frantz Fanon and the 'Problems' of Visual Representation," *Qui Parle* 13, no. 2 (Spring/Summer 2003): 91–117.

39. For related thoughts on Ligon's exploration of the fraught relation between individual and community, which I here extend, see Thelma Golden, "Everynight," in *Glenn Ligon: Unbecoming*, 44.

40. Mary Helen Washington, "Zora Neale Hurston: A Woman Half in Shadow," in *I Love Myself When I Am Laughing . . . and Then Again When I Am Looking Mean and Impressive: A Zora Neale Hurston Reader*, ed. Alice Walker (Old Westbury, NY: Feminist Press, 1979), 7–25.

41. See, for example, the commentary that introduces the essay in Walker, *I Love Myself When I Am Laughing*, 151.

42. Rosenzweig, *Glenn Ligon*, n.p.

43. Henry Louis Gates Jr. productively charts this history in "Literary Theory and the Black Tradition," in *Figures in Black: Words, Signs, and the "Racial" Self* (New York: Oxford University Press, 1987), 3–58. For a crucial analysis of the formulaic tropes that enable the slave narrative as genre, see James Olney's "'I Was Born': Slave Narratives, Their Status as Autobiography and as Literature," in *The Slave's Narrative*, ed. Charles T. Davis and Henry Louis Gates Jr. (Oxford: Oxford University Press, 1985), 154–157.

44. I think, say, of the 1851 volume *Sketches of the Life and Labors of James Quinn, Who Was Nearly Half a Century a Minister of the Gospel in the Methodist Episcopal Church.*

45. These episodes are recounted in Harriet Jacobs, *Incidents in the Life of a Slave Girl, Written by Herself*, ed. Jean Fagan Yellin (Cambridge, MA: Harvard University Press, 1987), 110–113 and 192–193, respectively.

46. Aliyyah I. Abdur-Rahman, "'The Strangest Freaks of Despotism': Queer Sexuality in Antebellum African American Slave Narratives," *African American Review* 40, no. 2 (Summer 2006): 223–237.

47. Kobena Mercer charts these developments in "Dark and Lovely: Black Gay Image-Making," in *Welcome to the Jungle: New Positions in Black Cultural Studies* (New York: Routledge, 1994), 221–232.

48. Rosenzweig, *Glenn Ligon*.

49. Meyer, "Borrowed Voices," 15.

50. Rosenzweig, *Glenn Ligon*.

51. The advertisement is reproduced in John Hope Franklin and Loren Schweninger, *Runaway Slaves: Rebels on the Plantation* (New York: Oxford University Press, 1999), 283.

52. Franklin and Schweninger, *Runaway Slaves*, 285.

53. Franklin and Schweninger, *Runaway Slaves*, 217.

54. Franklin and Schweninger, *Runaway Slaves*, 210–213.

55. Franklin and Schweninger, *Runaway Slaves*, 224.

56. Snead, "Repetition as a Figure of Black Culture," 220.

57. Meyer, "Borrowed Voices," 17.

58. Rosenzweig, *Glenn Ligon.*

59. On the historical transformation of site-specific practices, see Miwon Kwon's crucial essay, "One Place After Another: Notes on Site-Specificity," *October* 80 (Spring 1997): 85–110.

60. Michel de Certeau, "'Making Do': Uses and Tactics," in *The Practice of Everyday Life*, ed. and trans. Steven Rendall (Berkeley: University of California Press, 1984), 37.

61. Here I refer specifically to Orlando Patterson, *Slavery and Social Death: A Comparative Study* (Cambridge, MA: Harvard University Press, 1982), 1–14.

62. Henry "Box" Brown, *Narrative of the Life of Henry Box Brown, Written by Himself* (1851; repr., Oxford: Oxford University Press, 2002), 62.

63. Elizabeth Alexander, "'Can You Be BLACK and Look at This?': Reading the Rodney King Video(s)," in *Black Male*, 92.

64. Wood, *Blind Memory*, 106–107.

65. Daphne A. Brooks stunningly charts Brown's performances in "The Escape Artist: Henry Box Brown, Black Abolitionist Performance, and Moving Panoramas of Slavery," in her *Bodies in Dissent: Spectacular Performances of Race and Freedom, 1850–1910* (Durham, NC: Duke University Press, 2006), 66–130.

66. As quoted and described in Jeffrey Ruggles, *The Unboxing of Henry Brown* (Richmond, VA: Library of Virginia, 2003), 94, the most comprehensive account to date of Brown's life and work.

67. On this score, see Cynthia Griffin Wolff, "Passing beyond the Middle Passage: Henry 'Box' Brown's Translations of Slavery," *Massachusetts Review* 37, no. 1 (Spring 1996): 23–44.

68. William Pietz, "The Problem of the Fetish, I," *Res* 9 (Spring 1985): 9. For two opposing interpretations of how Brown's box should be understood—as tomb, womb, coffin, or merely a parcel—see Wood, "'All Right!,'" 91, and Samira Kawash, "Freedom and Fugitivity: The Subject of Slave Narrative," in Kawash, *Dislocating the Color Line: Identity, Hybridity, and Singularity in African-American Narrative* (Stanford, CA: Stanford University Press, 1997), 68–72.

69. Karl Marx, *Capital: A Critique of Political Economy*, trans. Ben Fowkes (1867; repr., London: Penguin, 1990), 1:176–177.

70. Fred Moten, *In the Break: The Aesthetics of the Black Radical Tradition* (Minneapolis: University of Minnesota Press, 2003), 11.

71. Jean Baudrillard, "Fetishism and Ideology: The Semiological Reduction," in *For a Critique of the Political Economy of the Sign*, trans. Charles Levin (St. Louis, MO: Telos Press, 1981), 92.

72. For an excellent analysis of the cube and its vicissitudes, see Benjamin H. D. Buchloh, "Conceptual Art, 1962–1969: From the Aesthetic of Administration to the Critique of Institutions," *October* 55 (Winter 1990): 105–143.

73. Kimberly Paice, "Catalogue," in *Robert Morris: The Mind/Body Problem* (New York: Guggenheim Museum, 1994), 256.

74. Paice, "Catalogue," 104.

75. Traces of Brown's narrative can be located in a range of African American cultural production, from James Weldon Johnson's *Autobiography of an Ex-Colored Man* (1912) to Melvin Van Peebles's 1971 film *Sweet Sweetback's Baadasssss Song*. For accountings of Brown's more

recent reincarnations—including a film by Charles Burnett and a performance by historian Anthony Cohen—see Richard Newman, in his introduction to Brown, *Narrative of the Life of Henry Box Brown*, xxix–xxxi; and Suzette Spencer, "Henry Brown, an International Fugitive: Slavery, Resistance, and Imperialism," in *Black Geographies and the Politics of Place*, ed. Katherine McKittrick and Clyde Woods (Toronto: Between the Lines, 2007), 115.

76. The "Box" Brown display was designed and curated by museum cofounder, Dr. Elmer P. Martin. Joanne Martin, email to the author, July 27, 2010. For an extended meditation on the institution's tactics of display, see Marcus Wood, "Atlantic Slavery and Traumatic Representation in Museums: The National Great Blacks in Wax Museum as a Test Case," *Slavery and Abolition* 29, no. 2 (June 2008): 151–171.

77. Glenn Ligon, conversation with the author, December 21, 2006.

78. Kellie Jones, "Pat Ward Williams: Photography and Social/Personal History," in *Pat Ward Williams: Probable Cause* (Philadelphia: Moore College of Art and Design, 1992), 7.

79. In these lines, I refer, of course, to another of Benjamin's well-known dicta: "There is no document of civilization which is not at the same time a document of barbarism. And just as such a document is not free of barbarism, barbarism taints also the manner in which it was transmitted from one owner to another." Walter Benjamin, "Theses on the Philosophy of History," 256.

80. Stephen M. Best, *The Fugitive's Properties: Law and the Poetics of Possession* (Chicago: University of Chicago Press, 2004).

81. On the differences between Brown's first narrative, which was overdetermined by the editorial influence of abolitionist crusader Charles Stearns, and the second, more autonomously authored edition, published in 1851, see Ruggles, *The Unboxing of Henry Brown*, 59–65, 128–132.

82. As Newman notes, this image also appeared on the cover of an 1854 book written by the runaway Anthony Burns. See Richard Newman, "Illustrations," in *Narrative of the Life of Henry Box Brown*, xxxix.

83. Michael A. Chaney, *Fugitive Vision: Slave Image and Black Identity in Antebellum Narrative* (Bloomington: Indiana University Press, 2008), 2–13.

84. Best, *The Fugitive's Properties*, 16.

85. My reading of Ligon here resonates with Kawash's interpretation of Brown. See her "Freedom and Fugitivity," 71.

86. My immediate reference here is to Michel de Certeau's "Reading as Poaching," in *The Practice of Everyday Life*, 165–176; though his "Walking in the City" in the same volume is again germane. In that essay, de Certeau suggests that the gridlines of New York provide a kind of text, a *langue* that only comes to mean through the movement of the pedestrian whose walking is a kind of speech act or *parole* (97–98); I would argue that this same logic applies to Ligon's installation.

87. Jacques Lacan, "The Line and Light," in *The Seminar of Jacques Lacan*, book 11, *The Four Fundamental Concepts of Psychoanalysis*, ed. Jacques-Alain Miller, trans. Alan Sheridan (New York: Norton, 1981), 91–104.

88. Gwendolyn Brooks, *To Disembark* (Chicago: Third World Press, 1981).

89. Saidiya Hartman, *Lose Your Mother: A Journey along the Atlantic Slave Route* (New York: Farrar, Straus and Giroux, 2008), 234.

5 Strangers in the Village

Hilton Als

1.

In the village of his mind, was the writer James Baldwin always a stranger?

2.

An essay—*essai* in French, meaning "experiment" or "attempt"—is a proposal or inquiry bound together, generally, by a writer's sensibility, his or her strengths and weaknesses, and, often, an irrefutable desire to say "I." *I feel this way. Why? I had this thought. Why? I imagined this. What does it mean?* On the page, the essayist is this "I" after "I" after "I," but the essay rarely comes to a single conclusion about its primary subject: the self, that "I" that no pen can shut up.

3.

In the landscape of James Baldwin's sensibility, we see it time and again: the author as the ultimate *étranger*, navigating a world no one invited him into, maybe wearing a white shirt. He is alone. He is, let's say, in his early thirties, black-skinned, living in Paris or Corsica—or in Loèche-les-Bains, a tiny hamlet in the Swiss Alps, the setting of his 1953 essay "Stranger in the Village." In that piece, Baldwin picks at his difference in every line but without ever exposing much; in that piece, Baldwin hides in plain sight.

4.

Essays—certainly the best ones—don't end so much as die. Think of Virginia Woolf's 1941 meditation "The Death of the Moth," where the

Figure 5.1 Glenn Ligon, *Stranger in the Village #13,* 1998. Enamel, silkscreen ink, oil and acrylic paint, gesso, and coal dust on canvas, 76 × 132 inches. Collection of the Art Institute of Chicago. Gift of The Peter Norton Family Foundation. © Glenn Ligon. Digital image © The Art Institute of Chicago / Licensed by Scala / Art Resource, NY.

author's thoughts end when her title character dies, thus filling her mind with moths of thoughts. That's what the essayist is after—ideas that flutter in and out of the mind's eye, words that capture something of a writer's experience before it's time to move on to record other experiences, the way one's "I" changes shape from paragraph to paragraph in a world where nothing is fixed. More than any other literary genre, essays try, overtly, to approximate life as it's lived—the hard bustle of existence, made to take on the shape of words.

5.

Look at any James Baldwin essay, and you'll find its author standing in the middle of it. There's anthropological Baldwin (1948's "The Harlem Ghetto," about pre- and postwar Harlem and the relationship between Jewish storekeepers and black patrons); literary Baldwin (1954's "The Male Prison," about André Gide's relationship to his sexuality and male exoticism); dishy Baldwin (1961's "The Black Boy Looks at the White Boy," about Baldwin's relationship to novelist Norman Mailer); queer Baldwin (1985's "Here Be Dragons," about Baldwin's relationship to, among other things, a Puerto Rican pimp who loved him). In "Stranger in the Village," we see several of these various Baldwins standing side by side, but it's queer Baldwin who captivates our imagination. And yet, queer Baldwin never tells us how he got to Loèche-les-Bains in the first place: he was in love with Lucien Happersberger, a Swiss boy being raised in Paris, where the two met.

6.

Baldwin lived with Happersberger in Loèche-les-Bains—also called Leukerbad—for three months in the winter of 1951–1952. Baldwin was just twenty-eight years old; Lucien was six years younger. Happersberger's mother had been born in the town, and the family kept a chalet there, where Lucien and Baldwin holed up for the winter alone together, and where Baldwin finished his first novel, *Go Tell It on the Mountain.* He'd brought the manuscript with him when he left his native New York in 1949. (It was finally published in 1953, after a decade of struggle.) In his 1961 essay "The Discovery of What It Means to Be an American," Baldwin recalls how he went to icy Switzerland armed with his typewriter and some Bessie Smith records; Smith helped him recall the "pickaninny" he had once been—the better to finish his book, which centers on the Harlem of Baldwin's youth. But where, in either "The Discovery" or "Stranger," is Lucien? Where is *his* strangeness—his full, pink lips on Baldwin's brown ones? Where is the story of Lucien casting off his heterosexual impulses—for a time—to be with Baldwin, or the story of Baldwin's interest in men who weren't entirely "gay"? Where was the story of the poverty Baldwin and Lucien shared, and of Lucien's desire to bring his lover to meet his family—his youthful desire to bring love home to show his parents?

7.

In some ways, Baldwin's "Stranger in the Village" is a kind of fable. And, like most fables, it reads as realistic and fantastic all at once. At the beginning of the piece, we learn that Baldwin has been invited for a stay in Switzerland. He writes: "From all available evidence no black man had ever set foot in this tiny Swiss village before I came." He goes on:

> I was told before arriving that I would probably be a "sight" for the village; I took this to mean that people of my complexion were rarely seen in Switzerland, and also that city people are always something of a "sight" outside of the city. It did not occur to me—possibly because I

am an American—that there could be people anywhere who had never seen a Negro.

8.

Fiction can and often does add luster to the essayist's persona, thus making him seem both innocent and heroic in ways that real life does not, unless a historic action or event occurs to dress up life's backdrop for a while. Some writers are ashamed of their relative isolation and perceived ineffectualness, their small nook of being in the vast ocean of events that take place as they carry on living, cultivating their "I." So they make up a different "I," one more actively engaged in world events: Lillian Hellman wrote about her friend "Julia" and their joint fight for freedom during World War II—but while Julia was based on a real figure who did lose her life fighting fascism, Lillian Hellman didn't know her personally. Appropriating "Julia's" history for her own ends made Hellman both less and more than what she was: less her writer self, and therefore more than a mere "I"—it made her an actor, doing good in the real world.

9.

In "Stranger in the Village," Baldwin lies so that he can come across as the quintessential stranger—so he can have a piece to write. The first lie: he just shows up in this tiny, obscure village. How? Why? The second lie: being an American, it never occurs to him that other people in the world might never have seen a Negro before. Really? What world was Baldwin living in? Hadn't he, for a time, been *the* black man in another village called Greenwich? And in that other village, hadn't his body been ogled, derided, and under near-constant attack?

10.

For the most part, the people Baldwin describes in "Stranger in the Village" are heterosexual—or they enact heterosexuality. They look at Baldwin, at his queer blackness, and know he must be kept away so they can preserve their homogeneity, their shared think-speak. What would happen if they began to listen to this "*neger*" walking through their streets piled high with snow? Would his words seep in and make their hearts as black as Africa, too?

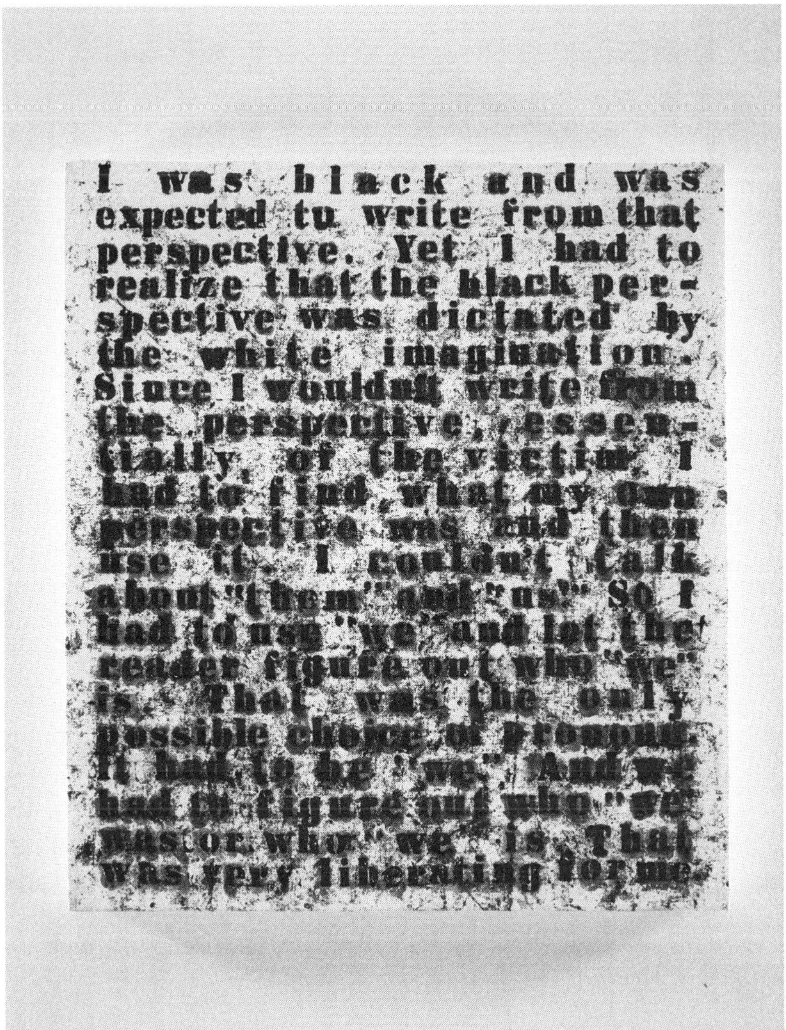

Figure 5.2 Glenn Ligon, *James Baldwin #2*, 1990. Oil stick, graphite, and gesso on canvas, 22 × 20 inches. © Glenn Ligon; Courtesy of the artist, Hauser & Wirth, and Thomas Dane Gallery. Photo Credit: Ronald Amstutz.

Figure 5.3 Glenn Ligon, *Stranger in the Village (excerpt) #10*, 1997. Oil stick and coal dust on linen, 96 × 144 inches. © Glenn Ligon; Courtesy of the artist, Hauser & Wirth, and Thomas Dane Gallery.

11.

The artist Glenn Ligon began his series of paintings inspired by Baldwin's "Stranger in the Village" (figures 5.1, 5.3, 5.4) in 1996, some forty-five years after his source material had become the symbol of Africa for Europe, a continent that treated the stranger in *its* village as living proof of that other, darker continent's impenetrability. Ligon's *Stranger* paintings, which use Baldwin's sentences (obscured and impenetrable) as a field, are dark and dense and can look like the very soul of blackness. They are essentially essayistic—or, more accurately, visual plays on the words that go into making Baldwin's essay, which tells us about his blackness and his maleness and his isolation straight off. Baldwin's themes are Ligon's great themes, too.

12.

Ligon's *Stranger* paintings also bring to mind certain icons of twentieth-century art history—specifically, the number and letter paintings that Jasper Johns created in encaustic on canvas in the early 1960s. But instead of carving them from wax, Ligon weighs down his words with coal dust, a black element that saturates the surface of Baldwin's black world.

13.

The *Stranger* paintings are weighed down, too, by the influence of these two masters—Johns and Baldwin, both of whom used language to reveal who they were and, at the same time, who they weren't. While the coolness of Johns's surfaces is part of his implicit meaning (Stay away! What does "intimacy" mean anyway? What does your interpretation mean? What is interpretation?), Baldwin made a show of rhetoric—and what is rhetoric but a kind of linguistic theater? The curtain rises on an "I" (figure 5.2). That "I" tells us something true about himself or herself, for a bit, but ultimately draws us in through the examination of a particular part of the world, one that calls into question our collective "I." The rhetorician is a master of this bait and switch—a show-off, always with another flourish at the ready.

14.

To make a painting is to create a visual flourish in the world—to wave a flag of difference. But, of course, it's more complicated than that. Like Baldwin's essay, Ligon's work—certainly in this series—is about being seen and not seen at the same time. The surfaces of the paintings, their layers upon layers of coal dust and handiwork, both draw you close and push you away (but where to? To the artist's imagination? And what would you find there, in that queer universe influenced by queers who belonged to a generation in which you could say who you were only through metaphor, if even then?) The best clue is in the phrases Ligon has elected to borrow from Baldwin—maybe he chose the ones that resonate most with his own "I," with his sense of being a stranger in the village known as the art world, the queer aesthetic world dominated by men who do not look like Ligon or make art like him, let alone know anything about the source of his *Stranger* paintings.

15.

To be a stranger is to be excluded from the quotidian, to be "unreadable." The surfaces of Ligon's *Stranger* paintings are "strange" because of their texture—at first readable but, upon closer inspection, collapsing into a mass of words that can look like a mass of blackness, either hard or soft depending on the angle of view. Ligon remakes Baldwin's language without changing the content. So, what is the relationship between the paintings and the essay? To understand Ligon, must one have read Baldwin? Or is it enough to read Ligon? Is each artist tapping into the same source—namely, how they're haunted by the house they both inhabit: their black maleness?

16.

Imagine Ligon taking one of his *Stranger* paintings to Baldwin in St. Paul de Vence, the village in the south of France where the writer ended up living and working until his death in 1987. Imagine Baldwin putting on his glasses to read the surface of Ligon's work. What words can he make out? "I"? Imagine him looking across at Ligon—his eyes peering through his spectacles as Ligon looks at Baldwin through his spectacles. What would Baldwin see? The ghost of his feelings for Beauford Delaney, the black abstract expressionist who helped him to see when he was, himself,

Figure 5.4 Glenn Ligon, *Stranger in the Village #16*, 2000. Acrylic, coal dust, oil stick, glue, glitter, and gesso on canvas, 48¼ x 56¼ inches. Collection of the Walker Art Center, Minneapolis. © Glenn Ligon; Courtesy of the artist, Hauser & Wirth, and Thomas Dane Gallery.

a young man, living in Manhattan? Would Baldwin be able to see his own history of running both toward and away from other queer black men, the better to see and not see himself? Or would he see Ligon for himself, which is to say, a self that finds its artistic self in others—in Baldwin (and, later, in Richard Pryor)? Is it fair to assume that Ligon sees himself in black men who won't let history ignore them?

17.

Sometimes Ligon's studio is filled with white canvases. One can imagine him being a stranger in that peculiarly white landscape—a landscape he gets to remake in his image, a landscape where white turns to black filled with layer after layer of philosophical and emotional investigation.

6 Black Skin, Black Masks: The Citational Self in the Work of Glenn Ligon

Lauren DeLand

"I am an invisible man": so declares an untitled work of 1991 by the American artist Glenn Ligon before the queasy text smudged across the paper gives way to illegibility (figure 6.1). A brief survey of Ligon's contemporaneous works reveals the sustained use of this declarative "I": another painting produced in 1990 states, "I feel most colored when I am thrown against a sharp white background" (figure 1.1). An untitled work of 1992 reads, "I'm turning into a specter before your very eyes." The form the works assume is unvarying and simple: each repeats its given phrase over and over, stuttering across the white surface and gradually bleeding into an indecipherable inky mass. Unencumbered by other visual cues, Ligon's paintings appear as a straightforward series of self-reflexive statements organized along the axes of racial and gender identification.

Yet for readers, a nagging sensation of familiarity may belie the apparently autobiographical nature of these texts. In fact they originate, respectively, from the writers Ralph Ellison, Zora Neale Hurston, and Jean Genet. In repurposing these textual fragments from seminal works on racial identity and socialization, Ligon charts a conversion of the particularities of racial experience into the generalities of fiction from which he selectively gleans to represent his own experience in a Black male body. The sources that comprise the "I" of Ligon's work are a multitude, appropriated from art and literature to suggest a series of racial, sexual, and gender particularities that resemble Ligon's own, an "autobiography" of which the subject has written not a single word. Even the appearance of Ligon's own body in his work does not constitute a simple act of self-reflexivity. This

Figure 6.1 Glenn Ligon, *Untitled (I Am an Invisible Man)*, 1991. Oil stick and graphite on paper, 30 × 17¼ inches. Collection of the Museum of Modern Art, New York. Gift of the Bohen Foundation. © Glenn Ligon. Digital image © The Museum of Modern Art/Licensed by SCALA / Art Resource, NY.

is deceptively true of a photo-serigraphic dyad of 1997, which initially appears to report the facts of Ligon's physical features with a simplicity bordering on banality (figure 6.2). For the inscrutable sameness of Ligon's *Self-Portrait Exaggerating My Black Features and Self-Portrait Exaggerating My White Features* exists to critique notions of racial "difference" put forth in a 1981 self-portrait in which conceptual artist Adrian Piper purported to exaggerate her "Negroid Features." In Ligon's work, identificatory declarations come from other lips, and the artist's body represents not a unitary self but a dialogic, citational, and wholly subjective being-for-others.

In coalescing a legion of voices into an approximation of a unitary speaking subject, Ligon both gestures toward and offers a means of navigating a problem endemic to "Black" art since its conception in the early twentieth century. "Black art," writes Darby English, "began its life as a component of a political program of uplift," as leaders such as W. E. B. Du Bois deemed "positive" representations of Black American life to be a central plank in the project of enfranchisement.[1] The development of the Black Arts and Black Aesthetics movements in the 1960s and 1970s imposed still more specific expectations upon Black artists tasked with "representing" on behalf of their race,[2] a responsibility compounded by external as well as internal pressures in the 1990s, as the politics of multiculturalism evolved into a central concern of a White-dominated art world suddenly interested in staging self-consciously the spectacle of racial difference within cultural forums. The presumption, and expectation, that the Black speaking subject represents always on behalf of bodies external to their own emerged at the same moment as the notion of the "Black artist" itself. When one takes into consideration also that the Black body constitutes, in English's words, "a black representational space par excellence,"[3] in that the actions of individual Black subjects are routinely scrutinized and judged to be indicative of qualities endemic to their race, the full weight of the burdensome, promiscuous task of developing Black subjectivities comes to rest.

By offering appropriated declarative statements on race in lieu of his own Black body, Ligon captures the sensation of being continually transformed into an object to be measured against competing definitions of what "Black is / Black ain't," while cannily slipping the bonds of surveillance and fetishism by which these scopic regimes operate.[4] Scholars of Ligon's work have celebrated his ability to trace the processes by which "authentic" Black subjectivities are postulated and constructed within the social, confounding the expectation to appear as a representative for others even as he

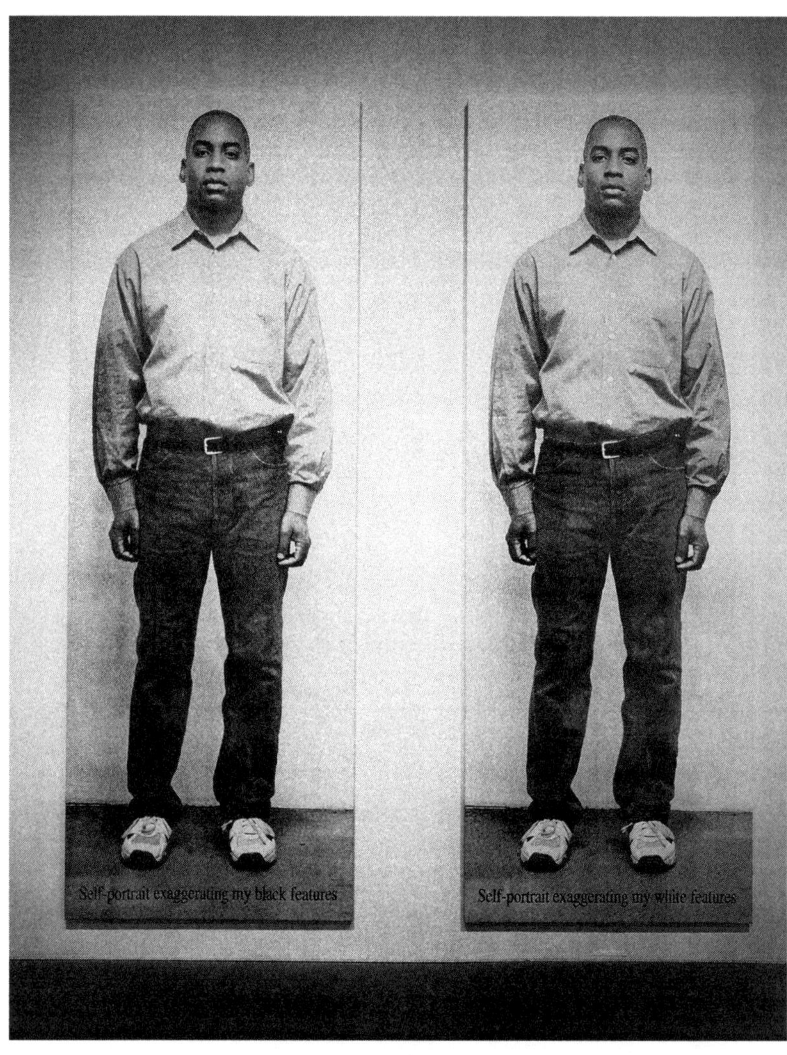

Figure 6.2 Glenn Ligon, *Self-Portrait Exaggerating My Black Features and Self-Portrait Exaggerating My White Features*, 1997. Silkscreen on canvas, two panels, each 120 × 40 inches, edition of 2 and 1 artist's proof. © Glenn Ligon; Courtesy of the artist, Hauser & Wirth, and Thomas Dane Gallery.

reveals this identificatory process to be foundational to the notion of Black identity. Highlighting the identificatory possibilities that the art opens up for viewers, English quotes the artist in declaring Ligon's work to be "*about* the desire" that compels viewers to engage with it.[5] In an educational video produced for *Glenn Ligon: AMERICA*, a comprehensive midcareer retrospective presented by the Whitney Museum of American Art in 2011, the artist Christine S. Kim echoes this sentiment about the dialogic nature of Ligon's art in simpler and more broadly optimistic terms, declaring "The title, 'America,' lets us know that this show speaks for everyone."[6]

Yet it is *A Feast of Scraps* (1994–1998)—a work that was notably absent from the Whitney retrospective—that bears most poignant witness to the messy, exhausting business of speaking to, and on behalf of, so broad a spectrum of desiring subjects. *A Feast of Scraps* is a photo assemblage in which Ligon maps the course of his own history and sexuality without ever picturing himself within the work (figure 1.8). Through this careful arrangement of a cache of creased and faded photographs on a few bound pages, he conjures something akin to a lovingly assembled family photo album, tracing a genealogy from the 1940s to the 1980s and touching on the familiar milestones of marriage, birth, military service, and family reunions.[7] Some of these photos feature Ligon's own relatives, gleaned from his family's archives.[8] Tenderly tucked among the pictures of couples and parties are pornographic images of Black men, some pictured within dimly lit and cluttered private interiors, and some deliberately posed in outdoor locations against clusters of trees, reinscribing the set of racialized stereotypes known colloquially by the term "jungle fever." Brief descriptive fragments of text, such as "Daddy" and "Brother" (figure 6.5), bring these disparate images into relation through punning and double entendre while leaving the viewer to question how these nude, solitary Black men fit with the wholesome images that record Ligon's family history.

The foundling photographs collected within Ligon's album belong, as most pornographic images do, to a category of media that quintessentially resists historicity. In the Greenwich Village bookstore Gay Treasures, the artist discovered a box provocatively labeled "Black Men," containing scores of photographs dating from the 1960s and 1970s: Polaroids, black-and-white snapshots, and even collectable six-packs of photos, all castaways from individual collections.[9] The unceremonious process of deaccession by which these photos came to reside in a secondhand porn shop is indicative of how such images are infused at every stage of their

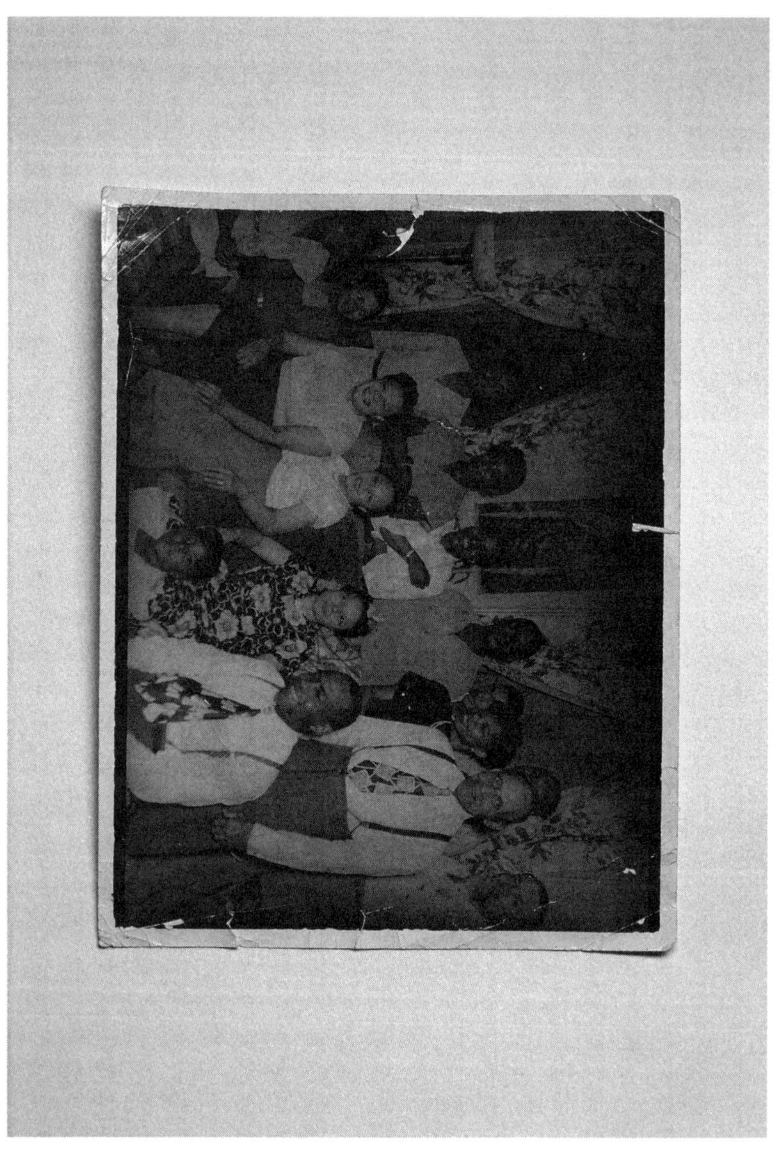

Figure 6.3 Glenn Ligon, *A Feast of Scraps* (detail), 1994–1998. Photographs and text, 20½ × 11½ inches. © Glenn Ligon; Courtesy of the artist, Hauser & Wirth, and Thomas Dane Gallery.

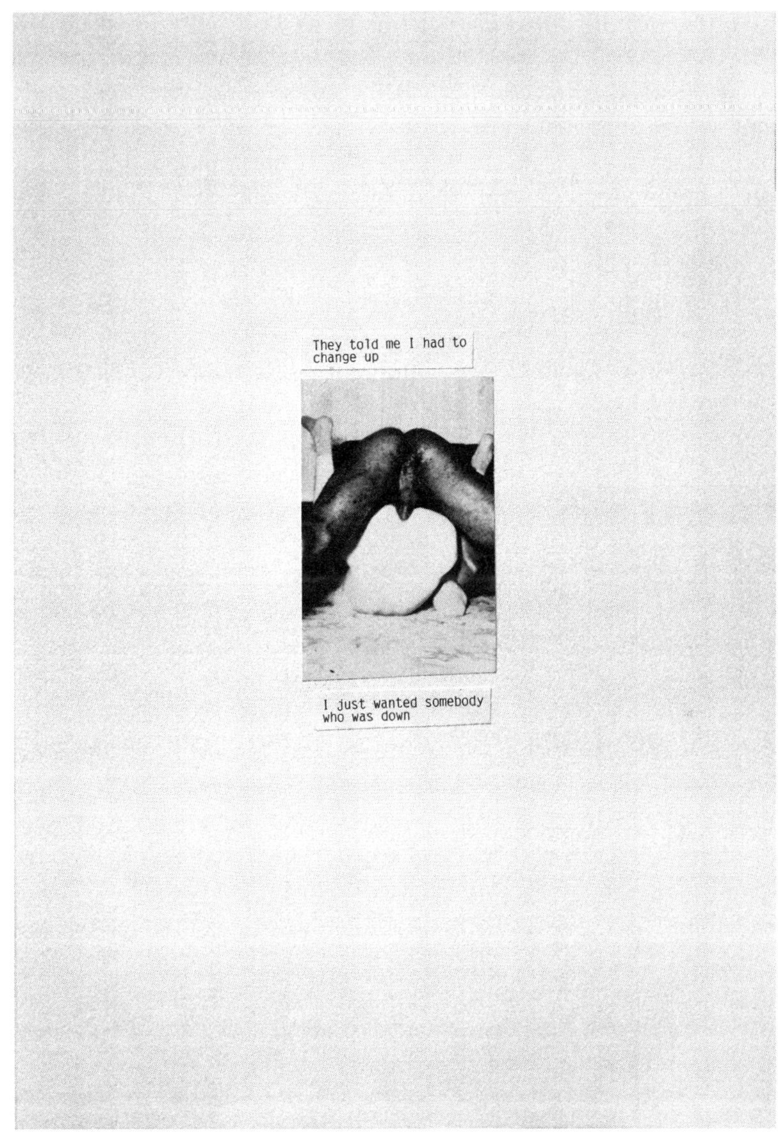

Figure 6.4 Glenn Ligon, *A Feast of Scraps* (detail), 1994–1998. Photographs and text, 20½ × 11½ inches. © Glenn Ligon; Courtesy of the artist, Hauser & Wirth, and Thomas Dane Gallery.

production, distribution, and consumption by anonymity. Produced via collaborations between nameless models and photographers and circulated within clandestine circles of connoisseurs, these photographs are impervious to the organizational methods of the archive. In their orphaned state—abandoned by their authors and then again by their audiences, and estranged from their models—the pictures are uniquely unfixed in their meaning, available to the interpretation of any number of individuals for any number of purposes.

From the enticing blankness that constitutes the material and narrative history of these images of Black men, Ligon extracts stopgaps for the holes in his own family history. "The photos of black men in Gay Treasures," writes Ligon, "are the photos left out of my family albums."[10] In Ligon's hands, the family album is a text dually marked by history and the ineffable: the vehicle through which the narrative of heteropatriarchal family unity is mobilized, and the end product of the excisions necessary to produce it. Ligon recalls albums full of family photos from the 1970s that document the "unkempt afros" and "flowery polyester shirts" of his teenaged self and his male cousins. Yet the most personally significant fact of the historical moment chronicled therein—Ligon's discovery of his sexual attraction to men, a desire awakened by his cousins—is precisely what these photos cannot reveal.[11]

While Ligon's essay on *A Feast of Scraps* seems initially to document the failure of the family album to record histories that go beyond the bounds of the rigidly defined nuclear family, in another statement he hints at the polysemous possibilities of the family archive. The artist recalls flipping through family albums as a child and asking his elders what must be the most commonly posed query regarding family photos: "Who's that?" He remembers "being told 'Oh, that's Uncle James's friend,' and I thought, 'What does that mean?' If you didn't know, you weren't supposed to know."[12]

The family album, as demonstrated by Ligon's anecdote, is not simply the illustrated genealogy of a single family; it is full of interlopers, friends, and relatives who have meandered in and out of the family's lives and collective memory. The passing of time both blurs these memories and places the photographic subjects in a kind of democratic equilibrium: the contextual knowledge necessary to discern one's own once-revered ancestors from anonymous "friends" of the family diminishes with each passing generation. In this way the family album does more to trouble the coherence of the nuclear family than it does to maintain it. In this essay I take Ligon's

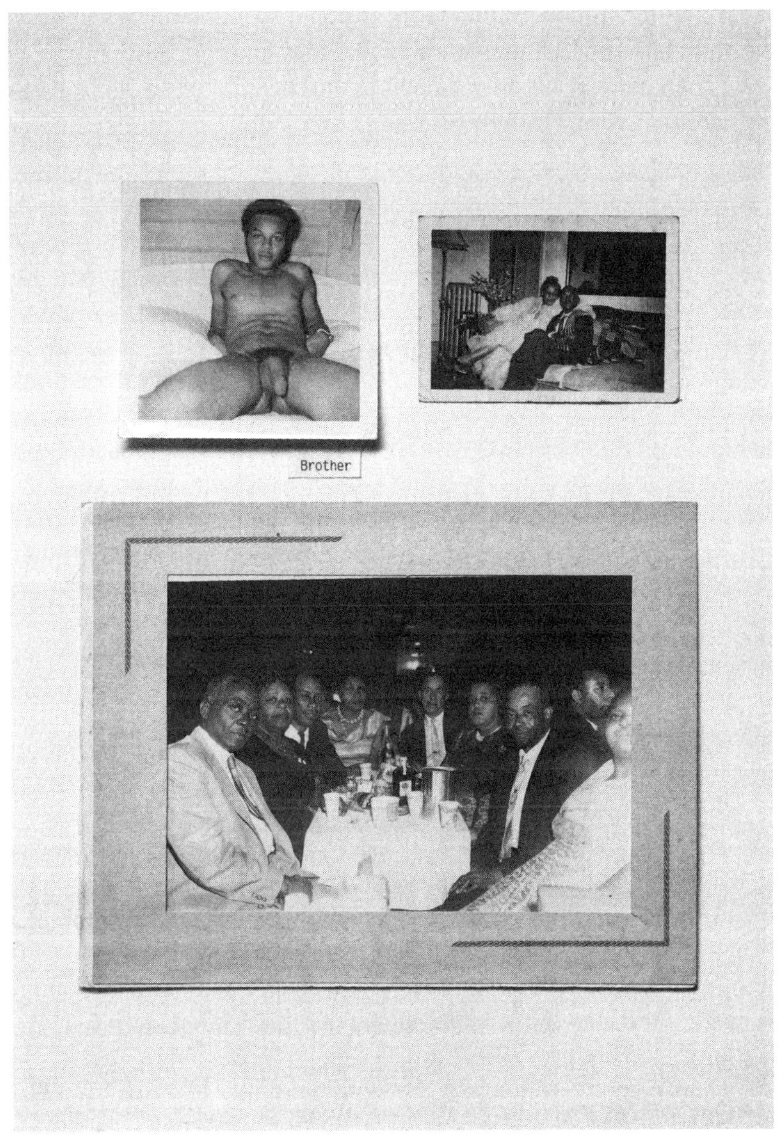

Figure 6.5 Glenn Ligon, *A Feast of Scraps* (detail), 1994–1998. Photographs and text, 20½ × 11½ inches. © Glenn Ligon; Courtesy of the artist, Hauser & Wirth, and Thomas Dane Gallery.

album, and the trouble that it makes, to explicate problems of identification and representation pertaining to that most overburdened symbol of America's social, sexual, and economic health: the Black American family.

Robert F. Reid-Pharr declares,

> The belief that the black family, the black home, is in crisis, in ruins, has been one of the most palpable realities of U.S. culture. It has been bemoaned and pronounced upon by both black and white, from both the left and the right. It has been used as an argument for the erection of the welfare state—and for its dismantling. . . . From at least the mid-nineteenth century, American social commentators have been announcing the death of the black family and administering last rites.[13]

As the inheritors of economic hardships wrought by generations of racial iniquity, and as the perennial subjects of the social and institutional scrutiny to which (potential) recipients of state benefits must submit, Black American families are reflexively configured as the symbolic family buckling under the strain of late-stage capitalism and the erosion of the welfare state.[14] Images of Black American family life are thus never interpreted solely as intimate personal chronologies; their subjects are converted into pieces of sociological evidence from the moment they begin to circulate publicly within economies of representation, though what this "evidence" points to depends upon the politics of the interlocutor.

The vexed and anxious sociological narrative of "progress" from the slave-era nadir of American history plays itself out compulsively through the trope of the Black family; the uneasy business of developing a cohesive identity for a people denied their humanity is thus conducted through attempts to formulate an archetypal *one* from *many*. In its uniquely generous open-endedness, *A Feast of Scraps* provides opportunities to reexamine seemingly antithetical political imaginings of the Black American family—such as the socially prescriptive goals of the 1965 Moynihan Report, on one hand, and the revolutionary and revisionist aims of Black liberation movements, on the other—because it both pictures and actively contradicts the ideal of the Black, male-headed, heteropatriarchal family to which both default. Liberationist groups such as the Black Panther Party promoted the Black family as a fortress from which Black Americans could together resist systemic racist oppression. Yet, as Roderick A. Ferguson argues eloquently in *Aberrations in Black: Toward a Queer of Color Critique* (2004), in asserting the primacy of the patriarchal, male-headed household as the Black liberationist ideal, the Panthers and others in fact reiterated and reinforced sexist and homophobic attitudes that ultimately dovetailed with White conservative social prescriptions for "the Negro problem."[15] The promotion of the productive, reproductive, and patriarchal Black family ideal necessitated the banishment of a host of diluting influences, both real and imagined: these included the formative contributions of queers of color to African American culture and the specter of female dominance and control encapsulated in the figure of the Black matriarch.

Ligon forges *A Feast of Scraps* from these discarded subjectivities, placing them in disquieting proximity to the unified front of the Black, heteropatriarchal family from which they have been culturally and personally excluded. The material reality of the scrapbook facilitates this unsettling reunion; prompted to read these seemingly incongruous subjects as members of the same family, we are reminded of Roland Barthes's statement that in viewing amateur photography we presume to extract the truth of an individual through the multitude; the *one* of the subject becomes comprehensible through the *many*: "the Photograph . . . sometimes makes appear what we never see in a real face . . . a genetic feature, the fragment of oneself or of a relative which comes from some ancestor. . . . The Photograph gives a little truth, on condition that it parcels out the body. But this truth is not that of the individual, who remains irreducible; it is the truth of lineage."[16]

The associative, identificatory affect of family photography thus intersects harmoniously with Ligon's methodology: both offer a means of discerning the individual subject through *other* subjectivities that have in some way shaped the individual. In Ligon's album the fraught image of the Black American family reads both as a place of respite—a shelter from the pressures of institutionalized racism, a place where the burden of "representing" one's race for the edification of outsiders may be temporarily released—and of suffocating responsibility, as one is expected not only to represent on behalf of oneself in the world, but also on behalf of one's kin. Across these pages Ligon charts the confrontations, disappointments, and revisions of expectations that define interfamilial dynamics through the figure of the Black gay man, who remains the most pernicious specter haunting the Black utopias prescribed by thinkers across the political spectrum. Throughout a wide array of literature on Black identity and the Black family, Black male sexuality emerges as a duplicitous and malevolent entity, regarded with deep suspicion by the authors who invoke it. Configured in social policy such as the Moynihan Report as a destructive force to be reined in and regulated, the sexuality of Black men fares little better in ostensibly radical texts on race and liberation from the critical period of the 1960s and 1970s. Here the crude and enduring fascination of some Whites with the ostensibly awesome sexual prowess of the Black male casts a pallor over the subject, as though mere consideration of the Black male as a sexual subject constitutes a kind of collusion with the fetishizing gaze of White racism.

Ligon elaborates on this problem in his accompanying essay to *A Feast of Scraps*: "Pornographic images of black men usually fall into a narrow range of types: black men as closer to nature, sexually aggressive, enormously endowed. Black men *as* phallus. [Frantz] Fanon and others have argued that these stereotypes allay the fears of whites while serving their needs and desires."[17] Here Ligon refers to an oft-quoted passage from *Black Skin, White Masks* (1967; published in the original French as *Peau noire, masques blancs* in 1952), the enormously influential anticolonial text by the author and revolutionary Frantz Fanon.[18] Fanon in this book famously analyses the doubling effects of institutionalized racism on the Black colonial subject, who exists simultaneously for himself and as a specularized Other for the dominant White "being." Fanon's framework thus proves ideal for parsing the dynamics of association, disassociation, and splitting of the subject that reoccur throughout Ligon's work. Moreover, I argue that in *Black Skin, White Masks*, Fanon is concerned particularly with the transformative effect of White hegemonic surveillance on the Black *male* body and psyche: the White spectator who views the Black subject through the distorting lens of racist projections "is no longer aware of the Negro but only of a penis; the Negro is eclipsed. He is turned into a penis. He *is* a penis."[19]

The collapse of Black man into phallic object is played out on Fanon's own body and psyche in his fifth chapter, "The Fact of Blackness": at the midpoint of the text, the authority of the author is disrupted and corrupted by a single, devastating declaration: "Look, a Negro!"[20] Fanon himself is the object of this exclamation, uttered by a White child frightened by Fanon's presence in a train car traveling across the French countryside. As the child continues to panic audibly in his presence, Fanon experiences the dissolution of his own subjectivity; pinned under the gaze of a squalling White child, Fanon the physician, the philosopher, the revolutionary is eclipsed. He feels himself dispersed across space and time: "In the train I was given not one but two, three places. . . . I was responsible at the same time for my body, for my race, for my ancestors."[21]

For Fanon, to be a Black person within a society historically and linguistically premised on the denigration of Black people is to be perennially incorporated into mythohistorical narratives that preexist one's self. The fundamental iniquities of slavery and colonialism, he argues, render the reciprocal dynamics between the Self and Other unavailable to the colonized subject. Under colonialism the "absolute reciprocity" which the Hegelian dialectic assumes cannot exist: "It is in the degree to which I go beyond my own immediate being that I apprehend the existence of the other as a natural and more than natural reality. If I close the circuit, if I prevent the accomplishment of movement in two directions, I keep the other within myself. Ultimately, I deprive him even of this being-for-itself."[22]

This refusal of recognition constitutes an insidious form of systemic racism that begins in the terrain of the imaginary and thus remains stubbornly impervious to the law and to mechanisms of social change. The Black subject is not reified via the gaze of the White Other, but rather fragmented, dislocated, "woven . . . out of a thousand details, anecdotes, stories."[23] The Black subject is consequently forced to enact a schizophrenic self-negation against the "crushing objecthood" imposed by the preconceptions of Whites.[24] In Ligon's work, we see a performance of this psychosocial conundrum, as his oeuvre presents a self that is constituted entirely through others. In *A Feast of Scraps*, this fragmentation of Black identity is reenacted through that most disruptive and dislocating medium: photography.

Fanon feels himself tripled under the pressure of surveillance, at once responsible for his race, his ancestors, and himself, and ultimately usurped as a subject by the White beholder's concept of "Negro." His description of this process of objectification, fragmentation, and finally self-effacement parallels strikingly with Barthes's description of the experience of posing for a photograph. From the assumption of the pose to the click of the shutter, four competing "image-repertoires" inform the final photographic product: "In front of the lens, I am at the same time: the one I think I am, the one I want others to think I am, the one the photographer thinks I am, and the one he makes use of to exhibit his art. In other words, a strange action: I do not stop imitating myself, and because of this, each time I am (or let myself be) photographed, I invariably suffer from a sensation of inauthenticity, sometimes of imposture."[25] For Barthes, to become a photographic subject is to experience a sensation of being "neither subject nor object but a subject who feels he is becoming an object."[26] In posing for a photograph, the subject anticipates the perceptions and judgments of others; while he may attempt to fix a desirable image of himself via the reality effect of the photograph, his very anticipation of the competing views of the photographer and other potential beholders distorts his own sense of self. To pose for a photo is thus always to submit to a process of self-fragmentation, and to risk the indefinite appropriation of one's image as proof to support any number of obscure and often oppositional convictions.

The subjects of Ligon's album are united in their common obligation to serve as "living proof," irrespective of the apparent differences between the pornographic models and the middle-class families that they contrast. While Fanon and, more recently, Kobena Mercer and Isaac Julien[27] have argued that the Black male body plays an overactive role in the sexual imagination of Whites, Ligon's album facilitates a conversation about the sociological practices that have long situated the African American family as a locus of social and sexual deviance. Roderick A. Ferguson, reflecting on over half a century of studies that posit the African American family as the de facto subject of American sociology, writes, "As figures of nonheteronormative perversions, straight African Americans were reproductive rather than productive, heterosexual but never heteronormative. . . . This construction of African American sexuality as wild, unstable, and undomesticated locates African American sexuality within the irrational, and therefore outside of the bounds of the citizenship machinery."[28] In *Aberrations in Black*, Ferguson traces the trajectory of twentieth-century sociological publications and concomitant public policy decisions that located the origin of the social and economic strife experienced by African Americans squarely within the Black body itself. He begins with the 1937 publication of *Caste and Class in a Southern Town*, in which American psychologist John Dollard argues that African Americans had inherited a joint lack of economic responsibility and sexual regulation under the sharecropping system, thereby fomenting sexual aggression and weakening the "monogamous family" among Black communities.[29]

This portrait of African American kinship structures as sexually uninhibited and inimical to the model of the American nuclear family established a pattern repeated over decades of sociological studies and joint political initiatives. In his 1944 book *An American Dilemma: The Negro*

Problem and Modern Democracy, economist Gunnar Myrdal famously maintains that female-headed households in African American communities bred familial dysfunction, which led to inner-city poverty and crime.[30] Following this hypothesis, New Deal social policy allocated benefits for women on the basis of their status as wives and mothers, thereby excluding a full fourth of African American households.[31] In his 1965 report *The Negro Family: The Case for National Action*, Daniel Patrick Moynihan marshals Labor Department data to cement the notion of the deviant Black matriarchy in the American consciousness. The Moynihan Report links problems such as poverty and poor performance by Black students in public schools to deficiencies in "the family structure," which, according to Moynihan, stem from a crisis of masculinity. Black men, argues Moynihan, were stripped of their earning ability and thus emasculated under institutionalized racism, thereby creating the "pathological" phenomenon of the Black matriarchy.[32]

These are the hypotheses by which the people pictured in Ligon's photo album were evaluated, submitted as evidence before the appraising gaze of the welfare state. Ligon has described the album as a site in which "the family represents itself to itself,"[33] yet the birth announcements and family gatherings that make up Ligon's album also carry the burden of proof for their subjects' race, and for their ancestors. Within the pages of Ligon's album, unidentified Black families gather again and again across a span of four decades to pose stiffly in their Sunday best. In these photos, the image of familial closeness and financial stability is compulsively created and re-created, underscoring the social narrative to which these photos point, compelling the viewer to look and believe.[34] It is the narrative of Progress: the treacherous process by which post-slavery Black American identities are forged, which sociological literature demands and much African American art and writing anxiously reiterates.[35] If the family photos gathered in Ligon's album function not only as personal keepsakes but also as sociological documents to be scanned by parties searching, for one reason or another, for proof of the subjects' humanity, the pornographic images that abut them threaten to undo this hard-earned veneer of social respectability, spotlighting and "proving true" sociological narratives designating the African American family as sexually deviant and intrinsically nonheteronormative.[36]

Ligon devotes two pages of the album to a collection of birth announcements and snapshots featuring infants. The babies appear strangely isolated, posed before plain backgrounds or propped against furniture sized for absent adults. The sole adult featured in these pages appears in the form of a nude, grinning Black man, gripping his erect phallus and reclining among the detritus of ashtrays and dirty clothes in what appears to be a slovenly bachelor pad. The man bears the suggestive label "The baby's father," yet his carefree manner renders him indifferent to the children populating the pages, and impervious to the viewer's efforts to search for similarities between his face and those of the babies pictured around him. Positioned as such, he assumes the stereotype of the absent Black father, which Moynihan identified as a present threat to urban peace and stability, and Black Panther Party Supreme Commander Huey Newton decried as a symptom of Black male rage and impotence in the face of the system.[37]

Apposite to the sociological myth of the absent father and the Black matriarchy is a page in Ligon's album labeled simply "Daddy," in which the majority of figures pictured are actually female (figure 6.6). Two snapshots aligned along the left side of the page each feature a solitary Black woman dressed formally in a good suit, gloves, hat, and pumps. The women clutch handbags as if to go out: it matters little whether they are destined for work or for leisure; either way, the photos gesture toward the sociological fantasy of the working-class Black woman, dangerously at liberty to both earn and spend her money as she chooses, in the absence of a "Daddy" to provide her livelihood.

The photo at the bottom of the page initially appears to depict a benevolent "sugar daddy" enjoying the company of five smartly dressed young women who cluster affectionately around him, ignoring a younger man situated at the left margin of the image. Yet a closer look reveals a flowered armchair and an upright lamp, identifying the setting as a living room and the older man as a beloved patriarch. If the stately gentleman pictured in this photo can thus be understood to represent the strong father figure that Moynihan and others believed to be lacking in African American families, the stridently sexual "Daddy" in the photo directly above—packing an impressive phallus beneath his trench coat and cowboy hat—may represent the type of man that Black women were presumed to be taking up with in their willfully deviant relationships. As Ferguson recalls, in the 1960s welfare aid to single Black mothers was offered on the condition that they submit to the surveillance of "welfare detectives" who would invade their homes in the middle of the night "to look through dirty clothes hampers and refrigerators in search of Black men."[38]

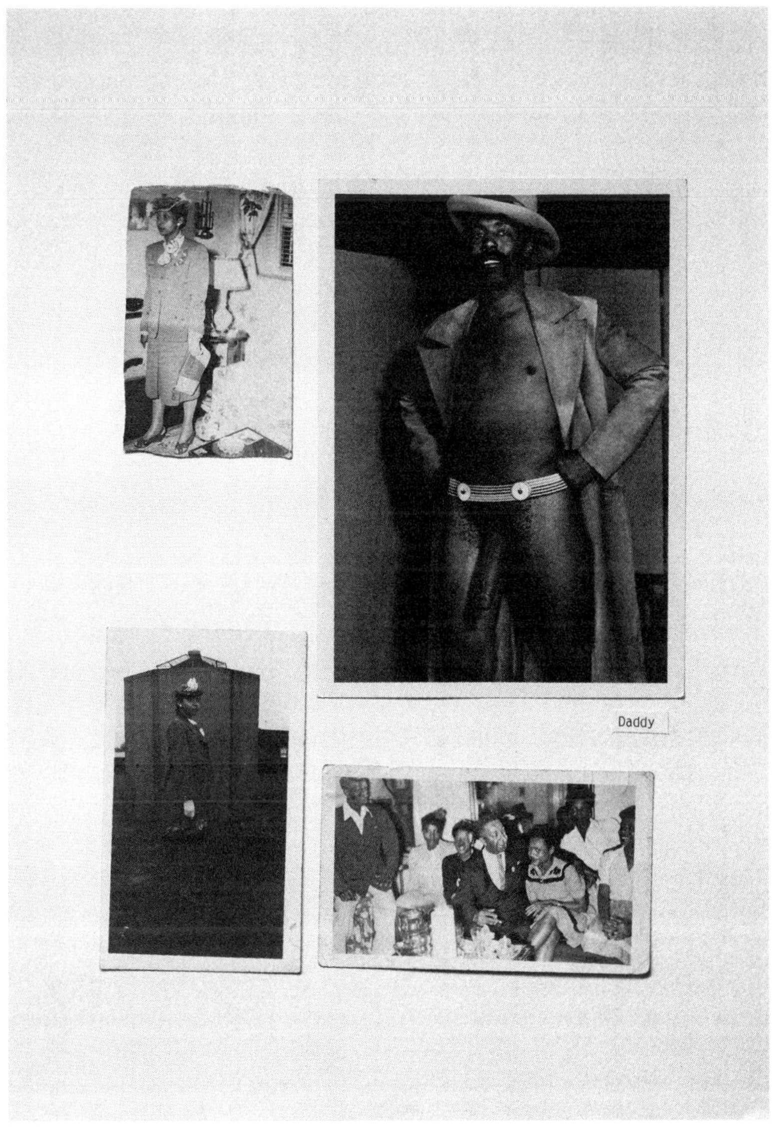

Figure 6.6 Glenn Ligon, *A Feast of Scraps* (detail), 1994–1998. Photographs and text, 20½ × 11½ inches. © Glenn Ligon; Courtesy of the artist, Hauser & Wirth, and Thomas Dane Gallery.

"The Photograph," writes Barthes, "reproduces to infinity [what] has occurred only once: the Photograph mechanically repeats what could never be repeated existentially."[39] For Barthes, this inherent contradiction is the essence of photography: it is the ultimate signifier of the Real, yet unrepeatable in reality. So do the photographs of Black families in Ligon's album gesture toward a vision of racial progress and familial cohesiveness against which the actual, human subjects of the pictures were constantly measured and found wanting. According to Barthes, to pose for a photograph is to actively transform oneself into an image and to file that image under the category of the Real.[40] This accounts for the uncanny power that the pornographic pictures collected in the album effect over the adjacent scenes of domestic tranquility; by agreeing to pose in porno tableaus that work to stimulate and satiate White fantasies surrounding the Black male body,[41] these models threaten to actualize sexualized racist preconceptions.

Fanon possessed both a heightened awareness of the oppressive weight of White racist fantasies and, as a close investigation of *Black Skin, White Masks* reveals, a deep suspicion of Black subjects whom he believed to be collaborationists in the formulation of these fantasies. In *Black Skin, White Masks*, the terrain of Black male sexuality is rendered as a minefield riddled throughout with the salacious projections of Whites, and Fanon's discomfort with this subject is not limited to his personal experiences as the target of this objectification. Insomuch as these fantasies invoke the possibility of interracial sex, and therefore the creation of biracial subjects, they likewise threaten Fanon's attempts to arrive at a watertight definition of "Negro" subjectivity. This is nowhere more evident than in the means by which Fanon extracted himself from that unbearable situation in the French train car. Fanon relates the comment of a woman, presumably the mother of the boy who initially objectified him, who attempts to rectify the situation by paying him an indirect sort of compliment: "Look how handsome that Negro is!" Thus submitted as an object for the aesthetic *appreciation* of the Whites in the car, Fanon retorts, "Kiss the handsome Negro's ass, madame!"[42]

Fanon will not be reassured of his physical beauty by a White woman; he feels it to be a reiteration, rather than a negation, of his own dehumanization. In delivering his retort, he refers to himself in his tormentor's terms, as if to amplify the theft of his subjectivity for her uncomprehending ears. If the woman's comment broaches the forbidden possibility of cross-racial sexual attraction, Fanon's reply renders it explicit, provoking her shame even at the expense of denigrating his own Black body.

Nor is this the first place in the text where Black male sexuality emerges as the locus of White racist fantasies; Fanon dedicates two entire chapters of *Black Skin, White Masks* to the topic of Black sexuality, organizing chapters 2 and 3 according to the heteropatriarchal pairings: "The Woman of Color and the White Man" and "The Man of Color and the White Woman."[43] The fact that sexual and romantic relationships between Black men and Black women are never discussed—much less investigated as a potential site of liberation and resistance—is indicative of the degree to which Fanon in *Black Skin, White Masks* presumes Black sexuality to be not merely overdetermined by White racist fantasies, but fundamentally corrupted by colonialist perversions. Fanon locates the root of this corruption within the Black woman, who he presumes possesses a fundamental desire to breed her own race out of existence by partnering with and bearing the children of White men. In his second chapter he excoriates the Antillean memoirist Mayotte Capécia as an avatar of this desire, denouncing her work *Je suis Martiniquaise* (1948) as "a sermon in praise of corruption."[44]

The subject of sexuality proves to be an especially fraught one for Fanon in his efforts to sketch out a schema for postcolonial Black identities, for, as Reid-Pharr notes, the sexual unions that produced the inhabitants of places such as Fanon's native Martinique in the wake of colonization demand that one recognize in the dark face "not simply the slave but the slaver," making it difficult to distinguish "the torturer from her victims."[45] Fanon's suspicion of Black colonial subjects whom he presumes seek to "whiten" their way out of abjection through sexual alliances with colonizers is not, however, directed solely toward the reproductive acts by which this deracination is presumed to occur. Fanon's brief remarks on homosexuality in *Black Skin, White Masks* are remarkable, particularly for the ways in which he conflates the subject with the dynamics of coercion and iniquity that he identifies as intrinsic to interracial heterosexual relationships within a colonial setting; indeed, in his first reference to homosexuality, Fanon simply swaps one for the other. Speculating whether "Negrophobic" women are justified in their fears of sexually rapacious Black men, he concludes, "the Negrophobic woman is in fact nothing but a putative sexual partner—just as the Negrophobic man is a repressed homosexual."[46]

The ease with which Fanon parallels the fear that the White racist woman harbors for the imaginary, sexually avaricious Black male with the

White racist man's desire for the same archetype demands further scrutiny. In Fanon's schema, homosexuality in the colonial world specifically connotes the one-sided desire of a White man for a Black man; the consummation of this desire fulfills an appetite for self-degradation on the part of the former, and revenge on the part of the latter.[47] Moreover, Fanon reads these desires as a more virulent manifestation of the White subject's failure to recognize Black subjects—or, more precisely, to misrecognize them as embodiments of and outlets for forbidden passions.[48] The desire for interracial sex on the part of the White subject can thereby signal only as perversion, a type of masochism reliant upon the social strictures of racism itself, a point that Fanon makes clear by contrasting what he perceives to be the desires of "passive" European homosexuals with those of "Negrophobic" White women who nonetheless "putatively" desire interracial intercourse.

For Fanon, homosexuality constitutes simply another infectious European disease imposed upon unwilling colonized peoples with deleterious effects.[49] It is, indeed, Fanon's failure to imagine Black sexualities outside of the dynamics of coercion and imposition that limits so severely his articulations of Black sexual subjects. Speaking only of, and to, White racist tropes of the sexually excessive Black man, the sexually sycophantic Black woman, and the coveted fetish of the Black male homosexual, Fanon is distressingly in the thrall of the racist imagination that he purports to criticize. The hypersexualized Black Other of the White imagination—the only Black sexual being present in Fanon's text—must, by the logic of his critique, be eradicated if the Black subject is to recuperate a unitary sense of selfhood from the dislocating impositions of White racist projections.

Given the delimited and, as Kobena Mercer claims, disappointing scope of Fanon's writings on Black sexuality,[50] the regularity with which Fanon emerges as a source cited by scholars addressing the topic of Black male sexuality is startling. Mercer, Isaac Julien, Reid-Pharr, Charles I. Nero, Charles Johnson, and, notably, Ligon himself have each in turn grappled with Fanon's fragmented musings on Black male sexuality, as if attempting to complete an unfinished but nonetheless foundational chapter in the writing of Black subjectivity. Stuart Hall notes that much of the attention in this relatively recent spike of interest in Fanon's work focuses on issues of identity and difference raised in *Black Skin, White Masks*.[51]

The urge to return to the unfinished business of Black sexuality in Fanon's work might not have resonated so strongly with contemporary theorists had sexual politics not proven, in Mercer's words, to be "the

Achilles heel of the black liberation movement."[52] Fanon's concept of homosexuality—exclusively male, inherently sadomasochistic, and always a product of European colonial impositions—echoes throughout Black liberationist literary dispatches of the 1960s and 1970s, perhaps most notoriously in the work of the Black Panther Party's Minister of Information, Eldridge Cleaver.

In his 1966 essay "Notes on a Native Son," Cleaver attacked James Baldwin for what he perceived to be the author's "fanatical, fawning, sycophantic love of the whites"—an act of "race-betrayal" which, according to Cleaver, was both motivated and encapsulated by Baldwin's homosexuality.[53] The Black homosexual, writes Cleaver, is "a white man in a black body," and his putative desire for White male bodies signifies nothing less than a self-annihilating drive to extinguish his race, a deliberate turning away from "the sacred vehicle of life and love" by which Black Americans would supposedly be sustained by consolidating their powers in heteropatriarchal unity.[54]

Comparing Baldwin to Yacub, the mythical Black scientist whom followers of the Nation of Islam believe selectively bred the White race into existence out of a mad desire to obliterate the "original" Black inhabitants of Earth, Cleaver rages that Baldwin and his work constitute an attack on Black masculinity—the "stud" power by which Cleaver clearly believed the revolution would be achieved.[55] Cleaver's condemnation of Baldwin's "little jive ass,"[56] according to Rudolph P. Byrd, thus "legitimized homophobia in Black public discourse" at a crucial turning point in African American history as the goals and ideologies of various Black liberationist movements began to coalesce.[57]

While different manifestations of the Black Power movement continued to multiply, as ideological differences caused Black activists to gravitate variously toward Afrocentrism, the Black Panther Party, the Nation of Islam, or the burgeoning field of Black studies, individuals central to all of these movements advocated for the purging of Black homosexuals from their ranks. Cleaver's conviction that homosexual desire in Black men constituted a "racial death wish" reached audiences via a diverse body of African American literature and activism, from Black liberationist poet Imamu Amiri Baraka's tirades against "faggots" to African American studies pioneer Molefi Asante's declaration that homosexuality "is a deviation from Afrocentric thought."[58] The notion that homosexuality constituted a present threat to the very survival of African American communities was reiterated in the fiery pronouncements of ministers Louis Farrakhan and Khalid Abdul Muhammad, and couched in clinical terms in the writings of psychologists Frances Cress Welsing and Nathan and Julia Hare.[59] The work of creating an Afrocentric history from which Black Americans could draw sustenance thus became a simultaneous exorcism of the contributions of Black gay Americans, from the Harlem Renaissance onward; their excision reverberates still, just as abrupt and painful as Fanon's separation from his own, specularized body while trapped in that French train car.[60]

In *A Feast of Scraps*, language is the thread that sutures together these disparate histories, allowing for a host of multiple meanings that permit points of contact and overlap between the seemingly irreconcilable lives represented therein. "To speak," writes Fanon, "means above all to assume a culture, to support the weight of a civilization."[61] As a colonial subject, Fanon conceives of language in terms of imposition and loss, expressing a nostalgic yearning for a precolonial state of linguistic cohesiveness, a desire to name something outside of the oppressor's lexicon. Yet in *A Feast of Scraps*, Ligon reveals the polysemous potentialities of the master's language, utilizing terms that denote the relative positions of authority within the heteropatriarchal family structure—"Father," "Brother," and so on—and using double entendre to establish alternative relationships beyond the hegemonic kinship structures that these terms officially represent. This quick-witted transformation of meaning is encompassed within Henry Louis Gates Jr.'s concept of *signifying*. "Signifying," writes Gates, is "the black term for what in classical European rhetoric are called the figures of signification" or "the indirect use of words that changes the meaning of a word or words."[62] Charles I. Nero adds, "As a rhetorical strategy, signifying assumes that there is shared knowledge between communicators and, therefore, that information can be given indirectly."[63]

It is the indirect conveyance of multivalent meanings that bring the erotics of *A Feast of Scraps* to life; the words Ligon has chosen resonate within both Black and queer idioms, establishing an implicit understanding between the figures of Black middle-class respectability and their subaltern relations who have been officially disappeared from the community. Above the label "Brother" lies a young Black man sporting an Afro that periodizes him roughly within the context of the debates over Black identity that consumed Afrocentric movements of the 1960s and 1970s—a period that overlaps with Ligon's own sexual awakening. Like Fanon experiencing the division of his self into three under the invasive gaze of the White spectator, the suggestive coupling of the caption with the intimate photo bestows a triple meaning upon the subject: he is the child of your mother, your blood brother; a "brother" in racial solidarity, the child of Mother Africa; and, finally, a "down-low brother"—a slang term for a sexually discreet Black man who is attracted to men. Below, Ligon has placed a photo of a group of solemn-faced elders gathered at a long table. Only a single, younger man smiles slightly and winks suggestively at the camera, anticipating and desiring the viewer's understanding. In this way, Ligon's album both compels the viewer to look and catches them in the act. The surreptitious wink becomes a tacit acknowledgment of the spectator's not entirely disinterested contemplation of the photographs' subjects: it is as if he knows what thoughts these images may provoke in the viewer's mind, and wants them to know that he knows.

This polysemic discourse between text and image, photographic subject and beholder, gives the images collected within *A Feast of Scraps* the photographic quality that Barthes identifies as "pensive": a photograph is only truly subversive, he writes, "when it thinks," or when it encourages associations that go beyond the straightforward, "unary"[64] image that the photograph initially appears to offer.[65] Though the family photographs collected in Ligon's album may seem to fall under Barthes's definition of unary photography, reproducing the ideal of familial harmony without doubling or disturbing the generative scene from which they derive, it is the inclusion of pornographic images that imbue the album with Barthes's *punctum*: the detail that at once seduces and distracts the beholder from the self-evident content of the photograph and encourages them to imagine "a whole life external" to what the photograph purports to show.[66]

The photographic *punctum*, according to Barthes, is that which "pricks" the viewer, a partial detail that piques the imagination.[67] To discover the punctum is to abandon disinterested contemplation and recognize certain desires, repulsions, tendencies, and prejudices. For Barthes, "there is no *punctum* in the pornographic image"; nothing, he claims, "is more homogeneous than a pornographic photograph . . . [it] is completely constituted by the presentation of only one thing: sex."[68] Yet like the punctum, "dirty" pictures compel the viewer to "give [themselves] up," if only to themselves; the feelings of excitement, disgust, or disinterest they inspire emerge heedless of the viewer's sense of "morality or good taste."[69] To be swayed by the punctum is to abandon the Kantian state of detached aesthetic judgment and tread into the dangerous territory of the emotional, the corporeal, and of that nebulous concept in obscenity law, "prurient interest."[70]

A Feast of Scraps overflows Barthes's definitions of both the punctum and pornography: in its pages the meanings of discrete words and images shift in response to one another, inspiring the reader to imagine ulterior narratives beyond what the individual photographs initially appear to show. The punctum in Ligon's work is mobile, multifaceted, and changeable, and despite Barthes's insistence on the monofunctional nature of pornographic images, the album makes it significantly difficult for the viewer to concentrate on sex. Confronted with the coupling of images that play to primitivizing fantasies of virile Black men and others which reproduce and enshrine the aspirational ideal of the Black nuclear family, the viewer is compelled to contemplate the very last thing one wishes to consider in taking the image of another as the subject of one's fantasy: Who is this model, and where did he come from? Do the family photos clustered nearby afford a glimpse of his origins, and, if so, how does he reconcile them with the image he now presents?

Whether pornographic or prosaic, the photographs collected in *A Feast of Scraps* ultimately cast doubt upon the potential for representational images—"positive" or otherwise—to counteract the derogatory, anti-Black tropes perpetuated through White supremacist discourse. Didactic representations of Black familial stability ultimately do little to dislodge these attitudes, as the Black family remains the constant subject of social surveillance, and thus always outside of the heteropatriarchal norms against which it is measured. The people pictured in the family photos are not so dissimilar from the pornographic models pictured nearby in the sense that both are subjugated by White preconceptions of Black sociosexual realities and possibilities, irrespective of whether they seek to effect "respectable" visions of the Black family and Black masculinity. Through Ligon's intervention, these images appear no longer disparate but linked, albeit through a history of conflict, schisms, and separations: in short, a portrait of a family.

The substance and verve of the queer desires that animate the album manifest through familial terms; it is the power and protectionism implicit in the patriarchal household that make the word "Daddy" attach itself so seductively to a lover. Yet this queer deployment of kinship terms also points toward a sober reality experienced by many Black gay subjects, rejected by their families and forced to seek new support structures within predominantly White gay communities. "They told me I had to change up," declares a block of text pasted opposite a page containing a single, well-worn photo of an extended family gathering. "I just wanted somebody who was down" is the cocky conclusion to this statement, punningly positioned beneath a blown-out snapshot of a Black man topping a White bottom (figures 6.3, 6.4). The sheer multiplicity of smiling faces in the portrait of the intergenerational family throws the picture on the adjoining page into stark relief: cropped tightly around the legs and asses of the two men, the photograph at once consigns them to anonymity and expels any other potential figures from the scene, underscoring the couple's isolation from the reproductive family presented in the photo opposite. Presumably, the members of this family have withdrawn their collective support as a punishment for the behavior they expected their deviant relative to "change up"—namely, wanting a man, and a White man in particular, to get "down" with him.

Cast out of the family circle, this anonymous Black man is presented without a genealogical lineage, a history, even a face: in the photograph, the facts of his individuality are reduced to the color of his skin, and the White man impaled beneath him. Casting the Black gay male in the role of executioner to his own race, Eldridge Cleaver conflates homosexuality and interracial sex into a selfsame threat to the survival of Black people: "It seems that many Negro homosexuals are outraged and frustrated because in their sickness they are unable to have a baby by a white man. The cross they have to bear is that, already bending over and touching their toes for the white man, the fruit of their miscegenation is not the little half-white offspring of their dreams but an increase in the unwinding of their nerves—though they redouble their efforts and intake of the white man's sperm."[71]

The strange formation that Cleaver employs to express his vitriol toward Black male homosexuality warrants close investigation. Cleaver performs a classic fetishistic disavowal: leaving aside that he "knows very well" that no offspring, "mixed" or otherwise, are generated by sex between men, Cleaver "just the same" projects this fantasy onto the mind of the Black gay man, bizarrely invoking the White supremacist bogeyman of "miscegenation" in the service of his supposedly liberationist philosophy of Black masculinist resistance. Cleaver in one breath condemns both homosexual and heterosexual acts of interracial sex, and for the same reason: both fail to reproduce "authentic" Black subjects under the aegis of the Black male–headed household. In this way, both of the aforementioned photographs fail to meet Cleaver's ideal: the smiling faces in the family photo present a wide range of skin tones, testifying to interracial sex as a reality that has shaped American families for centuries. Yet the vast white gulf of the page gutter that separates this family gathering from the scene of queer, interracial sex just opposite makes plain how heteropatriarchal ideologies like Cleaver's have changed the makeup of Black families: not all acts, nor all individuals, are allowed to become a matter of family record.

"Necessity is a *mother*," proclaims the text positioned beneath a photo of a muscular nude Black man standing against a stark, pale background, his fists balled at his sides as if in determination (figure 1.7). This dual play on the expression "Necessity is the mother of invention"—and, more provocatively, "Necessity is a motherfucker"—raises the question of the necessity to which Ligon's subjects are bound. The institutions of marriage and the military represented on this page suggest that the heteronormative lifestyle does indeed inspire a particular kind of invention in subjects compelled to participate by a sense of necessity rather than desire: namely, the wholesale reinvention of one's persona in order to "pass" in a heteropatriarchal world.

Yet at the same time, Ligon allows that this passing may not always be necessary—or convincing. "Mother knew," declares the text accompanying a photo of a sweetly smiling young Black man who leans coquettishly toward the camera, his robe hanging suggestively open, imparting a sense of the unspoken truth that "Mother" has intuited. More than any other junction in the album, this convergence of text and image reminds one of *who* is typically responsible for the creation of the family album, and the author of the family history that it encapsulates. One also may be spurred to consider this by how something about viewing *A Feast of Scraps* in its various iterations never feels quite right, whether the work is presented in a gallery context or reprinted in an exhibition catalog. To view the pages of a scrapbook disgorged and presented at a respectable distance in a glass vitrine is to view it uncomfortably outside of the context in which one normally absorbs the pictorial history of a family. *Console* (1995), an installation work produced concurrently with *A Feast of Scraps*, partially reconstructs the settings in which family albums are typically perused (figure 6.7). Ligon provides a mock-up of a family room, with various markers of middle-class comfort (a cocktail set, a souvenir Disneyland mug, copies of *Jet* magazine) arranged as fastidiously as dollhouse furniture atop an entertainment console. The open pages of a scrapbook included amongst these objects remind one that the invitation to familiarize oneself with these intimate histories

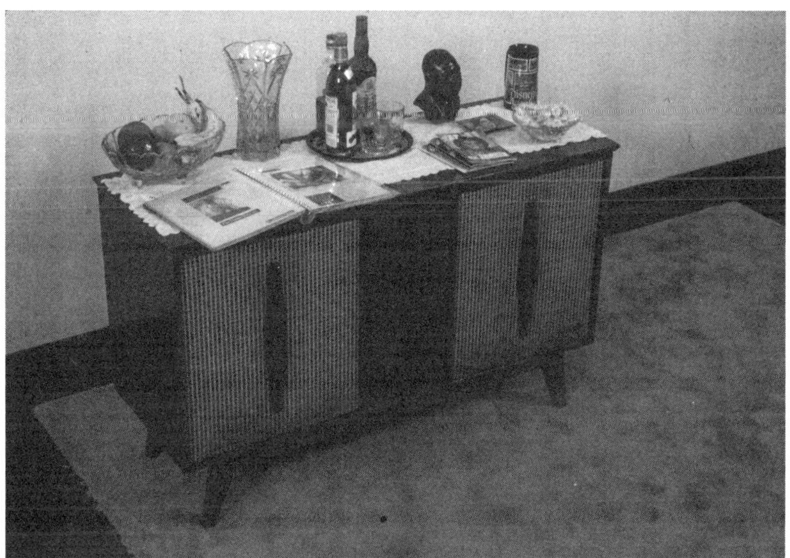

Figure 6.7 Glenn Ligon, *Console*, 1995. Mixed media, variable dimensions.

usually extends from an invitation into the home itself, which is typically issued by the keeper of both the family home and history: the mother. Her overture opens up possibilities for both intimacy and embarrassment, threatening to disclose details of personal histories that the subjects would sometimes rather leave behind. By engaging in the gendered labor of scrapbooking, Ligon poses a similarly chiding corrective to heteropatriarchal, revisionist narratives of Black American history, reuniting them with the queer, effeminate brethren that they tried to excise from the cultural record.

The mother-author of the family album is doubly responsible for the family reproduced therein: as the progenitor and the axis around which the family coalesces, she is responsible both for the subjects themselves and for building their histories through her archive. If the album that she assembles is meant to project and reify the impression of familial stability, the mother first bears the responsibility for reproducing a narrative of familial cohesiveness through her own body—a body that, in its potential for promiscuity and unregulated reproduction, simultaneously threatens the undoing of this institution. Reid-Pharr traces the roots of what he declares "a constant misogyny embedded within Black American radicalism" to the pernicious cultural expectation that Black mothers are uniquely responsible for "maintain[ing] a fiction of black unity" by bearing and raising ideal Black subjects. This expectation, Reid-Pharr notes, is attended and undercut by a parallel conviction in the perfidiousness of Black female sexuality that exists in the Black American imaginary. Citing Angela Davis's claim that "the enslaved woman is understood to be treacherous precisely because of her centrality to the reproduction and maintenance of the slave family," Reid-Pharr reminds us that the Black American woman carries the evidence of White "colonialism" in her body and, by extension, in her offspring, the lighter skin tones and pale eyes serving as a constant reminder of Black Americans' subjugation—and of the Black woman's supposed complicity.[72]

A symmetry between the reproductive Black female subjects and the queer Black male subjects of Ligon's album thus emerges: in certain strains of Black liberationist thought, both are suspected of collusion with the oppressor; of taking in "prodigious amounts of the white man's sperm" and perhaps referring to these unions, and any offspring produced thereof, by the term "love." Cleaver's bizarre choice of reproductive figures of speech in his condemnations of Black gay men thus comes into focus: in accusing Black gay men of trying to do the "job" of women, he simultaneously evokes the figure of the traitorous Black woman who sleeps with the enemy in her efforts to produce a "half-white offspring" through which, in Reid-Pharr's words, she might "displace the white father from his seat of victory."[73] The Black woman is the target of such vehement antipathy in Black liberationist discourse because she threatens the system of self-replicating patriarchy that it (futilely) demands. In a peculiar echo of the divine right of European kings, the ideal of Black Power put forth by certain Black male theorists is passed from Black male subject to Black male subject without the messiness of women, reproduction, or the insecurity about paternity and miscegenation that the Black female body signifies in this discourse. It is she who produces these bastard subjects—pale, queer, or otherwise outside of the essentialist racial ideal—and she who ensures their inclusion in familial and cultural histories by way of her acceptance and love. "Mother knew."

In assembling the ragtag family presented in *A Feast of Scraps*, Ligon becomes the mother to this multitude: it is he who compels us to see these mismatched figures as a unit, prompting us to compare the genteel faces of the members of middle-class Black families with those of the pornographic models—searching here for a distinctive profile, there for a similar smile—and he whose subjectivity is consolidated and reflected in their collective image.[74] Black, male, and gay, Ligon's profile matches those of the subjects deliberately excluded from Black heteropatriarchal discourse. He thus finds a means of actualizing himself through bastard subjects picked from archives of dubious pedigree, filling in the gaps where information has been deliberately effaced, displaced, or disappeared by creating a queer lineage informed by speculation, fantasy, and desire.

The final words of Ligon's album articulate succinctly the risks and potential pleasures inherent in regarding queer, Black subjects—rejected in conservative Afrocentric rhetoric as dupes to the White fetishistic imagination—and recognizing them as kin. Sandwiching a photo of four nude Black men posing in front of a thicket of brush, a pair of captions tease out the phrase: "It's a process—It's not natural." The image is flanked across two pages by a series of photos that effectively chronicle the African American quest for social dignity and economic stability. The noble pursuits of marriage, childrearing, and brotherhood are reinscribed throughout these snapshots, notably in an image of what appears to be a sizable family reunion composed largely—but not exclusively—of Black people, proud to gather under the nationalist banner of the "Yankee Doodle Lodge." Yet this pointed juxtaposition reminds us how the perennial demand that African Americans demonstrate their "progress" in overcoming the long history of their own subjugation has both facilitated a culture of scopophilic surveillance around the Black family and compelled some Black subjects to disavow others, whose very being was interpreted as incompatible with the process of attaining respectability.

This fraught history weighs particularly heavily upon the image of the four nude Black men, grinning and jostling one another against a "naturalistic" backdrop. The picture seems to vindicate the deep suspicion harbored by Fanon and others toward eroticized Black male bodies: the photo rehearses a White fantasy, the twisted desires of a racist imagination. Such an image is truly not "natural," but a perverse reenactment of a long process of colonialist imposition. Yet it is through the productive reuse of these discarded ciphers of desire that Ligon makes apparent the psychic weight that the subjects of these photos share with those featured in the family photographs, who likewise find the intricacies of their social, sexual, and familial lives subject to invasive scrutiny. In so doing, he produces a kind of

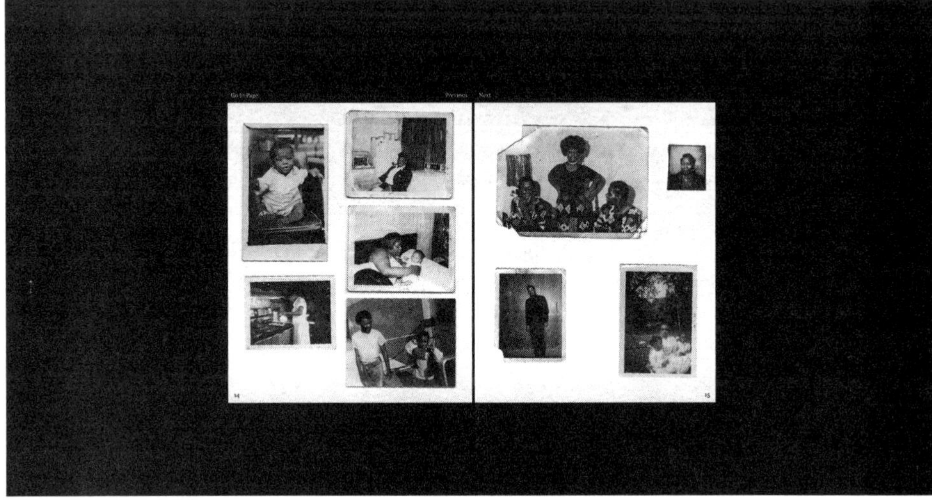

Figure 6.8 Glenn Ligon, *Annotations*, 2003. Dia web project. © Glenn Ligon; Courtesy of the artist, Hauser & Wirth, and Thomas Dane Gallery.

solidarity: a network of tenuous, prodigal bonds, approaching something like family (figure 6.8).

Notes

1. Darby English, *How to See a Work of Art in Total Darkness* (Cambridge, MA: MIT Press, 2007), 9. As English notes (54–55), "'a revival of art and literature' ranked second in the itemized program for black uplift" that W. E. B. Du Bois published in 1915 in the magazine he founded, *The Crisis: A Record of the Darker Races*. Du Bois's investment in the development of a quintessentially Black American culture of arts and letters is examined at length in English's first chapter, "Beyond Black Representational Space" (27–70).

2. As English notes, the expectations imposed by proponents of the Black Arts and Black Aesthetics movements demanded even that Black artists develop an "ethnic consciousness" through their work by dedicating "special attention to the accurate rendering of black physiognomy"—as the stability of this concept was assumed to be self-evident (*How to See a Work of Art*, 64).

3. English, *How to See a Work of Art*, 32.

4. "Black is / Black ain't" is both a phrase from Ralph Ellison's *Invisible Man* (1952) and the title of a 1994 film directed by Marlon Riggs. *Black Is, Black Ain't* is also the title of an exhibition organized around the subject of Blackness that appeared at the Renaissance Society at the University of Chicago in 2008, in which Ligon exhibited a work (see Krista Thompson's essay reprinted in this volume). My thinking on "voyeurism and fetishism" is indebted

to Peggy Phelan's skeptical reinvestigation of the power dynamics of visibility politics in *Unmarked: The Politics of Performance* (London: Routledge, 1993), 6.

5. English, *How to See a Work of Art*, 223. Ligon's statement appears in Byron Kim, "Interview with Glenn Ligon," in *Glenn Ligon: Unbecoming*, exh. cat., ed. Judith Tannenbaum (Philadelphia: Institute of Contemporary Art, 1997), 52.

6. Christine S. Kim, "*Glenn Ligon: AMERICA*," vlog, Whitney Museum of American Art, accessed April 15, 2013, https://whitney.org/media/428.

7. *A Feast of Scraps* was commissioned for the exhibition *The Masculine Masquerade: Masculinity and Representation*, which was presented at the MIT List Visual Arts Center in 1995. The first iteration of the work appears in the exhibition catalog with an accompanying essay by the artist. It is to this initial presentation of the work that my essay refers. In subsequent exhibitions in which *A Feast of Scraps* was included, the photos were presented in conventional albums, or a copy of the *Masculine Masquerade* catalog was provided for viewers to peruse. I am grateful to the artist for clarifying these points for me in a conversation on July 20, 2010. See also Glenn Ligon, "A Feast of Scraps," in *The Masculine Masquerade: Masculinity and Representation*, ed. Andrew Perchuk and Helaine Posner (Cambridge, MA: MIT Press, 1995), 89–99.

8. Conversation with the artist, July 20, 2010. I will here stress that some of the photos feature Ligon's relatives while others do not, and Ligon is (perhaps strategically) cagey about which is which.

9. Ligon, "A Feast of Scraps," 89.

10. Ligon, "A Feast of Scraps," 89.

11. Ligon, "A Feast of Scraps," 89.

12. Conversation with the artist, July 20, 2010.

13. Robert F. Reid-Pharr, *Black Gay Man: Essays* (New York: New York University Press, 2001), 62.

14. As Samuel R. Delany reminds us, the modern concept of the "family" itself is a fairly recent invention. Urging caution against the assumption that the family is "a transcultural absolute, arcadian in origin, . . . an 'authentic' form of sociality that is somehow battered and undermined by 'inauthentic' forces of urbanism, industrialism, and modernism," Delany parses Philippe Ariès, arguing: "The family is specifically a bourgeois institution that originates in the upper middle class. . . . When times are bad, it crumbles from the bottom up" (Samuel R. Delany, foreword to Reid-Pharr, *Black Gay Man*, xiii–xiv).

15. Roderick A. Ferguson, *Aberrations in Black: Toward a Queer of Color Critique* (Minneapolis: University of Minnesota Press, 2004).

16. Roland Barthes, *Camera Lucida: Reflections on Photography*, trans. Richard Howard (New York: Hill and Wang, 1981), 103.

17. Ligon, "A Feast of Scraps," 89.

18. Frantz Fanon, *Black Skin, White Masks*, trans. Charles Lam Markmann (New York: Grove Press, 1967). Because in this essay I read *Black Skin, White Masks* in conjunction with writings on Black male sexuality produced by American Black liberationist thinkers of the 1960s and 1970s, I refer to the 1967 English translation that would have been available to Black American revolutionaries at the time instead of the more recent translation of 2008 by Richard Philcox.

19. Fanon, *Black Skin, White Masks*, 170.

20. Fanon, *Black Skin, White Masks*, 109.

21. Fanon, *Black Skin, White Masks*, 112

22. Fanon, *Black Skin, White Masks*, 217.

23. Fanon, *Black Skin, White Masks*, 111.

24. Fanon, *Black Skin, White Masks*, 109.

25. Barthes, *Camera Lucida*, 13.

26. Barthes, *Camera Lucida*, 13–14.

27. See Kobena Mercer, "Looking for Trouble," *Transition* 51 (1991): 184–197; as well as Mercer (with Isaac Julien), "Black Masculinity and the Sexual Politics of Race: True Confessions," and Mercer, "Reading Racial Fetishism: The Photographs of Robert Mapplethorpe," both in Mercer, *Welcome to the Jungle: New Positions in Black Cultural Studies* (New York: Routledge, 1994), 131–170, and 171–219.

28. Ferguson, *Aberrations in Black*, 87.

29. Ferguson, *Aberrations in Black*, 75.

30. Ferguson, *Aberrations in Black*, 88–89.

31. Ferguson, *Aberrations in Black*, 37.

32. Ferguson, *Aberrations in Black*, 119–122.

33. Lauri Firstenberg, "Neo-archival and Textual Modes of Production: An Interview with Glenn Ligon," *Art Journal* 60, no. 1 (Spring 2001): 44; quoted in Darby English, "Glenn Ligon: Committed to Difficulty," in *Glenn Ligon: Some Changes*, ed. Thelma Golden and Wayne Baerwaldt, exh. cat. (Toronto: Power Plant, 2005), 70.

34. "The Photograph," according to Barthes, "is never anything but the antiphon of 'Look,' 'See,' 'Here it is'; it points a finger at certain *vis-à-vis*, and cannot escape this pure deictic language" (*Camera Lucida*, 5).

35. Ligon has observed that literature has served a "treacherous" function for Black Americans, as "literary production has been so tied with the project of proving [Black American's] humanity through the act of writing"; see English, "Glenn Ligon: Committed to Difficulty," in *Glenn Ligon: Some Changes*, 68. Henry Louis Gates Jr. expresses similar sentiments in *Figures in Black: Words, Signs, and the "Racial" Self* (New York: Oxford University Press, 1987). Gates argues that scientific racism and dominant eighteenth-century theories on the inferiority of the African intellect spurred African Americans to point to their own literature as proof of the "progress and perfectibility of man" and of "the artistic potential of a 'race'" (see xxiv). See also English, *How to See a Work of Art*, 2–70.

36. Ferguson, *Aberrations in Black*, 87.

37. Huey Newton argued that urban Black men suffered from a crisis of masculinity under American "colonization" and that this crisis asserted itself in the form of certain pathologies; for instance, the ghettoized Black man "may even father several 'illegitimate' children by several different women in order to display his masculinity." Yet, Newton predicts, the Black man will soon see that his actions have no effect on the White superstructure that dictates the conditions of his being; he is thereby condemned to live in "a constant state of rage." See David Ray Papke, "The Black Panther Party's Narratives of Resistance," *Vermont Law Review* 18 (1993–1994): 659–660.

38. Ferguson, *Aberrations in Black*, 123.

39. Barthes, *Camera Lucida*, 4.

40. Barthes, *Camera Lucida*, 10.

41. Ligon asserts that the images he collected from Gay Treasures were "definitely intended for a White [male] audience" (conversation with the artist, July 20, 2010).

42. Fanon, *Black Skin, White Masks*, 114.

43. Fanon spends chapter 2 denigrating the memoirist Mayotte Capécia as a prime example of the Antillean woman's supposed urge to "whiten," to get outside her race by partnering with and bearing a child by a White man. He dedicates chapter 3 to abrading the fictional character Jean Veneuse, whose relationship with a White woman is derailed by his own feelings of self-loathing, and whom Fanon reads as a transparent stand-in for his author, René Maran (*Black Skin, White Masks*, 41–82).

44. Fanon, *Black Skin, White Masks*, 42. I am indebted on this point to Robert Reid-Pharr, who notes that Fanon's "difficult relationship to the questions of blackness and Americanness . . . is mediated through Fanon's hostility to the productive black female, the bad black mother." Unwilling to recognize Mayotte Capécia as his "intellectual peer" in the common goal of exposing "the lie of racial difference," Reid-Pharr writes, Fanon instead turns her into a sick subject to be analyzed, a "bad mama" desiring a mixed-race child; see Reid-Pharr, *Black Gay Man*, 69–71.

45. This problem, Reid-Pharr believes, proved too complex for Fanon's tastes, prompting a shift in his scholarship following his relocation to Africa: "The Fanon of *The Wretched of the Earth* [1961] and *A Dying Colonialism* [1959] . . . is a man considerably less troubled by the intricacies of racial difference than the one we see represented in *Black Skin, White Masks*" (*Black Gay Man*, 79). Produced in the context of colonized Martinique and of France, where Fanon was surrounded by the products of "racial mixing," *Black Skin, White Masks* is itself a sort of reluctant hybrid, which Fanon would abandon in favor of a tidier philosophy of racialism and unity in his later works.

46. Fanon, *Black Skin, White Masks*, 156.

47. Fanon, for instance, claims knowledge of "men who go to 'houses' in order to be beaten by Negroes; passive homosexuals who insist on black partners" (*Black Skin, White Masks*, 177). Fanon mentions desire between women only once, and only to dismiss the mere idea of such attraction as ridiculous. In a scalding retort to Michel Salomon's writings on the "prodigious vitality of the black man," Fanon declares, "M. Salomon, I have a confession to make to you: I have never been able, without revulsion, to hear a man say of another man; 'He is so sensual!' I do not know what the sensuality of a man is. Imagine a woman saying of another woman: 'She's so terribly desirable—she's darling'" (201). Fanon, reacting to Salomon's racist sexualization of Black men, is compelled to declare the very concept of male sensuality to be unthinkable. Lesbian sexuality is invoked to further underscore the preposterousness of this idea.

48. Fanon declares that the figure of the maleficent Black man inspires in the White man "regression to and fixation at pregenital levels of sexual development. . . . The Negro is taken as a terrifying penis" (*Black Skin, White Masks*, 177).

49. For instance, while he claims to have never detected the "overt presence of homosexuality" in his native Martinique, Fanon is quick to add that he has known "several Martinicans" who "became" homosexuals after arriving in Europe. Even in these circumstances, he argues, Antillean men remain fundamentally different from their "passive" homosexual European partners, stooping to homosexuality only "as a means of livelihood," rather than out of any particular "neurosis" (*Black Skin, White Masks*, 180n44).

50. See Kobena Mercer, "Decolonization and Disappointment: Reading Fanon's Sexual Politics," in *The Fact of Blackness: Frantz Fanon and Visual Representation*, ed. Alan Read (London: Institute of Contemporary Art and Bay Press, 1996), 115–129.

51. See Mercer, "Looking for Trouble"; Mercer and Julien, "Black Masculinity"; and Mercer, "Reading Racial Fetishism." See also Reid-Pharr, "At Home in America," in *Black Gay Man*, 62–84, esp. 69–80; Charles I. Nero, "Toward a Black Gay Aesthetic: Signifying in Contemporary Black Gay Literature," in *Brother to Brother: New Writings by Black Gay Men*, ed. Essex Hemphill (Boston: Alyson, 1991), 229–252; Charles Johnson, "A Phenomenology of the Black Body," in *Traps: African American Men on Gender and Sexuality*, ed. Rudolph P. Byrd and Beverly Guy-Sheftall (Bloomington: Indiana University Press, 2001), 223–235; and Stuart Hall, "The After-life of Frantz Fanon: Why Fanon? Why Now? Why *Black Skin, White Masks*?," in Read, *The Fact of Blackness*, 12–17, quotation on 14.

52. Mercer, "Decolonization and Disappointment," in Read, *The Fact of Blackness*, 116.

53. Eldridge Cleaver, "Notes on a Native Son," in *Soul on Ice* (New York: McGraw-Hill, 1968), 99. While it should be noted that Cleaver was an avid reader of Fanon's, declaring *The Wretched of the Earth* to be the "Bible" of the Black liberationist movement, he does not cite Fanon as a formative influence on any of his sentiments regarding Black homosexual men despite numerous similarities between the two authors' writings on the subject, which I note in this essay. See William L. Van Deburg, *New Day in Babylon: The Black Power Movement and American Culture, 1965–1975* (Chicago: University of Chicago Press, 1992), 60.

54. Cleaver, "Notes on a Native Son," 103. Judging by his remarks that "Negro homosexuals" attempted to indulge their "racial death-wish" through a prodigious "intake of the white man's sperm," Cleaver, like Fanon, was unable even to conceive of intimacy between Black women (see 102).

55. Cleaver, "Notes on a Native Son," 109.

56. This, along with "Sugar," is but one feminizing (and thereby, to Cleaver, derogatory) nickname given to James Baldwin in "Notes on a Native Son" (100, 106).

57. Rudolph P. Byrd, "Prologue: The Tradition of John: A Mode of Black Masculinity," in Byrd and Guy-Sheftall, *Traps*, 16. It should also be noted that Cleaver's opinions, while obviously enormously formative for the Black Panther Party's philosophy, did not go unopposed within the Party itself. In 1970, no less than Huey Newton, the Minister of Defense and Supreme Commander of the Black Panther Party, urged Black revolutionary support for and collaboration with feminist and gay activists. In a distinct departure from Cleaver, Newton declared that "maybe a homosexual could be the most revolutionary" in the ongoing struggle to transform American society. See Huey Newton, "A Letter from Huey to the Revolutionary Brothers and Sisters about the Women's Liberation and Gay Liberation Movements," *Black Panther Party Community News Service*, August 21, 1970, p. 5. That same year, white queer French novelist Jean Genet (whose words are replicated in Ligon's 1992 work *Untitled [I'm Turning Into a Specter before Your Very Eyes and I'm Going to Haunt You]*) illegally entered the United States and accompanied Black Panther Party officials on a multi-university tour, advocating on behalf of Bobby Seale and other Black political prisoners before audiences of mostly White students and academics. For a recent interpretation of this show of unity, see Lindsay Zafir, "Queer Connections: Jean Genet, the Black Panther Party, and Coalition Politics in the Long Sixties." *GLQ: A Journal of Lesbian and Gay Studies* 27, no. 2 (2021): 253–279.

58. Byrd, "Prologue," 18–19.

59. Byrd, "Prologue," 17-19; on Welsing and the Hares, see also Nero, "Toward a Black Gay Aesthetic," 231.

60. "Unmercifully imprisoned" by the White Other, Fanon wishes to slip the bonds of his body altogether: "What else could it be for me but an amputation, an excision, a hemorrhage that spattered my whole body with black blood?" (*Black Skin, White Masks*, 112).

61. Fanon, *Black Skin, White Masks*, 17.

62. Henry Louis Gates Jr., *The Signifying Monkey: A Theory of African-American Literary Criticism* (New York: Oxford University Press, 1988), 81.

63. Nero, "Toward a Black Gay Aesthetic," 230. For a useful discussion of signifying as it pertains to Ligon's oeuvre, see Okwui Enwezor, "Text, Subtext, Intertext: Painting, Language, and Signifying in the Work of Glenn Ligon," in *Glenn Ligon: AMERICA*, ed. Scott Rothkopf, exh. cat. (New York: Whitney Museum of American Art and Yale University Press, 2011), 51–63.

64. Here Barthes deploys a rather obscure term, meaning "having, consisting of, or acting on a single element, item, or component: monadic"; see Merriam-Webster.com, August 31, 2011, www.merriam-webster.com/dictionary/unary.

65. Barthes, *Camera Lucida*, 38–41.

66. Barthes, *Camera Lucida*, 40–42, 57.

67. Barthes, *Camera Lucida*, 51.

68. Barthes, *Camera Lucida*, 59; 41. Barthes does allow that the punctum may manifest in certain sexualized images, though he does so through an ultimately unsatisfying attempt to differentiate between "pornography" and "erotic photography":

> Pornography ordinarily represents the sexual organs, making them into a motionless object (a fetish), flattered like an idol that does not leave its niche; for me, there is no punctum in the pornographic image; at most it amuses me (and even then, boredom follows quickly). The erotic photograph, on the contrary (and this is its very condition), does not make the sexual organs into a central object; it may very well not show them at all; it takes the spectator outside its frame, and it is there that I animate this photograph and that it animates me. The punctum, then, is a kind of subtle beyond—as if the image launched desire beyond what it permits us to see: not only toward "the rest" of the nakedness, not only toward the fantasy of a praxis, but toward the absolute excellence of a being, body and soul together. (57–59)

This distinction between pornography and erotica, like all others I have read, is determined entirely by the author's personal definition of eroticism and is thus of little empirical use.

69. Barthes, *Camera Lucida*, 43.

70. See *Miller v. California*, 413 US 15 (1973).

71. Cleaver, "Notes on a Native Son," 102.

72. Reid-Pharr, *Black Gay Man*, 67–68.

73. Reid-Pharr, *Black Gay Man*, 72.

74. In his essay on *A Feast of Scraps* Ligon writes, "Many of the images I'm looking at replay [racist] stereotypes, yet as I try to put them aside I find I can't. A look, a face, a body, keeps bringing me back to them. The images are somehow familiar, like portraits of long-dead relatives you never met but in whose faces you can trace the contours of your own. I look closely and I begin to remember" ("A Feast of Scraps," 89).

7 "Negro Sunshine": Figuring Blackness in the Neon Art of Glenn Ligon

Krista Thompson

The phrase "negro sunshine," wrought in deceptively polite American font typescript, greeted visitors to the *Black Is, Black Ain't* exhibition at the Renaissance Society at the University of Chicago (figure 7.1). Sixteen feet long and three feet wide, the words radiated a clear ambient white light against a darkened wall. The piece, by artist Glenn Ligon, seemed from afar the familiar illumination of neon lighting—a script of letters forged through industrial tubing—appearing both singular and soldered together, hand- and machine-made, free-standing and plugged in. Indeed, approaching viewers might even have anticipated that buzz, that sonic static, which sometimes accompanies the visual electricity of neon signs that have been part of the American landscape since 1923. But as viewers neared the silent work, titled simply and suggestively *Warm Broad Glow* (2005), they might have observed that the two words were not lighted neon, but its obverse. In fact, the letters themselves were black, spray-painted in a dark-colored industrial compound known as Plasti Dip, which produces a matte finish that is the opposite of shine. Only the back of the neon tubing was not subsumed in the rubber coating, allowing a gentle white light to emanate against the wall behind it.

What viewers of Ligon's work, in fact, saw were the contours of black letters made visible by a tempered glow of light behind them, a kind of haloed silhouette. At first glance, the work appears to make blackness—the absence of light—legible. The work interestingly reverses the "optics of seeing" from Isaac Newton's studies of light and the color spectrum in 1666.[1] It was Newton who first surmised that "It was white light that

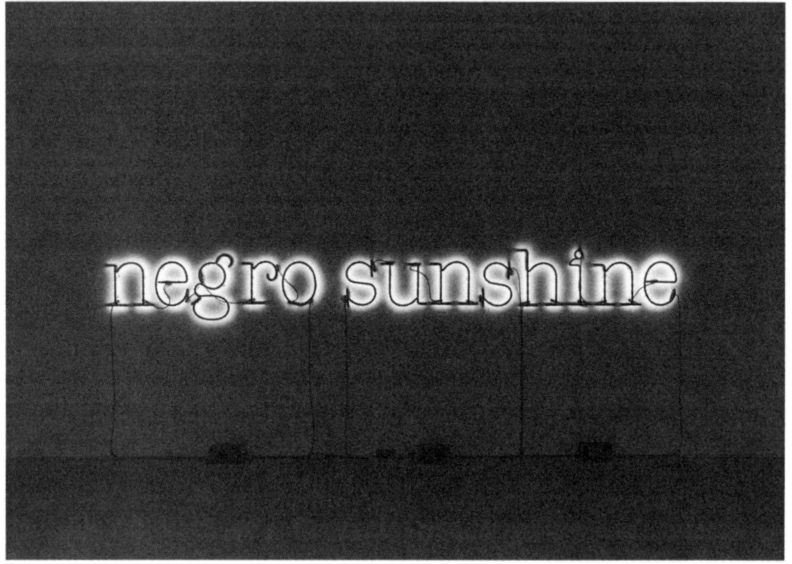

Figure 7.1 Glenn Ligon, *Warm Broad Glow*, 2005. Neon and paint, 36 × 192 inches. © Glenn Ligon; Courtesy of the artist, Hauser & Wirth, and Thomas Dane Gallery. Photography credit: Thomas Barratt.

contained all other colors, rather than, as had been believed before, black."[2] Thereafter, through Newton's and others' studies, as film theorist Richard Dyer maintains, light was associated with whiteness, universality, and visibility, and blackness with absence and invisibility.[3] What do we make of Ligon's black neon and its representation of blackness and light? What form of visibility does it reproduce, reflect, and refuse? What might it reveal more broadly about the representational context in which contemporary African-American artists create their work and its reception and legibility in the twenty-first century?

Warm Broad Glow is the first neon piece by Ligon, an artist well known for his text paintings, works that quote—through the thick materiality of paint—the words of writers and orators as diverse as Richard Dyer and Richard Pryor. In this essay, I consider Ligon's neon turn and his specific choice of medium: light and Plasti Dip. Ligon's use of black light and his production of shine, I maintain, highlight the historic and contemporary conditions and technologies, the always allusive processes, through which blackness is seen. More specifically, the work spotlights how blackness comes into view through commodification—how it becomes visible as it is packaged for consumption.

Ligon's particular form of neon and the ways it plays with the relations of visibility and invisibility also may speak specifically to the status of blackness in the contemporary art world. Currently, African-American artists, as Ligon notes, have unprecedented visibility—precisely at the moment when interest is waning in the politics of identity and race in mainstream American art.[4] Ligon's work inhabits and reflects the ambivalent status of blackness, its spotlighting and elision in contemporary art and, one might argue, in the United States more generally.

Standing before the wall-mounted letters of *Warm Broad Glow*, which announce themselves in that insistent way that neon invades the perceptual field, viewers might naturally try to understand the relation between "negro" and "sunshine." In small caps, and without so much as the now mandatory quotation marks surrounding the antiquated "negro," suspended on the wall above loosely hanging wires, the words seem polar opposites brought into uneasy proximity. How did these words come to be brought together, as if they flowed sequentially from an author ardently at work at a typewriter? If the neon phrase were a commercial sign, what product would "negro sunshine" be? What would it do? What would it cost, and who would buy it? How would or could such intangible things take commodity form?

The words, which immediately put into play the possibilities and impossibilities of their meaning and materiality, in fact issued from the pen, if not the typewriter, of early twentieth-century author Gertrude Stein. They appear in Stein's "Melanctha," published as one of three stories in her first book *Three Lives* in 1909.[5] Understanding something of how "negro sunshine," as well as the term "warm broad glow," were brought together in Stein's writing allows us to begin to outline how Ligon approaches the figuration of blackness in his neon work.

"Warm broad glow" and "negro sunshine" appear three times in Stein's book and are used to describe African-American characters. In the introductory paragraphs of the novella, Stein describes Melanctha's friend Rose Johnson, who had been raised by a white family, as "never joyous with the earth-born, boundless joy of negroes." The author elaborates, "Rose laughed when she was happy but she had not the wide, abandoned laughter that makes the warm broad glow of negro sunshine."[6] Stein's text is interesting in that the words she uses to characterize her figures never quite represent her subjects.

More specifically, Stein's efforts to define her characters' racial traits, their blackness, are constantly defeated and exceeded in the text. This is evident in her opening sketch of Rose. Stein describes the "joy of negroes" as "boundless" and then moves to offer laughter as representative of this unlimitable quality. Then, almost immediately, Stein frames laughter, the sonic utterance, itself this intangible thing, as emblematic of blackness, but concedes that it does not characterize Rose. The type of blackness she tries to construct is not applicable to the very figure she aims to bring to fictional life.

One of the other instances in which Stein introduces the term "warm broad glow" comes late in the text. Stein describes Jeff Campbell, the protagonist's suitor, as "a robust, dark, healthy, cheery negro. . . . He always had a warm broad glow, like southern sunshine."[7] In this instance, she describes the man as "always" displaying this sunny temperament (connected here to geography as well as to a cheery negro character). Stein immediately goes on to describe a scene in which Campbell is "scorning" and "bitter," again undermining the habitual claim asserted a few sentences earlier.[8] Blackness in "Melanctha" constantly eludes literary capture.

Ligon's *Warm Broad Glow* seems to represent Stein's efforts to represent blackness. The glowing words embody his interpretation of what negro sunshine would look like. Precisely what temperature of light would best characterize it? Would it be a warm glow or a stark glare? Taking up and recasting Bruce Nauman's neon signs from the 1960s through 1980s (some of which Nauman obscured with paint, oil, or fiberglass) and his *Neon Templates* (1966–1967), Ligon plays with the materiality of language, its literalization, its perception, and its role in the surrogation of the body, particularly of bodies seen as black.[9] By reproducing Stein's text in two parts, with "negro sunshine" occupying the wall and its title taking up the more modest space of the work's label, the relation and disjunction of language and image, word and the thing described, sign and signifier, is further highlighted. Viewers encountering Ligon's interpretation of Stein's words in the gallery space engage in their own efforts to understand the work, to fix its meaning in place (whether or not they are familiar with Stein's use of the term). *Warm Broad Glow* in all these ways spotlights what the artist refers to as the "fugitivity" of blackness, the attempts to give it a form that highlights its unfixity and intangibility.[10]

We might see the neon signage as a metaphor for these efforts, literary and otherwise, to give blackness a delineated and fixed shape. Neon lighting functions precisely by trapping an inert gas, which is otherwise invisible to the human eye, nor detectable through smell or taste, for that matter, in glass tubing. Its outer structure—which, in the case of Ligon's work, is handmade blown glass—gives neon gas a physical structure and visual form. Under low pressure, when an electrical current passes through the gas in the glass tubing, it emits a bright orange-red light. Typically, the exterior of the glass may be painted to give the appearance of different colors. The artist's specific use of neon tubes spray-painted black highlights the processes through which black joy—negro sunshine—which has no singular, definite, or detectable form, comes to be visualized and materialized through the optics and technologies used to give form to ideals of race.

Ligon also specifically highlights the commercial conditions that structure how blackness comes into view—how blackness comes spectacularly to light. His use of Stein's "negro sunshine" quotation, with its relationship in her mind to black cheer and laughter, calls attention to the longstanding use of jovial black figures to sell consumer goods—from pancakes to novels—in, and beyond, the United States. Through such images, blackness became visible in popular culture only if in a palatable, consumable, form. In a sense, Ligon's *Warm Broad Glow*—which uses neon, the visual language of advertising—spotlights the fact that when blackness began to appear in mainstream media and commercials, it did so only if it fit into a sunny, happy mold.

We might also consider Ligon's attention to Stein's writing on the jovial negro against the background of Saidiya Hartman's scholarship on the concept and legal definition of enjoyment during slavery and post-emancipation.[11] Hartman notes how notions such as the one that blacks were filled with "boundless joy" were intrinsic to the erasure and normalization of the structures of violence that often governed everyday life for blacks during and after slavery. Spectacles of black enjoyment seemed evidence that slaves and their descendants were not only satisfied with, but also derived pleasure from, their stations. Ligon's eclipsing of the neon in dark Plasti Dip produces this visible invisibility of blackness, highlighting what the spectacularization of blackness banished from perception the moment it appeared to put blackness most plainly on view.

For Hartman, this right to enjoy slaves defines what blackness is.[12] Anyone identified as black was legally designated as property that could be enjoyed, which, according to *Black's Law Dictionary*, meant "to have, possess, and use with satisfaction; to occupy and have the benefit of." As

Hartman puts it, "Indeed, there was no relation to blackness outside the terms of this use of, entitlement to, and occupation of the captive body, for even the status of free blacks was shaped and compromised by the existence of slavery."[13] Intriguingly, she views the popularity of blackface minstrelsy, the performance tradition in which white performers donned shiny black paint and mimicked black characters, as another example of the way blackness was a fungible commodity, an abstract thing that could be enjoyed or possessed. Hartman's work offers an interpretative framework in which Ligon's neon may be understood not only as calling attention to the shape blackness took through commercial goods, but also as highlighting how, in some legal formulations, the very notion of blackness gave visual form to the idea that blacks were property—commodities to be consumed. The black Plasti Dip compound, made out of a flexible synthetic rubber compound that can be molded into an array of things, seems to materialize that malleable blackness that Hartman describes, which can be enjoyed for all purposes.

But what of the relation between these modes of visibility/invisibility and light? Why does light shine, glow, becoming the means through which Ligon explores the commodification and materialization of blackness? One could make the case that blackness has taken commercial and visual form precisely through light—in particular, through shiny blackness—which Stein partly invokes in her characterization of negro sunshine. Ligon has long been attentive to the relation between the objectification of blacks—their visual consumption—and shininess. In a study for his *Notes on the Margin of the Black Book* (1991–1993), Ligon took a book of highly homoerotic black-and-white photographs of black male subjects taken by the artist Robert Mapplethorpe and wrote, with the magic-markered authority of a school teacher, comments on the borders of the pages (figure 10.3). Above a photograph of a head shot of a black male pictured with his dark skin aglow, the handwritten words "why are we always greasy?" appear. Below the image, another question: "why are we always shining?" How greasiness and shininess (and glow and shine, for that matter) relate to each other, or how Ligon thinks of these degrees of glossiness, is unclear. What these questions call our attention to, however, is the seemingly habitual way that shininess (or its various permutations), which Dyer identifies as particular to the representation of non-white bodies in advertising,[14] accompanies the form and production of a consumable blackness.

One could make the case that if we were to somehow muster a response to Ligon's question, if we were to track, in a way the artist didn't seriously intend, a prehistory of black shine, it might start during slavery itself. Indeed, it was not uncommon for slaves to be greased, to have their bodies covered with a substance known as sweet oil, at the point of sale—the moment at which their status as exchangeable goods was especially pronounced. Slave sellers had multiple reasons for wanting their human property to shine. It covered up, for one, malnutrition, and glossed over any wounds or scars. Slave owners sought to increase the salability of their slaves, to heighten, and even perfect, their status as commodities.[15] Shininess, of course, was also the physical attribute of minstrel makeup—whether pomatum and burnt cork or black greasepaint—which heightened the visibility of minstrel characters, especially after gas lighting illuminated theatres in the nineteenth century.[16] While I do not want to overdetermine the multiple meanings of shine, this earlier history reiterates the point that people defined as black, and blackness more generally (as manifest in minstrel paint), were seen and actively produced as commodities through the optics of light.

Although Ligon's *Notes on the Margin of the Black Book* underscores shininess, and his illumination of the words "negro sunshine" exudes this quality, *Warm Broad Glow* reveals how efforts to package blackness never quite succeed in doing so. The soft luminous light, for one, notably exceeds the bounds of the sign's glass structure, becoming most visible on the back wall and in the surrounding space. Ligon's choice of lighting ultimately did not reproduce the harsh glare of some neon, the cool crisp light of commercial photography, or the stark, glistening, almost liquid white light of Mapplethorpe's photographs. The work's warm glow creates a more organic-seeming light. While not quite the natural glow of sunshine, its softness recalls the glamour lighting used in Hollywood films since the 1920s—the back-lit, haloed effect long reserved for white movie stars.[17] Ligon's neon also tempers the more spectacularized forms of blackness with the use of the black Plasti Dip. The dull rubber compound does not shine, and indeed, inhibits the perception of glass's shininess.[18] While invoking the historic ways blackness has been confined to a "shellacked shine" structure, Ligon's work casts light on the structures of visibility that typically bring blackness into view, producing a new optic—a visual space through which blackness may be differently perceived.

Warm Broad Glow will alter over time, like constructions of blackness itself. Subject to the changing conditions and environments in which it is placed, to time, and to its particular physical configuration, its fragile glass structure might fracture ever so slightly—or it might produce sound, which, the artist explains, happens when the piece's wiring is not working properly.[19] Sound signals the dysfunction of the visual. This mutability of the physical object itself, as well as the changeable way it is experienced, this shifting ground between visibility and invisibility and the visual and the sonic reflects the artist's interrogation of the fluctuating visual frame of blackness in the work: what appears most spectacularly visible disappears, what seems the most plastic dematerializes, what looks white is black, what pronounces shine is matte, what gives the impression it is delimited exceeds its representational structure.

I want to conclude by shifting and broadening the focus. I aim to suggest that *Warm Broad Glow* might also provide the backdrop against which we might catch a glimpse of the ever-changing social, political, and aesthetic contexts in which African-American art appears to be seen and consumed. I want to take this wider purview on Ligon's new neon work, in part based on his own writings on light and contemporary art practice, and more specifically, on his exploration of the work of artist David Hammons.

In "Black Light: David Hammons and the Poetics of Emptiness," Ligon reads what he describes as the "lightness" of Hammons's work in the early twenty-first century as related to a moment in which the elder artist felt less constrained by expectations "policed from both sides of the fence" that often surround African-American art—namely, that it should figure, represent, and address African-American culture.[20] My concluding inquiry is this: If Hammons's use of light responded to the lessening burdens of representation felt to be placed on African-American artists, how might we understand the contemporary moment, the movement toward light, in Ligon's neon work? Is it speaking from the same space of representational freedom in which Ligon situates Hammons's work, or does it differently reflect on the strictures surrounding African-American art in the twenty-first century?

Hammons is an interesting figure to introduce into this discussion. Once an ad man, trained in commercial art, he has steadily produced work that plays with the form, materiality, and salability of objects. As he put it in an interview with Deborah Rothschild in 1993, he was interested in producing art where there was "no object in the transaction." He went on to explain, "I'll dabble in it, but I'm not in it exclusively in that European way of art as commodity."[21] Since the early 1980s, Hammons produced work that dematerialized the art, as in his 1983 work *Bliz-aard Ball Sale*, for which the artist peddled snowballs on the streets of New York City, or *Cold Shoulder* (1990), composed of blocks of ice with coats thrown over them. The artist is also widely known for taking disregarded objects and turning them into highly regarded works of art, as in his *Higher Goals* of the 1980s, which he composed using bottle caps on utility poles.

Intriguingly, as Ligon notes in his article, when discussing issues of art commodification in the Rothschild interview, Hammons maintained that he "was not free enough yet" to use light to make art. As Hammons elaborated more fully:

> There's other ways of doing it. Like [James] Turrell, he's on a different wavelength. . . . But it's beautiful to see people who have a vision that has nothing to do with presentation in a gallery. I wish I could make art like that, but we're too oppressed for me to be dabbling out there. . . . I would love to do that because that also could be very black. You know, as a black artist, dealing just with light. They would say, "How in the hell could he deal with that, coming from where he did?" I want to get to that, I'm trying to get to that, but I'm not free enough yet. I still feel I have to get my message out.[22]

Eleven years later, after expressing earlier hesitation about dealing with light, Hammons created *Concerto in Black and Blue* (2002), which Ligon regards as emblematic of Hammons's ongoing process of "radical dematerialization" in his work. *Concerto*, which took place at the Ace Gallery in New York, consisted of a vast, empty, darkened gallery space into which visitors wandered with tiny, touch-activated flashlights. Entrants formed and co-produced the work as they navigated through the 20,000-square-foot venue, searching with flashlights that cast a blue shaft of light. All viewers became equal participants in, and navigators of, a collectively and socially produced blackness—a public and perpetually changing construction of the concept.[23]

Hammons's use of darkened space and light is both striking and pertinent to this essay's look at blackness and its visual forms. *Concerto* figures blackness outside of the production of objects or marketable products, representing blackness as not bound, not lit up, not visually accessible, not tangible, not confined, not obtainable, not commodifiable in the way, for Hartman, blackness has been. In this respect, the word "free" in Hammons's Rothschild interview can be interpreted as referring to that which is not bound in space, transactional, and exchangeable for money.

So, given Hammons's influence on Ligon, the elder artist allows for a broader historical perspective on Ligon's taking up of neon light as a medium. It is fitting to interpret Ligon's new interest in light, as he views Hammons's, as emerging at a moment in which African-American artists are working outside of certain representational constraints that have structured the reception of African-American art since at least the 1920s. In one of the earliest scholarly articles addressing *Warm Broad Glow*, art historian Richard Meyer views Ligon's neon work precisely in these terms, examining them in the context of "post-blackness."[24] Ligon, of course, coined the overused—and often mischaracterized—term in conversation with curator Thelma Golden in the 1990s. "Post-black" characterized "artists who were adamant about not being labeled 'black' artists, though their work was steeped, in fact deeply interested, in redefining complex notions of blackness."[25] While I do not aim to venture into the debates that surround the term, in light of Meyer's contextual framing and Ligon's writings, I do want to consider how *Warm Broad Glow* may speak to particular forms of visibility and marketability that surround African-American art in the contemporary art world.

More specifically, the black neon may reflect what Ligon identified in the *Washington Post* as the increased visibility of African-American artists—the way their work has been spotlighted.[26] This era has also coincided with a waning interest in, if not distaste for, art that explicitly deals with racial politics. As Meyer perceptively points out, Ligon was producing his neon when critics like Holland Cotter were pronouncing explicitly race-engaged art as "out at the moment."[27] While detailing or gauging the shifting investments in racial politics in the art world is beyond the scope of this essay, I want to outline the complex and ambiguous ground that African-American art occupies (especially for artists who might not have subscribed to the argument that racial politics were "out"). This new visibility for African-American artists—with the concurrent invisibility of race as subject matter—seemed evident, for example, in the 2008 exhibition of the Rubell Family Collection in Miami titled simply *30 Americans*, which featured the work of African-American artists, including the neon piece *Untitled (Negro Sunshine)* (2005) by Ligon, without mentioning the race or ethnicity of any of the artists. I do not want to analyze the merits or pitfalls of such exhibitions. But I do want to suggest that Ligon's black neon highlights the complex status of blackness in relation to the art object—blackness's visible invisibility, the way it is accentuated yet disappeared, spotlighted and yet eclipsed, in contemporary art. Unlike Hammons's unbound use of blackness and light and his representational freedom, Ligon's neon work takes a decidedly material and commercial form, one that calls attention, both historically and in the present day, to the forces of commodification that continue to bring blackness in and out of view.

Notes

Thanks to Glenn Ligon for taking the time to reflect on his work with me and to Huey Copeland for his thoughtful comments on an early draft of this essay.

1. Isaac Newton, *Opticks: Or, A Treatise of the Reflections, Refractions, Inflections and Colours of Light* (1704; New York: Dover Publications, 1979), 1–4.

2. Richard Dyer, *White* (London: Routledge, 1997), 109.

3. Dyer, *White*, 103–116.

4. Glenn Ligon, quoted in Blake Gopnik, "Race Issue a Two-Edged Sword for Black Contemporary Artists," *Washington Post*, January 24, 2010, http://www.washingtonpost.com/wp-dyn/content/article/2010/01/21/AR2010012105249.html.

5. Gertrude Stein, *Three Lives* (1908; New York: Modern Library, 1933).

6. Stein, *Three Lives*, 47.

7. Stein, *Three Lives*, 113.

8. Stein, *Three Lives*, 114.

9. Joseph D. Ketner II, *Elusive Signs: Bruce Nauman Works with Light* (Cambridge, MA: MIT Press, 2006).

10. Glenn Ligon, in discussion with the author, New York, September 27, 2010. See Huey Copeland, "Glenn Ligon and Other Runaway Subjects," *Representations* 113 (Winter 2011): 72–108, for an insightful discussion of fugitivity as it relates to Ligon's work (reprinted in this volume).

11. Saidiya V. Hartman, *Scenes of Subjection: Terror, Slavery, and Self-Making in Nineteenth-Century America* (New York: Oxford University Press, 1997), 23–32.

12. Hartman, *Scenes of Subjection*, 23.

13. Hartman, *Scenes of Subjection*, 25.

14. Dyer, *White*, 122–142. Dyer also explains how white women are represented through "glow," not "shine."

15. For a more detailed discussion, see Krista A. Thompson, "The Sound of Light: Reflections on Art History in the Visual Culture of Hip Hop," *Art Bulletin* (December 2009): 481–505.

16. Thanks to Tara Rodman for this information on minstrel makeup.

17. Dyer, *White*, 82–144.

18. See Margo Natalie Crawford, "Black Light on the Wall of Respect: The Chicago Black Arts Movement," in *New Thoughts on the Black Arts Movement*, ed. Lisa Gail Collins and Margo Natalie Crawford (New Brunswick, NJ: Rutgers University Press, 2006), 41. The industrial compound's matte finish brings to mind efforts by photographers, artists, and poets working in the Black Arts Movement, as art historian Margot Crawford details, who explored the representational and metaphysical properties of a black light. Chicago-born poet Margaret Danner, for one, aimed to conceive of blackness outside of the furniture-polished, shellacked-shine variety, speaking poetically of a velvety blackness instead.

19. Glenn Ligon, in discussion with the author, September 27, 2010.

20. Glenn Ligon, "Black Light: David Hammons and the Poetics of Emptiness," *Artforum* 43, no. 1 (September 2004): 244–245.

21. David Hammons, quoted in Deborah Menaker Rothschild, *Yardbird Suite* (Williamstown, MA: Williams College Museum of Art, 1994), 51.

22. Hammons, in Rothschild, *Yardbird Suite*, 51.

23. See Darby English's characterization of the piece in Darby English, *How to See a Work of Art in Total Darkness* (Cambridge, MA: MIT Press, 2007), 1–7.

24. Richard Meyer, "Light It Up, or How Glenn Ligon Got Over," *Artforum* 44, no. 9 (May 2006), 241.

25. Thelma Golden, in *Freestyle: Studio Museum in Harlem* (New York: Studio Museum of Harlem, 2001), 14.

26. Ligon, quoted in Gopnik, "Race Issue a Two-Edged Sword."

27. Meyer, "Light It Up," 241.

8 How to Hear What Is Not Heard: Glenn Ligon, Steve Reich, and the Audible Past

Janet Kraynak

In 2015, on the occasion of the Venice Biennale, Glenn Ligon prominently installed a large neon sign sculpture atop the façade of the Central Pavilion, one of the buildings in the historic exhibition's *giardini* (figure 8.1). The visibility of its site, however, stood in contrast to its muted presence and enigmatic message. Crafted from translucent neon and white paint and mounted on a horizontal scaffolding, the work comprised just three detached words ("blues," "blood," and "bruise") that obscured the existing sign (for "la Biennale"). Extending an idiosyncratic welcome to visitors, the three words, at any moment, were illuminated or not, yielding a playful, if nonsensical semiosis. Fragmented from any semantic context, the words were bound together only by the rhythmic sound pattern suggested by their repeating *b-b-bs*. *A Small Band*, as the work is titled, that silently plays.[1]

Ligon has used this strategy—of simultaneous citation and deletion—many times before, most notably in text paintings where he appropriates language only to subject it to processes of distortion and fragmentation, so that words succumb to illegibility. As Huey Copeland eloquently describes, Ligon's visualizing of absence functions strategically as a form of historical intervention, whereby the "selective occlusion of the past continues to falsify our imagining of the present."[2] Consistent with this approach, the words found in *A Small Band* have a charged history. Taken from a recorded interview with Daniel Hamm, one of six youths—the "Harlem Six"—arrested for a murder they did not commit, the texts testify to the "long hot summer" of 1964, when the African-American community of Harlem erupted into visible and audible rebellion.[3] Hamm's

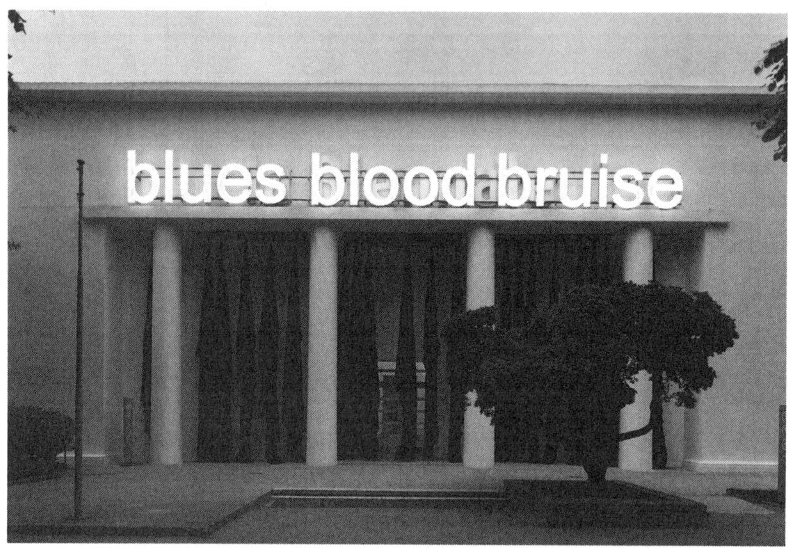

Figure 8.1 Glenn Ligon, installation view of *A Small Band* (2015), Fifty-Sixth International Venice Biennale, 2015. Neon, paint, and metal support, approx. 74¾ × 797½ inches. Collection of the Virginia Museum of Fine Arts, Richmond. © Glenn Ligon; Courtesy of the artist, Hauser & Wirth, and Thomas Dane Gallery. Photography credit: Roberto Marossi.

interview, one of a series conducted by social worker Willie Jones from the community services organization Harlem Youth Opportunities Unlimited (HARYOU; now defunct), took place in the basement of the Friendship Baptist Community Center—under the occasional watch of the police peering through the windows.[4] Resulting in ten reels of audiotape totaling about seventy hours, the tapes stand as direct records of the young men's otherwise silenced voices—one instance of a brutal, repetitive history of auditory occlusion.[5]

How and why Ligon came to borrow or appropriate Hamm's speech is part of the story I want to explore here, where questions of the place of aesthetic manipulation—of radical fragmentation and decontextualization—face the materiality or, to be more precise, the aurality of political struggle. Ligon's repurposing and the multiplicity of his production—with differing versions of *A Small Band*, as well as a series of paintings again featuring Hamm's words—come at a secondary remove, as they were first borrowed by minimalist composer Steve Reich in his now well-known experimental tape work from 1966, *Come Out*. The dialogue between Ligon and Reich, as well as numerous other actors and multiple remediations of the original recordings, reveal a complex narrative: of black resistance, silent accused, pleading mothers, a white civil-rights activist and a white avant-garde composer, a black social worker and a black journalist. And a pile of reel-to-reel audiotapes.

★

It all started with an upturned fruit cart. On the afternoon of April 17, 1964, a local shopkeeper's fruit cart was accidentally knocked over by some schoolchildren, who then tossed around some of the fruit, prompting a call to police. Yet the police of Harlem had recently been armed in riot gear—a militarization of law enforcement that consistently follows the struggle for civil rights—and proceeded to pummel the children. Hamm, along with two other boys (Wallace Baker and Frederick Frazer) and two men (Fecundo Acion and Frank Stafford), heard their moans and came to their aid, leading to their arrest in what came to be called the "Little Fruit Stand Riot."[6] After they were taken into custody, the five experienced brutal beatings from police, who charged them with "incitement to riot and assault," as Hamm's mother recounted at the time.[7] Because they were refused treatment unless they were visibly bleeding, Hamm proceeded to "open the bruise up and let some of the bruise blood come out to show them that I was bleeding," as he notes in the interview. A short time later, on April 25 of that year, a local shopkeeper, Margit Sugar, was murdered, and Hamm and Baker, along with four others (Walter Thomas, Willie Craig, Ronald Felder, and Robert Rice), were wrongly accused of the killing.[8] The six, denied legal counsel of their choice, were subsequently found guilty the following year and sentenced to life in prison, sparking protests and a call for a retrial.

At the time, the case of the Harlem Six attracted prominent voices of protest, including those of Louis Aragon, Amiri Baraka, Ossie Davis, and James Baldwin, a number of whose names appear in a series of advertisements titled "Georgia Justice for Harlem Six" that appeared in the *New York Times* and the *Village Voice* in July 1967 after the youths' retrial had been denied.[9] Shortly after their arrest, fifteen-year-old James Powell was killed by Thomas Gilligan, a white lieutenant in the New York Police Department, further fueling the community's simmering anger over police brutality and mistreatment, sparking six nights of protests and rioting that would extend to Bedford Stuyvesant, another center of black life and culture in New York City.[10] "So, last week, the 'long hot summer' of Negro discontent began," one *New York Times* article reads. "In Harlem, in Brooklyn and upstate in Rochester there was rioting, shooting, charges and counter-charges. The race struggle had reached a climax and no immediate way out was indicated."[11]

Soon dubbed the "Harlem Race Riots," the events of the summer of 1964 brought the turmoil of southern battles into the symbolic heart of African-American culture. "The police responded with live bullets," Michael W. Flamm writes in a reflection on the incident's legacy. He goes on to cite James Farmer of the Congress of Racial Equality: "'I saw New York's night of Birmingham horror,'" Flamm quotes Farmer as saying, adding that the latter was "referring to the water cannons and police dogs used against black children in Alabama a year earlier."[12] Similarly, news anchor John Rolfson reported from the scene that "bricks, bottles and flaming Molotov cocktails" were "answered with live ammunition and night sticks," and Langston Hughes later described "listen[ing] to gun fire" and "hear[ing] cries sharper than any words speakers speak."[13] Baldwin adds additional urgency to this chorus, writing of his experiences with "the thunder and fire of the billy club" and "the paralyzing shock of spittle in the face."[14] Threading through all of these accounts is a dissonant, polyphonic soundtrack of racial strife: "Now, Harlem be nice! Harlem behave yourself," Hughes writes with biting sarcasm. "Kill me! Go ahead, kill another one of me! You killed James Powell! I have been killed before."[15]

But despite the case's notoriety, the events of the summer of 1964—a simmering stew of racial antipathy, police brutality, and media irresponsibility—largely faded from collective memory. "The Harlem Riot of July 1964 was soon forgotten," Flamm remarks, "overshadowed by more deadly rebellions and other 'long hot summers' in Los Angeles, Newark and Detroit. But in an important sense, James Powell was the first casualty in a larger conflict that has subsequently done great harm to generations of African-Americans."[16] To Powell's name, we can add Hamm's and those of his codefendants, whose saga will continue for a decade more until they are all (with one exception) finally released from prison in 1973: their release precipitated by another tape recording—this one recorded in secret by the men's attorneys—of a witness who had refused to testify in the original trial.[17]

To what ends, therefore, does Ligon revive these pains of the past in 2015—and in the center of contemporary art's global spectacle, no less? In

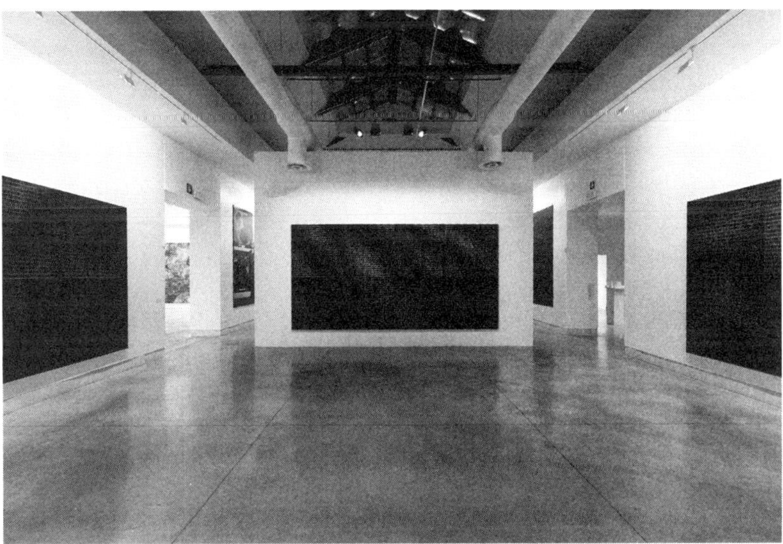

Figure 8.2 Glenn Ligon, installation view of paintings from the *Come Out* series (2014–2015), Fifty-Sixth International Venice Biennale, 2015. Photo credit: Roberto Marossi.

addition to *A Small Band*, Ligon also exhibited a series of quasi-monochromatic text paintings featuring the phrase "*come out to show them*"—again taken from Hamm's testimony—repeated over and over in tightly scripted lines (figure 8.2). For the *Come Out* paintings, rendered only in blacks and grays, Ligon divided the canvas into a series of grids, laying individual screen prints one atop another so the text builds into moments of dense black, as if being stamped out through superimposition. From afar, the paintings' surfaces appear as luminescent, undulating shadows carrying only the faintest traces of the words, which demand close viewing to be read. In a similar fashion, in the neons, during the bright light of day, *A Small Band*'s white letters almost disappear into the monochromatic pale of the white façade, their blank neutrality simultaneously succumbing to acts of marking and erasure.

Given the volatility of their subject matter, Ligon's works seem reductive, even constrained, but there is something brutal in this constraint. Their neon reflections and monochromatic passages of abstruse, fragmented text echo words once spoken but now visually silenced. Ligon's pieces, while mute, nonetheless constitute an "aural aesthetic" (*A Small Band* announces so in its title), to borrow Fred Moten's phrase, or a "phonographic rewriting" of signs.[18] While Western thought privileges the visual, sound—including dissonance—and its discursive partner, silence, represent an important, if underrecognized, index of social and political hierarchies. Sounds, like images, function to extend policies of racial, ethnic, and political oppression, acting on subjects and history. They act on what Jonathan Sterne terms the "audible past," where the conflictual terms of modernity reside in modes of sonic differentiation that valorize particular modes of listening.[19] If, as he contends, "sound media emerged in the tumultuous context of turn-of-the-century capitalism and colonialism," then the audible past exposes mechanisms of power. The advent of recording technologies exacerbated these tendencies, arising from particular sets of beliefs regarding modernization, progress, and cultural superiority.[20] In this "'maelstrom' of modernity," he notes, citing Marshall Berman, "the white man" is positioned "at the pinnacle of world evolution."[21]

Who, then, possesses the means to inscribe the auditory field, and who does not—and which sounds are listened to, admitted into, and preserved by the acoustical archive? If recording technologies do not in and of themselves usher in new modes of listening, but rather further preexisting "habits . . . dispositions, and tendencies," then *hearing* and *being heard* tarry in the realm of the political, amplifying cultural mores and practices.[22]

And so we return to the tapes. The recording of Hamm's speech was first borrowed by minimalist composer Steve Reich for his 1966 phase-shifting tape piece *Come Out*. Along with *It's Gonna Rain*, *Come Out* represents one of Reich's "race works," as Sumanth Gopinath describes them, created during the heady days of civil rights unrest and political revolution.[23] In both, through extreme condensation, Reich emphasizes the metrical and musical qualities of speech, the latter deployed in lieu of conventional notes or musical tones. During the opening bars of *Come Out*, we hear an unadulterated fragment of Hamm's sentence: "I had to like open the bruise up and let some of the bruise blood come out to show them." After repeating the phrase three times, it is then further truncated into two isolated motifs—"come out" and "to show them"—recorded on separate tape loops and set into competing tracks. "Come out / To show them / Come out / To show them / Come out / To show them / . . ." played over and over in rebellious repetition. As the piece progresses, the two loops swiftly become engaged in a back-and-forth, with one gradually getting ahead of the other and thus moving out of sync. Oscillating in a reverberating echo, the loops generate a score of constantly shifting

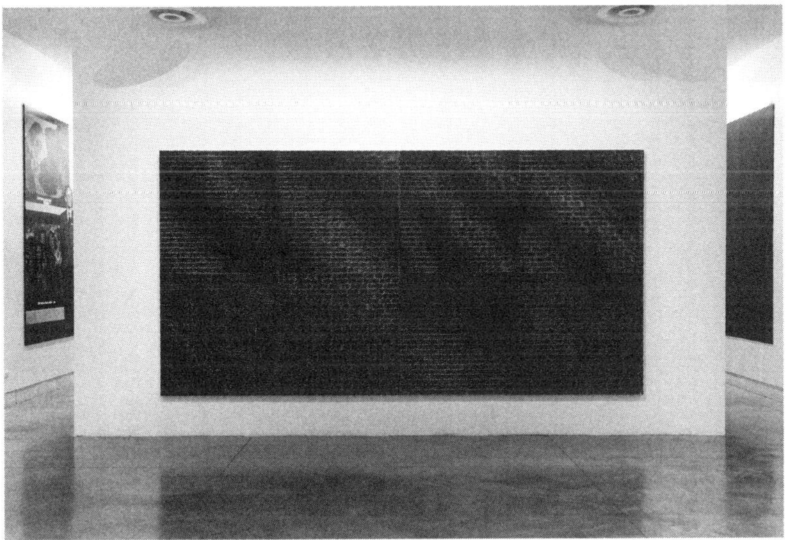

Figure 8.3 Glenn Ligon, *Come Out #14* (2015). Silkscreen on canvas, 95 × 192 inches. Installation view, Fifty-Sixth International Venice Biennale, 2015. Photo credit: Roberto Marossi.

yet equivalent patterns: a noise collage of sound, bound to the irritants of repetition.

Despite its charged origins, *Come Out* is exemplary of how contemporary, electroacoustical sound challenges musical norms. Through the reverberating echoes yielded by the phase-shifting process, it embraces the "noise sounds" prevalent in modernism that came to dominate the early experiments with electronic sound, given the potentialities of reverberation, feedback, and technical mediation. *Come Out*'s focus on the "speech melody," as Reich terms it, however, both preserves and disrupts the semiotic content of Hamm's words, emphasizing a slip of the tongue—a linguistic flaw: in his nervous recollection, Hamm seems to pronounce the word *bruise* as "blues." As a result, "signal" (or meaning) and "noise" (or nonmeaning) are conjoined in a necessary, if uneasy alliance.[24] Preserving Hamm's speech pattern while shattering it semantically, *Come Out* purges the original words into a liminal space of ambiguity, materializing the tension between *formalism* and *hermeneuticism*, to cite Joanna Demers, that characterizes electronic music.[25] By providing the listener with abstracted fragments offering multiple interpretive directions (including, potentially, a lack of comprehension),

Reich's *Come Out* yields a conflictual play of compositional disruption, technical experimentation, and conceptual radicality.[26]

★

The raw material—the recorded interview—that Reich used for *Come Out* was one of a series of interviews whose original purpose was to be submitted as evidence in a case of police brutality: a move preempted by the boys' subsequent arrest after Sugar's murder. Instead, the tapes ended up in the hands of Truman Nelson, a white civil-rights activist who, in the wake of the turmoil, wrote a full-length book, *The Torture of Mothers*, based on detailed accountings of the case. The book, written without literary polish, offers a somewhat confusing account, including snippets from news reports of the time, among which are a series of articles that consistently criminalize the young men in unsparing language.[27] Failing to find a publisher, Nelson self-published the book in 1966 through his own Garrison Press, and an excerpt was released in *Ramparts* magazine in July of that same year.[28]

Nelson relays how the mothers of the boys were offered plea deals to a lesser charge that carried a sentence of one to five years. The women rejected the deals after "the sleepless nights of the trial period," without consulting their offspring. For their part, the young men, "standing mute . . . in the exacerbating presence of a defense felt by them to be neither skillful, compassionate, nor just, rose at one point to collectively announce their conviction that they could not get justice in 'this white man's court.'"[29] As Nelson adds, the result of this collective statement—a rare audible interjection in their otherwise silent hearing—was the youths' transfer to the insane ward of a nearby hospital.

In addition to Nelson's prose, *The Torture of Mothers* includes transcriptions of the taped interviews of the young men and their mothers: what the author describes as "testimony of open resistance."[30] For Nelson, the tapes offered particularly powerful evidence—of mistreatment, of innocence—and he sought out Reich's technical expertise to produce an edited excerpt that could be featured at a benefit at New York's Town Hall to raise funds for the youth's retrial.[31] Reich's personal participation in the racially charged case thus came about unexpectedly, with the composer not recalling how the activist knew of or found him—only that "he knew I worked with tapes, he was a James Brown scholar."[32] Reich adds, "My real job was not making [*Come Out*], my real job was splicing bits of this and that—you know, to make an audio documentary of that material."[33] Reich agreed to do this tape editing for a separate work if he could, in turn, use the same material for "a piece."[34]

As a musical object of protest—a "civil rights piece," Reich has called it—*Come Out* is thus highly idiosyncratic.[35] In contrast to the revolutionary poetics and urgent testimonials of writers at the time (as Baldwin argues, Nelson's book stands as "an extraordinary moral achievement in the great American tradition of Thomas Paine and Frederick Douglass"), Reich's treatment is spare and experimental, demanding a form of intellectual engagement that seems at odds with the communicative transparency typically mandated by socially engaged art.[36] If Nelson's and the others' contributions stand as acts of visceral resistance, with the intent to garner an affective response, *Come Out*'s looped repetitions of prerecorded speech emphasize rhythm over tonal harmonies, disrupting conventions of musical authorship and the sense of "touch" afforded by live instrumentation. Charged with the task of filling in holes, the listener also must come to terms with the seeming disconnect between the abject horror the words describe and their musical treatment.

Exacerbating these tendencies is the very selection of text. Across the hours and hours of tape are extensive passages of brutal assault, many of which appear in Nelson's book, where they are transcribed in an almost poetic form, as Gopinath observes, which adds to the dramatic pacing of the retelling.[37] To cite one selection from Hamm's testimony,

> We went to the precinct and that's where they beat us.
> For nothing at all.
> They like turned shifts on us,
> Like six and twelve at a time would beat us,
> And this went on practically all day we were at that station;
> They beat us till I could barely walk and my back was in pain.
> My friends they did the same till they bled.
> All the time they were beating us they never took the handcuffs off.[38]

Given that mediation is never neutral, one might ask if *Come Out*'s editorial selection and format, as well as its place within the legacy of postwar noise aesthetics, serves to diminish the material force of the words. Does Reich's remediation mitigate racial conflict and, in so doing, (again) render black subjectivity *inaudible*? For musicologist Lloyd Whitesell, the aesthetic gestures Reich deploys (of appropriation, fragmentation, and rerecording) amount to a double violation, where the youth's subjectivity is again negated under the manipulations of a white composer: his "music mov[ing] toward an abstract, metaphorical whiteness, mesmerizing in its unfathomable remoteness from the material black vocality of the opening."[39] *Come Out*, he adds, follows modernist principles of negation—from painterly monochromy to Cagean silencing—where whiteness symbolically encompasses the norm (if not the absolute), while blackness is perpetually marked as "the figures of contrast" that "colors" the relative abstractness of music.[40]

Come Out was composed at the height of revolution and social upheaval, when questions regarding artistic responsibility vis-à-vis material conditions were paramount. In these ways, *Come Out* seems exemplary of the perceived axiomatic relationship between electronic sound and contemporary social concerns. As Robert Adlington writes, during the 1960s, "there was the question of whether novel approaches to musical language and technology could be meaningfully considered 'revolutionary' when very real struggles against authoritarian state and economic systems were being visibly waged around the world."[41] As a result, many critics charge avant-garde music of the period with a willful "rejection of worldly engagement." Reich's piece is placed in a seemingly contradictory position: at once providing testimony to racism's bodily assaults while seemingly distancing itself from these very concerns.

Yet this interpretation is overly simplistic, as it fails to gauge how "worldly engagement" enters into and is negotiated by acts of representation (beyond referentiality), as well as how structures of reduplication and recurrence figure in historical production. Michel-Rolph Trouillot writes, "narratives are made of silences," adding, "not all of . . . [these] are deliberate or even perceptible as such within the time of their production."[42] "Silencing" here refers not to a literal quieting but to the operations of obfuscation and willful forgetting that fuel historical representation. The unknowability of the Haitian Revolution is his ostensible subject, but Trouillot provides a broader methodological précis on the production of knowledge—how narratives are made and then remade through retellings. By identifying fissures and elisions, new narratives and new archives can be produced. In the process, originary events are not simply recounted but revised, so that "the past" is never complete, always in a state of becoming.[43]

The question ensues, what constitutes an "originary" event? Reich notes that during the "world premiere" (as he wryly puts it) of *Come Out*, the audience at the Town Hall benefit (a group of activists and sympathizers, one can assume) did not consider—or "hear"—*Come Out* as music at all; rather, it functioned as a "pass-the-hat" soundtrack with the express intent "to stir people's emotions."[44] As music, *Come Out* might be reductive, but as something else (and this is speculation, as no firsthand accounts exist of its playing at the benefit), its unnerving repetitions of speech exploit the visceral aspects of linguistic embodiment—or the power of the performative to effect a material response. That is, the very experimental qualities that led *Come Out* not to be heard as music at the time it premiered (it was largely "ignored," others have noted) allowed it to function effectively while "the hat was being passed" due to this very misrecognition.[45] As Reich adds, emphasizing the work's nonmusical context, "[The benefit] was not a concert, and I don't think anybody thought [*Come Out*] was a piece of music. I think they thought it was some type of sound effects to help raise money." He continues,

> When it was recorded on CBS Odyssey, then people understood, hey this is a very important piece of music. . . . If the music wasn't good, then all of the message and all the politics would go down in the drain, ok; that's the first principle. Good music makes things possible. Bad music just takes the bad subject, takes the good subject-matter and throws it away. [That] the piece works as a piece of music has *preserved* the content of it as well. And that's why we remember Guernica even though otherwise it would be completely forgotten.[46]

Here, I want to take Reich's words seriously—or, more succinctly, I want to *listen* to them rather than simply accept them at face value, in particular with regard to the mnemonic operations of historical recovery: what Sigmund Freud calls deferred action or *Nachträglichkeit*.[47] Historical meaning comes from a scaffolding, whereby multiple layers of reception accrue. Rather than detract from the pain of any singular instance or event, such an accumulative process amplifies it—even its forgetting. In the case of the Harlem Six, the object at issue is an artistic representation, an aural aesthetic, whose legacy of remembrance and retelling starkly contrasts with that of the forgotten relics of the long hot summer of 1964—of the evidence *not heard*, to take poetic license with Baldwin's "the evidence of things not seen."[48]

And so we return to the tapes. Hamm's nervous alliteration ("bruise"/"blues") heard in the recorded interview can clearly be discerned in the opening bars of *Come Out*, which emphasize this linguistic static before being abandoned to the rhythmic play of the fluctuating phases. Yet this flaw is undetectable in the interview's transcribed form. Ligon's *A Small Band*, however, takes off from the wealth of associations stemming from this verbal misprision—an utterance outside the subjective agency of the utterer—suggesting Ligon has heard the tapes. Yet, as he notes, "Steve Reich's *Come Out* was the source material for the work, but that led me to the history of the Harlem 6 case and texts such as Baldwin's 'A Report from [the] Occupied Territory' as well as *There Is a Fountain: The Autobiography of Conrad Lynn*. . . . Reich was structure, Baldwin and Lynn were content."[49] Ligon here both confirms that he received Hamm's testimony at a secondary remove, via Reich's recording, while also alluding to a dialectical process. Remediations of cultural texts (i.e., literary tomes, poems, oral histories, slave narratives, music, protest signs, printed ephemera, and video and audio recordings) are set in relation to structures of multiplicity and variability, constituting political, artistic acts. These texts, moreover, are frequently marginal, often fragmentary, if not in content then in context, where artistic appropriation furthers a situational unmooring.[50] Through Reich's truncated record—his unofficial, artistic, and nondocumentarian retelling—Ligon "discovered" Daniel Hamm. But, as such, he found the events and select documents describing the "past."

Ligon locates the "retrospective significance," to borrow Trouillot's words, of Reich's *Come Out* in its fissures and elisions, and this cross-generational dialogue in turn serves to draw attention to the compromised archive of the Harlem Six, underscoring the "unevenness of historical power."[51] That the interviews of the six were recorded, but not by any institution of judicial, criminal, or legal authority, is further meaningful. Made by a volunteer social worker in the basement of a local church, the tapes at once serve as primary testimony to the terrible events *and* their own exclusion from the public sphere and, as such, from what Trouillot aptly describes as "archival power."[52] The recordings make manifest politics of racial marginalization and exclusion that resonate in the audible past, where sound "becomes a problem."[53] Reich's radically excised work materializes sonic conflict, while its survival—its ability to be heard—veers perpetually between manifest emptiness and plenitude.

★

Evidence. Tapes are direct traces of the real; they imprint the voice into a magnetic medium and thus putatively preserve it. At the time of its invention, recorded sound became highly popular in part due to its ability to preserve the voices of the dead, who go on to "live" in perpetuity through acoustical inscription. Reel-to-reel audiotape offers a warmth of sound, while capturing the naturalness of auditory noise, but it is a clunky technology, whose manipulations are tediously achieved. Moreover, far from being permanent, audiotapes disintegrate over time. But a social worker decided against all odds to record the boys and their mothers, and a white civil-rights activist in turn transcribed and self-published them and then handed them to an avant-garde composer. ("All of them?" Reich was asked. "Yes," he responded.)[54]

While the events were still unfolding, in the midst of the riots, arrests, and convictions, another activist took the tapes to the *New York Times* to play them for a reporter, Junius Griffin, who had a damaging role in the media representation—and conviction—of the Harlem Six. For Griffin, the racism at issue was not that of the police or of white citizens. Rather, what had led to the riots and uprisings that plagued the long hot summer of 1964 was black youths' own racist hatred. One article, titled "Whites Are Target of Harlem Gang," starts in exemplary fashion: "A gang of about 60 young Negroes who call themselves the 'Blood Brothers' is roaming the streets of Harlem with the avowed intention of attacking white people. They are trained to maim and kill."[55] Griffin was also African-American, a fact—as Nelson points out—that did not prevent him from committing "the major assault upon Harlem in the *Times*."[56]

Enter another civil rights worker who knew Griffin and was disturbed by his reporting. The unnamed worker convinced the HARYOU interviewer, who is again not identified, to bring the tapes for transcription to the *Times* as proof of the boys' innocence.[57] Griffin listened to—but did not hear—the tapes as he then proceeded to radically distort their content in his reporting. "Many of the quotes in the article were deliberate falsehoods. Some were evilly twisted in meaning," Nelson writes. "There was scarcely a point which the interviewer had put in defense and understanding of the slandered people of Harlem and the poor boys literally in the shadow of the executioner's chair that Griffin did not disfigure with error, either of principle or fact."[58] Infuriated, civil rights lawyer Conrad Lynn—one of four prominent attorneys who would represent the Harlem Six in retrial—demanded that the *Times* turn over whatever evidence they had supporting the allegations in Griffin's reporting, which was directly contradicted by the tapes, by the documented speech of the accused.[59] As

Lynn describes, "the cacophony of the newspapers drowned out the screams of the suspects at the station houses—which were known in Harlem as the 'meat grinder' and the 'slaughterhouse'—where the police supposedly were reciting their constitutional rights."[60] For its part, the *Times* never retracted the original reporting, nor did it correct Griffin's distortions, so the mythic gang (the "blood brothers") lived on, solidified in the public imaginary.[61]

Evidence. Add the relentless beatings of three of the defendants, including Hamm, by the police while they were incarcerated, leading to forced confessions whose existence further condemned them at trial: a phonographic sleight of hand entailing a silencing by other means, where transcription falsely reconstructs speech. The power of these fabulations, secured under extreme duress and physical suffering, is evidenced in Lynn's own questioning of the boys' innocence. "I was convinced that at least four of the defendants were innocent. . . . I was afraid Robert Rice and Daniel Hamm might be guilty." He continues,

> Each had signed a confession, and I knew I was almost as impressed by that fact as the jury had been. There is something about a confession—forget how it might be obtained—that carries great weight. Intimidation and fearsome physical force can be employed to obtain a confession, but when the punishment for murder can be electrocution there has to be a terrible reluctance to admitting a crime. With Robert Rice and Daniel Hamm, I simply was not sure.[62]

The story of the Harlem Six is inextricable from a set of tapes that represent a media hagiography of the accused. They went from hands to hands: from a social worker to a civil rights activist to another activist to a reporter to an avant-garde composer. Despite their significance, and the long journey they took, their fate is unknown. We now inhabit a digital world with the (often unquestioned) belief in an informational utopia: that technologies of reproduction assure the preservation and accessibility of the past, that they oversaturate us with all knowledge that is available—by extension, this means social ills, including racial disparities. But if the audible past shapes and excludes, carving out a particular framework of power that mimics societal habits and beliefs, then digitization is not immune. As of this writing, the tapes have not been found.[63] In addition, the location of Reich's audio documentary for the benefit is unknown. For his part, the composer has no idea what happened to the tapes after he returned them to Nelson, or what happened to his sound collage.[64]

All we have is *Come Out*.

A piece of avant-garde music assumes an outsize role in the historical narrative, made by a composer whose distortions have borne antithetical consequences to those made by a reporter, whose "truths" were circulated in print in the paper of record. The aural aesthetic (to cite Moten again) meets the graphic record, which is how not just Glenn Ligon but a host of others over the years have "found" Hamm and the Harlem Six. *Come Out* has become an archive—an originary event that, over the span of more than fifty years, has been cited, remade, and repeatedly sampled: from Captain Beefheart's early "Moonlight on Vermont" (1969), to tracks recorded by hip-hop artist Otis Jackson Jr. under the pseudonym Madlib (of the group Madvillain), among numerous others.[65]

★

Referring to the visual record of slavery, Stephen Best argues that "emptiness" lies "at the heart of the archive." Despite the vast corpus of iconic photographs and paintings, it is nonetheless woefully incomplete, as "it will always be lacking in works by slaves themselves." He continues, "For slaves are not the subject of visual imagination, they are its object. Slavery in the slaves' visual imagination remains foreclosed as a site of critical and historical metalepsis."[66] Given this set of conditions, the historian must, by necessity, "leap over the archive" or "take up" the subject "at a distance."[67]

While Best is concerned with *visual* documentation, his argument can be extended to auditory evidence. Ligon's returns are by proxy, accessed through a musical representation that functions as an "archive" of primary documentation now potentially lost. But what does it mean for Ligon to find history through an aesthetic fragment? For one, his own intervention into a story that is constantly being rewritten reveals the failures of history about which Sterne, Trouillot, and Best collectively write: a story that reveals the "silences" of narratives, the compromised ideals accompanying the "permanence" of recording, and the "emptiness" of archives. If Whitesell critiqued Reich's subjection of Hamm's voice to aesthetic manipulation, these "distortions" paradoxically perform a "critical metalepsis," a figurative act of representation-as-preservation that reveals sociocultural failure, where racial injustice is silenced or, at least, claimed for the "past." As Trouillot writes, "That U.S. slavery has both officially ended, yet

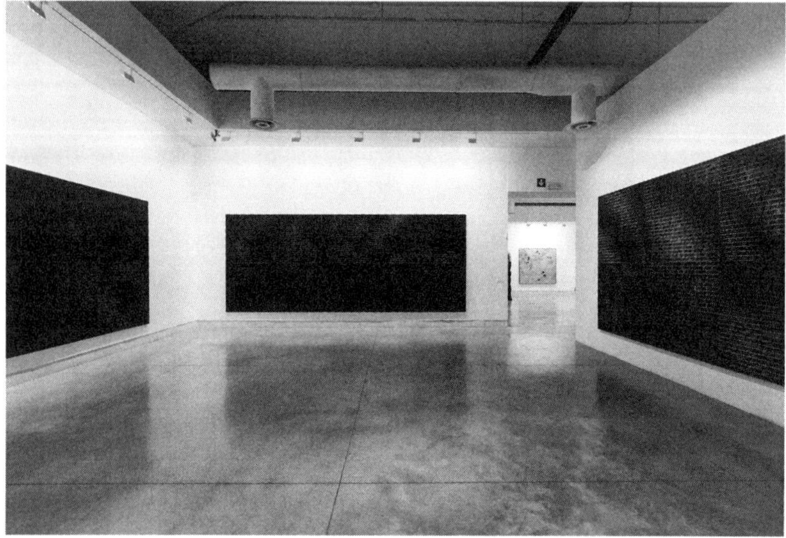

Figure 8.4 Glenn Ligon, installation view of paintings from the *Come Out* series (2014–2015), Fifty-Sixth International Venice Biennale, 2015. Photo credit: Roberto Marossi.

continues in many complex forms—most notably institutionalized racism and the cultural denigration of blackness—makes its representation particularly burdensome in the United States. Slavery here is a ghost, both the past and a living presence; and the problem of historical representation is how to represent that ghost, *something that is and yet is not*."[68] In Ligon's austere treatment, snippets of words, pieces of history, surface and resurface, oscillating between presence and voidness. Or rather, they point to the impossible burden of filling the void by neons, paintings, . . . or a piece of music. All will "fail": hence the bathos of their artistic treatment, the violence of their visual and auditory economy.

Ligon's series of paintings perform this feat most effectively. From a distance, they appear as nothing more than monochromatic grids containing gradations of black and gray due to the layering of individual screen prints set adjacent to each other (figure 8.4). Lines of repeating, overlapping text amass into dense accumulations, succumbing to illegibility. One's ability to properly "read" the words is thus sorely compromised, if not thwarted. Describing the development of his technique in his text-based paintings of the 1990s, Ligon once remarked, "The text has become more fragmented and abstract, and the work requires more effort to approach it. Text demands to be read, and perhaps the withdrawal of the text, the frustration of the ability to decipher it, reflects a certain pessimism on my part about the ability and the desire to communicate."[69] The smears, erasures, and accumulations of dense fields in the *Come Out* paintings give form to this "pessimism," their stymieing of communication more broadly pointing to the illegibility of history itself.

The *Come Out* paintings do not reveal much. If one is not already familiar with Reich's tape piece, they might mean nothing (they might just be ignored). Alternatively, given their manifest interest in abstraction, with surfaces that mimic screens of digital script, one might view them as instances of contemporary painting's post-Internet condition.[70] Their troubling of communication, however, suggests more is at stake (or that the surfeit of information now available still may serve to occlude rather than account for all subjectivities). The linguistic slip, where "bruise" (a violation of the body) becomes "blues" (a musical genre), amounts to a discursive construction of certain bodies, performatively enacted to sustain particular stereotypes (figure 8.5). Ligon consistently marks the aurality of black struggle, finding its clues through literary and cultural fragments that stand in contrast to "official" accounts that quiet modernity's racial burdens.

The blues, for Ligon, thread through this history: the color of sorrow and resistance makes an appearance, semiotically and artistically, in the series of *A Small Band* neons. Ligon indulges in the semiotic implications of assonance: sound (the blues) is tethered to physical violence (bruise and blood), the latter simultaneously suggesting a body that, to paraphrase Brian Massumi, is not "coded" but is "sensed," underscoring affect.[71] The scale of the letters—particularly in versions made as freestanding, sculptural works mounted on scaffolding or hanging from the ceiling, so that the beholder perambulates through them—add to this anthropomorphism. The words address us directly as subjects, as bodies, who in turn experience an uneven attraction to them. Whether rendered in white or azure, the color "blue" (as sign) assumes an auditory inflection that, paired with bodiliness, jumpstarts a host of associations. "I thought those words—bruise, blues, blood—went together like they were a small band," Ligon recently commented, discussing his curatorial project that considers the colors of racial violence, prompted by a "funny aural hallucination" he experienced of Louis Armstrong's version of Fats Waller's 1929 "(What Did I Do to Be So) Black and Blue?" playing in his head.[72]

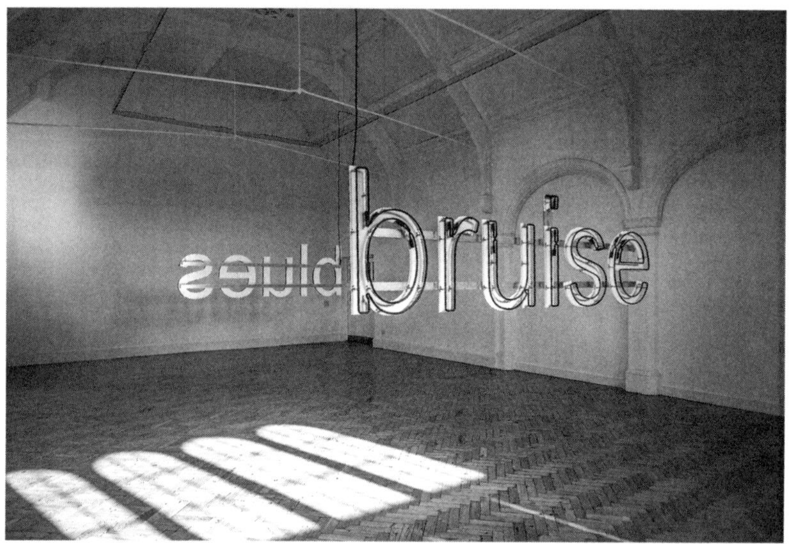

Figure 8.5 Glenn Ligon, *Untitled (Bruise/Blues)*, 2014. Neon and paint, two components: 115 × 32 inches; 101 × 32 inches, edition of 3 and 1 artist's proof. © Glenn Ligon; Courtesy of the artist, Hauser & Wirth, and Thomas Dane Gallery. Photo Credit: Valerie Bennett.

For Ligon, the blues connect sounds to black bodies—to the aural substance of black subjectivity.[73] Writing about David Hammons's *Concerto in Black and Blue* (2002)—where visitors, carrying small LED flashlights emitting a tiny dot of blue light, navigate a completely darkened, empty gallery space—Ligon remarks on the limitations of vision, marrying visual and acoustical tonalities. He writes, "How to reconcile the desire to be from nowhere, to have no identity and no personality, with the desire to make light 'very black,' when 'black' is suggestive of a particular history, culture, and practices?"[74] Invoking the work's title, he goes on to cite song titles and phrases that link sounds to states of physical and emotional suffering, underscoring the sitedness of meaning in the sensory body: "'What did I do to be so black and blue,' . . . or 'the blues,' or Amiri Baraka's 'Blues People,' or 'Kind of Blue,' or 'Say It Loud . . . ,' or 'Fugitive Blue . . . ,'" Ligon writes, suggesting that black subjectivity possesses both sounds and tones.[75]

The "blues people," Baraka argues, have always been defined as much by their *sounds* as by the color of their skin. And these sounds are mournful, soulful, atonal, "anti-assimilationist," Baraka contends, offering a covert form of rebellion. "As a folk expression of a traditionally oppressed people," he writes, "the most meaningful of Negro music was usually 'secret,' and as separate as that people were forced to be. ('The old blues remind me of slavery,' is the way many middle-class Negroes put it.)"[76]

Ligon has worked before on auditory secrecy and rebellion. In his exhibition *To Disembark*, the centerpiece is a series of wooden crates—mimicking the one that the slave Henry "Box" Brown used to ship himself to freedom in 1849. After remaining silent during transit, lest the sounds of his body reveal his presence, Brown emerged from the box in Philadelphia and broke out in song, his projected voice an audible emancipation. As Mark M. Smith writes, sound "serve[s] as an index of identity," and at no time was it more pressing than during slavery and colonialism.[77] As Smith adds, the "plantation soundscape" was a model of sonic difference and regulation, maintaining a quiet yet violent social order: as a concept, this soundscape references how only certain subjects were afforded the right to sound in the public sphere.[78] Ligon's installation breaks this regulative acoustics, as a series of otherwise hollow boxes, repeated at oblique angles on the floor, play a soundtrack of the "dissonant" traditions of jazz, spirituals, rap, and bebop music, which collectively function as a stand-in for the absent body of Brown, forever singing.

★

By means of conclusion, I want to return to Ligon's *A Small Band* at the Venice Biennale. Founded in 1895 with a mandate to glorify the cultural achievements (and superiority) of the nation-state, the biennale, the first of its kind, followed the "internationalist" world's fairs of the nineteenth century: outgrowths of European colonialism and empire where culture was an agent in the campaign of violence and geographical expropriation.[79] Through Ligon's work, the revolutionary, racial politics of the American 1960s confronts, even unwittingly, these histories: the subtle (or not so subtle) obscuring of the exhibition's name by the fractured words of Hamm suggesting as much. The work's aural substance confronts remnants of nationalism and universalism—or, rather, as Moten would have it, the "ongoing reconstruction [of the universal] in sound as the differential mark, divided and abundant, divided and abounding."[80] There is not so much distance from the past after all. Rather, there are ghosts. The conflict to which Ligon's works collectively allude is not singular but multiple:

colonialism, slavery, Reconstruction and Jim Crow, the struggles for civil rights and black autonomy, the policing of black communities through militarism and incarceration, as well as the ongoing drumbeat of all these legacies in the present, where silence loudly resonates. Forging archives from holes, Ligon's works suggest that the audible past is, in fact, the audible present. "*How to hear?*" they collectively ask, which remains an unresolved and pressing question.

Notes

1. In 2014, at the Camden Arts Center, Ligon exhibited an earlier version, with just two words (*blues* and *bruise*) rendered in bright, azure-like blue. Suspended from the ceiling, the neons were freestanding texts in the round, asserting a physical presence absent in Venice.

2. Huey Copeland, "Glenn Ligon and Other Runaway Subjects," *Representations* 113, no. 1 (Winter 2011): 73 (reprinted in this volume).

3. For an extensive discussion of the origin of the phrase "long hot summer" and an accounting of the events of the mid-1960s, see Malcolm McLaughlin, *The Long Hot Summer of 1967: Urban Rebellion in America* (New York: Palgrave Macmillan, 2014), 2.

4. "While I was interviewing these kids the sergeant was walking by the window and looking in. Another police officer kept glancing in, and after we had finished the interview and we came outside there was three or four of them on the corner, looking at us." Cited in Truman Nelson, *The Torture of Mothers* (Newburyport, MA: Garrison Press, 1965), 56.

5. In his book, Nelson refers to tape recordings made by Jones, as well as by himself, but does not provide further details.

6. Details of this history are taken from multiple sources: Nelson, *The Torture of Mothers*; Truman Nelson, "The Torture of Mothers," *Ramparts*, July 1966, 16–27; James Baldwin, "A Report from the Occupied Territory," *The Nation*, July 11, 1966, https://www.thenation.com/article/report-occupied-territory/; Conrad Lynn, "The Harlem Six," in *There Is a Fountain: The Autobiography of Conrad Lynn* (Brooklyn: Lawrence Hill Books, 1979), 3–33; Langston Hughes, "The Harlem Riot—1964," and Kenneth B. Clark, "HARYOU: An Experiment," in *Harlem: A Community in Transition*, ed. John Henrik Clark (New York: Citadel Press, 1964), 214–220 and 210–213, respectively; Harlem Youth Opportunities Unlimited (HARYOU), January 1, 1962–December 31, 1965, group V, series B, Administrative File, General Office File, Papers of the NAACP, Part 22: 1956–65, Library of Congress; and a series of articles from the *New York Times* cited in following notes.

7. Nelson, *The Torture of Mothers*, 17.

8. Conrad Lynn writes that the original arrest of the six was clearly in retaliation for their intervention into the Fruit Stand Riot. During his summation at the retrial, he noted, "These were marked black men and you can be sure in the kind of seething cauldron that was Harlem in the summer—in the late spring of 1964, just before the great Harlem riot—that the police would mark these boys as people who must be eliminated if they were going to maintain and enforce what they conceive to be law and order in 1964. So, when this murder happened, there was no problem on the part of the police finding or determining who should be charged with the responsibility for the crime. They just went back to those activists in

the Little Fruit Stand riot and they picked them up." Lynn, "The Harlem Six," 21. James Baldwin also notes that the police had tried to force the boys, with guns raised, to go to the precinct on another occasion, for no apparent reason. "But the boys put up a verbal fight and refused to go and attracted quite a crowd. . . . They refused to go to the precinct . . . and their exhibition of the spirit of '76 marked them as dangerous. Occupied territory is occupied territory, even though it be found in that New World which the Europeans conquered, and it is axiomatic, in occupied territory, that any act of resistance, even though it be executed by a child, be answered at once, and with the full weight of the occupying forces." Baldwin, "A Report from the Occupied Territory," n.p.

9. Untitled ad ("Georgia Justice for Harlem Six"), *New York Times*, July 16, 1967, 134; and *Village Voice*, July 20, 1967, 15.

10. "Mother Hysterical at Boy's Bier," *New York Times*, July 19, 1964, 54. Powell's murder happened on July 18, just a few months after the fruit stand incident. In a twist of historical fate, that very evening Barry Goldwater won the Republican nomination for president of the United States on a platform promising to restore "law and order" to the country: a slogan widely understood as coded racial language in response to civil rights unrest.

11. "'Hot Summer': Race Riots in North," *New York Times*, July 26, 1964, E1.

12. Michael W. Flamm, "The Original Long Hot Summer: The Legacy of the 1964 Harlem Race Riot," *New York Times*, July 16, 2014, A23.

13. Rolfson, cited by McLaughlin, *The Long Hot Summer*, 5; and Hughes, "The Harlem Riot—1964," 215.

14. Baldwin, "A Report from the Occupied Territory," n.p.

15. He continues the imaginary dialogue: "'Shut up Harlem!' BANG! BANG-BANG! 'I told you to be nice!' BANG! BANG-BANG! BANG! 'That for you! Take that, Harlem.'" Hughes, "The Harlem Riot—1964," 217.

16. Flamm, "The Original Long Hot Summer," A23.

17. The witness, Herman Joseph, approached Lynn and told him the prosecution's main witness, Ollie Roe, had lied, but Joseph stayed silent for eight years and refused to testify. Lynn and fellow attorney Lewis Steel invited Joseph to speak off the record and secretly tape-recorded their conversation, compelling him to speak to the judge, Joseph A. Martinis. See Lynn, "The Harlem Six," 26–29.

18. Fred Moten, "Black Mo'nin'," in *Loss: The Politics of Mourning*, ed. David Eng and David Kazanjian (Berkeley and Los Angeles: University of California Press, 2002), 66.

19. Jonathan Sterne, *The Audible Past: Cultural Origins of Sound Reproduction* (Durham, NC: Duke University Press, 2003).

20. Sterne, *The Audible Past*, 25 (see also ch. 4, "Plastic Aurality: Technologies into Media," for further discussion of these issues). While Friedrich Kittler also confronts questions of power, his examination of media, technological domination, and the place of the subject, as well as his interest in discourse analysis (and the linguistic encoding of media storage and communicative technologies), is distinct from Sterne's cultural account, which explicitly links sound recording technologies and modes of hearing to the sociopolitics of modernity from a postcolonialist perspective. For example, Sterne describes how, "after decades of pursuing genocidal policies toward Native Americans, the US government and other agencies began in the 1890s to employ anthropologists, who would use sound recording to 'capture and store' the music and language of native subjects." As he elaborates, this putative mechan-

ical act of preservation was bound to notions of Euro-American cultural superiority and its ideals of progress. "Phonography's much-touted power to capture the voices of the dead was thus metonymically connected to the drive to dehistoricize and preserve cultures that the US government had actively sought to destroy only a generation earlier. Permanence in sound recording was much more than a mechanical fact; it was a thoroughly cultural and political program." Sterne, *The Audible Past*, 17. See also Friedrich Kittler, *Gramophone, Film, Typewriter*, trans. Geoffrey Winthrop-Young and Michael Wutz (Stanford, CA: Stanford University Press, 1999).

21. Sterne, *The Audible Past*, 5, 9.

22. "To study technologies in any meaningful sense requires a rich sense of their connection with human practice, habitat, and habit. It requires attention to the fields of combined cultural, social, and physical activity—what other authors have called networks or assemblages—from which technologies emerge and of which they are a part." Sterne, *The Audible Past*, 8.

23. Sumanth Gopinath, "Reich in Blackface: *Oh Dem Watermelons* and Radical Minstrelsy in the 1960s," *Journal of the Society for American Music* 5, no. 2 (2011): 140. For an extensive analysis of *Come Out*, see also Sumanth Gopinath, "The Problem of the Political in Steve Reich's *Come Out*," in *Sound Commitments: Avant-Garde Music and the Sixties*, ed. Robert Adlington (Oxford, UK: Oxford University Press, 2009), 121–144. Created a year earlier, *It's Gonna Rain*, another phase-shifting tape work, exploits the songlike speech patterns of a street preacher, Brother Walter, warning of pending doom in the wake of the Cuban missile crisis.

24. According to communications theory, "signal" (as desired sound in the form of the message) and "noise" (as unwanted sound or auditory disruption) are at odds. As Norbert Wiener explains, the "signal" must be purged of "extraneous disturbances," which constitute "background noise." Similarly, John Peirce emphasizes the rationalistic basis of this understanding of noise, given that the integrity of the "message" is tantamount, resting on "efficient transmission" and the "resolution of uncertainty," which necessarily entailed eliminating "noise," defined as unwanted interference with the transmission of the code. See Norbert Weiner, *Cybernetics: Or Control and Communication in the Animal and the Machine*, 2nd ed. (Cambridge, MA: MIT Press, 1961), 10; and John R. Peirce, *An Introduction to Information Theory: Symbols, Signal, and Noise*, 2nd rev. ed. (New York: Dover, 1980), 8, 24. Both John Cage's reconsideration of noise and Pierre Schaeffer's tape music (*musique concrète*) are precedents for Reich and his fellow musical minimalists, although Reich's interest in preserving the semantic aspects of speech and the associative dimensions of sounds are distinct from both. In particular, Schaeffer's notion of acousmatics advocates the complete separation of sounds from their sources. See Pierre Schaeffer, "Acousmatics" (1966), trans. Daniel W. Smith, in *Audio Culture: Readings in Modern Music*, ed. Christopher Cox and Daniel Warner (New York: Continuum, 2004), 77.

25. Demers writes, "Unlike nonelectronic music, electronic music can transcend timbral limitations and just about every other existential limitation of traditional musical discourse. Electronic music can incorporate sounds of the outside world with ease and can generate new timbres that defy identification as music (or anything else). As such, electronic music can be mimetic and representational or abstract and obscure." See Joanna Demers, *Listening through the Noise: The Aesthetics of Experimental Music* (New York: Oxford University Press, 2010), 23.

26. For Gopinath, this "interpretive struggle" betrays the work's "politics." He writes, "Although Reich himself claims that the composition's structuring process intensifies the meaning of Hamm's recorded words . . . he also described his works as creating aural 'Ror-

schach test[s],' in which the listener has a great deal of freedom to interpret what is heard. Just as this hermeneutic flexibility makes *Come Out* less a text to decode and more a site of interpretive struggle, one that mimics the political contest itself, so Jameson's variant of the political resists the possible foreclosure of meaning found in representation and ethics, no matter how provisionally or contextually defined. To state the problem as simply as possible, the extreme variability of possible readings means that *Come Out* does not have a single, clearly defined politics." Gopinath, "Problem of the Political," 123.

27. For example, an article published in the *New York Times* on May 1, 1964, reads, "A detective disclosed that the attack on the storekeeper might have been the latest in a series of incidents in which militant and organized bands of Negro toughs have assaulted whites with seemingly no motive." Cited by Nelson, *The Torture of Mothers*, 53–54.

28. In an editorial note, the *Ramparts* editors write, "Truman Nelson wrote *Torture of Mothers* in the Autumn of 1964 in the aftermath of Harlem's 'long hot summer.' The bulk of the book consisted of tapes taken directly from the lips of mothers and children, the victims of the incidents he describes here. Despite considerable searching he was unable to find a commercial publisher who would take the book and decided to publish it on his own Garrison Press. Since then the book has made the rounds in a kind of private literary circuit but has received almost no attention from major reviews. We are publishing a short selection from this powerful book in the hope that it will attract the concern which it deserves." Editors' note, in Nelson, "The Torture of Mothers," 17.

29. Nelson, "The Torture of Mothers," 17.

30. As June Meyer, in a review of Nelson's book, adds, the mothers' testimony (which she suggests was recorded by Nelson), "becomes a voice for the reader; a voice quiet with outrage and bewilderment. Entry by the police in their homes was a terrorizing and inexplicable episode. All of them sat through cruel lengths of silence, denied access to their children held at the station house. These tapes provide powerful witness for the defense, a polyphony of pain heightened by memories of past humiliations." June Meyer, "Sons and Mothers: The Harlem Six," *The Nation*, April 25, 1966, 497.

31. The benefit took place on April 17, 1966, at New York City's Town Hall. Little mention of it exists in the press, outside of a brief article in the *New York Times*, "Benefit Aids Appeal of Six Convicted in Harlem Killing," *New York Times*, April 18, 1966, 21.

32. Steve Reich, interview with author, May 15, 2017.

33. Reich, interview with author.

34. In an interview with Ev Grimes, Reich repeats that Nelson had wanted him to produce a "dramatic sound collage" by editing down the tapes. "I explained to him that that was not my stock in trade, but that I would do it on one condition . . . that if I found something in all this mass of tape that I wanted to make a piece out of, he would let me do that." Gopinath, "Problem of the Political," 126–127, citing "Interview with Ev Grimes" (December 15–16, 1987), New York, NY, no. 186 a-1 OH V, tape and transcript, in Oral History of American Music, Yale University, tape 186-b.

35. Reich, quoted in Anastasia Tsioulcas, "Steve Reich at 80: The Phases of a Lifetime in Music," *NPR Music*, October 8, 2016, https://www.npr.org/sections/deceptivecadence/2016/10/09/496552301/steve-reich-at-80-the-phases-of-a-lifetime-in-music.

36. Baldwin, "A Report from the Occupied Territory," n.p.

37. He writes, "The testimony reads like a kind of postwar American poetry instead of transcribed depositions or interviews." See Gopinath, "Problem of the Political," 126.

38. Nelson, *The Torture of Mothers*, 14.

39. Lloyd Whitesell, "White Noise: Race and Erasure in the Cultural Avant-Garde," *American Music* 19, no. 2 (Summer 2001): 177.

40. Whitesell, "White Noise," 176. He adds, "From minstrel theater to the Jazz Age to youth culture since World War II, . . . white Americans have sought self-definition by way of black American culture. By appropriating or restaging aspects of black creativity, white people have pursued a rich, multiform aura of symbolic power, comprising the innocent, the authentic, the sensual, the uninhibited, the sophisticated, the edgy." Whitesell, "White Noise," 170.

41. Robert Adlington, "Introduction: Avant-Garde Music and the Sixties," in Adlington, *Sound Commitments*, 5.

42. Michel-Rolph Trouillot, *Silencing the Past: Power and the Production of History* (Boston: Beacon Press, 1995), 153.

43. Trouillot, *Silencing the Past*, 152.

44. Reich, interview with author.

45. As Keith Potter observes, the benefit featured "more familiar and more popular types of 'protest' music.'" As a result, "while contributions were being collected, [Reich's *Come Out*] was more or less ignored." Keith Potter, *Four Musical Minimalists: La Monte Young, Terry Riley, Steve Reich and Philip Glass* (Cambridge, UK: Cambridge University Press, 2000), 177. Gopinath takes issue with Reich's claim about the efficacy of *Come Out* as a motivator for donations, noting, "Whereas [Reich's] work for the benefit, including the sound collage, was not insignificant, the claim that *Come Out* performed its ostensible political function successfully despite being ignored seems odd, acting as an appropriation of the case for his own uses." Gopinath, "The Problem of the Political," 142n28. As I am exploring here, however, the conditions of the reception of *Come Out*—and its putative failure to register *as* music—complicates this critique, as it goes beyond authorial agency to consider the larger problematics of hearing.

46. Reich, interview with author; emphasis added.

47. As Trouillot emphasizes, historical narrativity operates through deferral, whereby an event is only ever completed through returns to it, representing the "fourth moment of historical production, the moment of *retrospective significance*." See Trouillot, *Silencing the Past*, 144; emphases added.

48. My use of this phrase ("evidence of things not heard") is preceded by Krista Thompson's compelling appropriation and extension of Baldwin's original concept in relation to photographic representation. Examining the temporal and conceptual coincidence of photography's invention and slavery's demise, Thompson analyzes the formation of the history of the African diaspora through what is missing in the photographic evidence, underscoring the corresponding power of photography's recording mechanism. See Krista Thompson, "The Evidence of Things Not Photographed: Slavery and Historical Memory in the British West Indies," *Representations* 113, no. 1 (Winter 2011): 39–71.

49. Glenn Ligon, email to author, May 19, 2017.

50. As Copeland argues, Ligon's focus on language and such "lost" writers as Zora Neale Hurston, as in his *Untitled* painting from 1990–1991, "stages the murkiness of racial thinking" that "runs headlong into the dilemma thrown up by [Frantz] Fanon's negative ontology of race: black being cannot be accessed rationally, though its affective contours can be inti-

mated in the gaps that structure hegemonic modes of speech." He adds that Hurston's works were subject to criticism, even the charge of racial stereotyping. See Huey Copeland, "Glenn Ligon and the Matter of Fugitivity," in Copeland, *Bound to Appear: Art, Slavery, and the Site of Blackness in Multicultural America* (Chicago: University of Chicago Press, 2013), 130.

51. Trouillot, *Silencing the Past*, 56.

52. Trouillot, *Silencing the Past*, 56.

53. Sterne, *The Audible Past*, 9.

54. Reich, interview with author.

55. Junius Griffin, "Whites Are Target of Harlem Gang," *New York Times*, May 3, 1964, 43. See also the following articles by Junius Griffin: "Forty Negro Detectives Investigate Anti-white Gang," *New York Times*, May 7, 1964, 28; "Police in Harlem Hunt Gang Chiefs: Two Adults Are Suspected of Preaching Hatred," *New York Times*, May 8, 1964; "View in a Harlem Street: 'Whitey' Won't Give Us a Job," *New York Times*, May 9, 1964, 13; "Grand Jury Investigation Urged into Anti-white Gang in Harlem," *New York Times*, May 10, 1964, 61; "N.A.A.C.P. Assails Reports of Gang," *New York Times*, May 11, 1964, 27; and "Harlem: The Tension Underneath: Youths Study Karate, Police Keep Watch, People Worry," *New York Times*, May 29, 1964, 1.

56. Nelson, *The Torture of Mothers*, 54–55.

57. Nelson, *The Torture of Mothers*, 55.

58. Nelson, *The Torture of Mothers*, 57.

59. Nelson, *The Torture of Mothers*, 58.

60. Lynn, "The Harlem Six," 7.

61. Soon after the riots, HARYOU disbanded. "In 1964, Harlem erupted in an urban rebellion after a white police officer fatally shot a 15-year-old black youth. Demonstrators, largely black youths, attacked their own community. Although HARYOU continued to promote its programs, it never did recover, nor did it achieve the results the organizers had intended. Shortly after, black youths instigated race riots in the urban ghettos in the North across the nation." Gladys L. Knight, *Race and Racism in the United States: An Encyclopedia of the American Mosaic*, vol. 2, ed. Charles A. Gallagher and Cameron D. Lippard (Santa Barbara, CA: Greenwood, 2014), 520–522.

62. Lynn, "The Harlem Six," 12–13.

63. The only material remnants that could be located by this author are in a recording of a WBAI radio broadcast from May 13, 1971: part of Pacifica Radio Archives' *American Women Making History and Culture: 1963–1982*, recordings that were digitally preserved from 2013 to 2016. The two-part program on the Harlem Six contains an interview from 1971 with Lynn, who at the time was still trying to free the incarcerated youths. The first part—approximately forty-five minutes long—includes an excerpted recording from the Town Hall benefit with, in addition to the music of the Freedom Suite and the narration of Ossie Davis, a reenactment of the Little Fruit Stand Riot, as well as edited excerpts from three of the interviews, which might come from Reich's "first" work, the audio documentary initially requested by Nelson. See "The Harlem Six: A Drama and Statements from the Trial," audiotape of radio broadcast on WBAI, May 13, 1971 (Los Angeles: Pacifica Radio Archives, 1971), available online in the *American Women Making History and Culture* series archive, University of California–Berkeley Library, http://oskicat.berkeley.edu/record=b23305811. Nelson passed away in 1987, and the literature contains no indication regarding the where-

abouts of the tapes. See Truman J. Nelson obituary, *New York Times*, July 14, 1987. Posthumously, an anthology of Nelson's writings, *The Truman Nelson Reader*, ed. William J. Schafer (Amherst: University of Massachusetts Press, 1989), was published. In a 1978 interview with Shaun A. McNiff (reprinted in the reader), only passing mention of the Harlem Six is made, and no mention of the tapes. Shaun A. McNiff, "Truman Nelson: An Interview," *Minnesota Review*, no. 10 (Spring 1978): 72–86. Nelson's surviving son, Garrison Nelson, in an e-mail exchange with the author (May 18, 2017) notes, "Truman and I were estranged during that period of time. He had moved to NY City while I was in graduate school at the University of Iowa. I never knew of these tapes." Garrison Nelson directed me to the Gottlieb Archives, Boston University, where Nelson's papers and other materials, including reel-to-reel tapes, are currently being archived. As this essay goes to press, however, I have not received confirmation that the Harlem Six recordings are part of this collection of tapes.

64. Reich, interview with author.

65. See "'Come Out' by Steve Reich," WhoSampled: Exploring the DNA of Music, May 28, 2025, https://www.whosampled.com/Steve-Reich/Come-Out/. Wikipedia names eight more samplings, including Orbital, "Time Becomes"; Prometheus, "Rush"; and Ben Vaughan on the album *Spike*. See "*Come Out* (Reich)," Wikipedia, May 28, 2025, https://en.wikipedia.org/wiki/Come_Out_(Reich).

66. Stephen Best, "Neither Lost nor Found: Slavery and the Visual Archive," *Representations* 113, no. 1 (Winter 2011): 151.

67. Best, "Neither Lost nor Found," 151.

68. Trouillot, *Silencing the Past*, 147; emphasis added.

69. Ligon quoted in Lauri Firstenberg, "Neo-archival and Textual Modes of Production: An Interview with Glenn Ligon," *Art Journal* 60, no. 1 (Spring 2001): 43.

70. While "post-Internet" has become a catchall (and controversial) term denoting objects beyond the computer or screen that nonetheless negotiate the digital, influential models of contemporary painting (largely abstraction) examine the medium in a postdigital age. David Joselit describes painting as "visualizing networks" that transitively extend to elements beyond their frames, forging surfeits of interconnected information. See David Joselit, "Painting beside Itself," *October* 130 (Fall 2011): 125–134.

71. Brian Massumi, "Introduction: Concrete Is as Concrete Doesn't," in *Parables for the Virtual* (Durham, NC: Duke University Press, 2002), 2.

72. Hilarie M. Sheets, "How Glenn Ligon Is Using Black and Blue to Begin a Dialogue," *New York Times*, June 4, 2017, 24.

73. Glenn Ligon, "Black Light: David Hammons and the Poetics of Emptiness," *Artforum* 43, no. 1 (September 2004): 249.

74. Ligon, "Black Light," 249.

75. Ligon, "Black Light," 249.

76. LeRoi Jones [Amiri Baraka], *Blues People: Negro Music in White America* (1963; repr., New York: Harper Collins, 1999), 176.

77. Mark M. Smith, "Listening to the Heard Worlds of Antebellum America," in *Ecologies of Hearing and Listening*, vol. 2 of *Sound Studies: Critical Concepts in Media and Cultural Studies*, ed. Michael Bull (London: Routledge, 2013), 179.

78. Smith, "Listening," 180–181.

79. The intertwined histories of nationalism and politics at the Venice Biennale, and their ongoing legacy in debates over globalization, are beyond the scope of this essay, but the exhibition's symbolic affirmation of European cultural superiority continues well into the postwar era when other challengers—first, the Americans in 1964, and more recently from countries outside the Euro-American axis—threaten its cultural (and political) dominance. For discussion of some of these issues, see Laurie J. Monahan, "Cultural Cartography: American Designs at the 1964 Biennale," in Serge Guillbaut, ed., *Reconstructing Modernism: Art in New York, Paris, Montreal, 1945–64* (Cambridge, MA: MIT Press), 369–415; Serubiri Moses, "The Venice Biennale and the Problem of Nationalism," Africa Is a Country, May 27, 2015, http://africasacountry.com/2015/05/thevenice-biennale-and-the-problem-of-nationalism/; and Caroline A. Jones, *The Global Work of Art: World's Fairs, Biennials, and the Aesthetics of Experience* (Chicago: University of Chicago Press, 2017).

80. Moten, "Black Mo'nin'," 66.

9 What's Black and White and Red All Over?

Helen Molesworth

Sometime during 1977, before the great blackout, and before Reggie Jackson hit three straight homers, my elementary school teacher at PS 219 sent us home with a permission slip requesting that our parents order daily delivery of the *New York Times* to our classroom. I remember the pitch: Dr. Butner (maybe it was Butler? I recall his reddish, late-1970s beard and tan wide-whale corduroy jacket as if it were yesterday) stood in front of the classroom and told us that the coupons in the newspaper would help offset the cost of the subscription, and that not only would we learn about local, national, and international events, we would also improve our vocabulary and sense of geography. The arrival of the newspaper fell under the rubric of "current events," and as such was structured by one of my favorite classroom assignments, so special in my eyes that it was alone in having a nickname: the Five Ws. The Five Ws were Who, What, Where, When, and the dreaded, because it was the most difficult, Why. Even at eleven, I struggled with the existential crisis provoked by the logic of cause and effect. The Five Ws was the matrix through which the *New York Times* would be read. Articles were meant to be dissected in No. 2 pencils, in big, fat elementary school penmanship, laboriously laid down on blue-lined paper. One of the things I remember loving most about the exercise was the use of the colon after each *W*, so gratifying, those two pencil dots, twirling the pencil around in your fingers to ground that little extra bit of graphite into the paper for emphasis.

When the day arrived, and everyone had a fresh newspaper in front of them, the air had the thick thrilling charge that came with not having

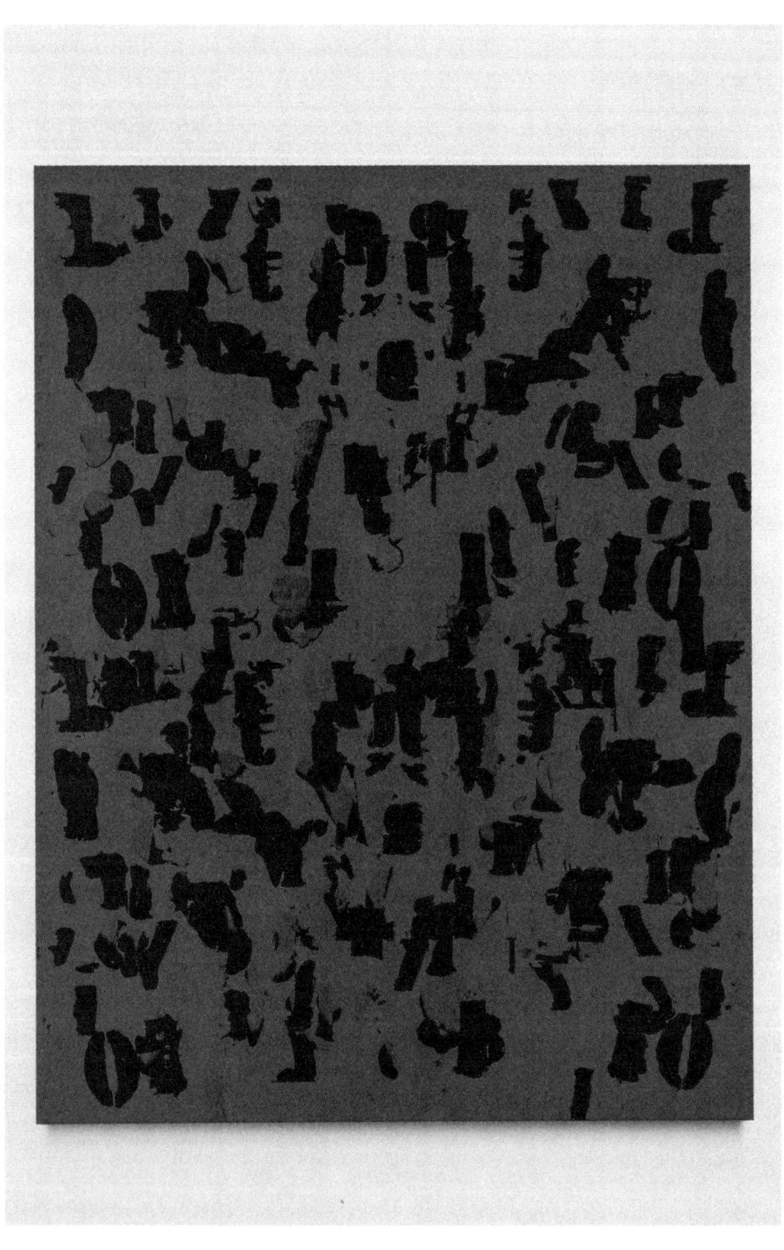

Figure 9.1 Glenn Ligon, *Debris Field (Red) #1*, 2018. Etching ink and acrylic on canvas, 114 × 88 inches. © Glenn Ligon; Courtesy of the artist, Hauser & Wirth, and Thomas Dane Gallery. Photo Credit: Joshua White.

to share. Standing in front of the class, Dr. Butler/Butner launched into a short lecture about the difference between the *New York Times* and its sister papers, the *Daily News* and the *New York Post*. Those newspapers could be read sitting down on the subway; they were, the implication was undeniable, simple that way. The *Times*, on the other hand, could not be read on the subway like that because it would be rude to your fellow passengers. Long before anyone had a word for manspreading, a bunch of eleven-year-olds in Queens were learning not to take up more than their fair share of room. What happened next was one of the greatest magic tricks of civics I have ever witnessed. Dr. Butler/Butner opened the *Times* to full width, and, with what I can only describe as smug verve, began to fold the paper first in half vertically, and then in half vertically again until it was a quarter of its unfolded width, and then, with a bit of snap, the whole thing was folded in half horizontally until it was tight and compact and ideal for reading both standing up and sitting down. Called "the subway fold," this democratic origami allowed you to read an article that started on A1 and continued on A22 with an equally deft opening and refolding, without ever once again opening the paper to its full width. Many years later, when the *Times* still ran classified ads, I deployed the subway fold, a deli coffee held precariously between my knees, as I circled open calls for waitressing jobs in the Village.

I encountered my first painting by Glenn Ligon sometime in the mid-to-late 1990s. I wasn't waitressing anymore; instead, I was leading public tours at the Whitney Museum as a way to pay for grad school. I was generally involved in a full-time, full-body crash course when it came to all things contemporary. My first encounter with Ligon's early, signature oil-stick paintings featuring a quotation from Zora Neale Hurston sent me directly to the library. I had not had an education in which I had encountered Hurston, so, for me, "I feel most colored when I am thrown against a sharp white background" was not the critical gambit of folklorist-*cum*-novelist, but rather a clever retooling of race along the fundamental Western pictorial tradition rooted in figure-ground relations. Later, when Ligon began adding coal dust to paint, I loved the way simple black paint was transformed into something iridescent and ragged. So too I was haptically engaged by the way it smudged through the stencil—liberally appropriated from Jasper Johns—ultimately becoming so clotted as to make the words indecipherable. The painting's accretive blackness was as redolent of Robert Rauschenberg's *Black Paintings* (an implicit nod to the closeted art history of the day, in which the great love affair between Johns and Rauschenberg was handed down to art students like so much samizdat in the old Soviet Union) as it was of the residual ink that often layered a subway rider's hands no matter how well-folded her copy of the *New York Times*. It was around this time that I remember having a plaintive, troubled conversation with a white male friend of mine. Sitting on a stoop in SoHo, he lit a cigarette and told me that he had found himself in a racist loophole earlier in the day. "What happened?" I asked. On the subway coming to meet me, he realized he was surprised to see a black man reading the *New York Times*. We both looked at one another and laughed the very specific laughter produced by the mixture of self-revelation and shame. Then we just hung our heads, and he said something like "Fuck." And I said something like "Man, they really did teach us some crazy shit."

Sidebar: Of course, "they" didn't ever teach "us" anything explicitly; indeed, it was the totalizing nature of structuring absence that codified the low hum of liberal racism that formed the intellectual and emotional groundwater for my white friends and me. The only redress was to engage in a lifetime's worth of study, a profound making up for lost time. I felt deeply fortunate to be catalyzed by a handful of contemporary artists, and, in order to meet them on their own terms, I set about educating myself. Because: Never. And, not only that, I didn't even realize it until I was fifty-two years old. Never. I never had a non-white teacher. Twelve years of New York City public school, and never. Four years of undergraduate schooling at two different public universities: SUNY Albany and UC San Diego, and never. A year at the Whitney Independent Study Program, never. Two years of part-time graduate study in art history at the City University of New York, never. Five years of a Ph.D. at Cornell University, and still never. I never once sat in a classroom and saw anybody but a white person. For sure, I have attended many lectures by people of color. The first one was in 1988 when Amiri Baraka came to speak at UCSD my senior year of college. (I don't remember anything about the lecture save for the following: when asked by a young, white male student if Baraka was "worried" about the "fate" of his work in the canon, Baraka scoffed and said he wasn't because he knew "my people will take care of that." It was a glimmer of rage, and it laid bare for me the concept, the notion, the reality, that some folks take care of other folk's stuff . . . I hadn't thought about that yet. I was twenty-one.) Never. I never sat in a lecture hall, week after week, and looked to the podium and saw a black man or woman be the figure of authority and the repository of knowledge. I never submitted my ideas for judgment to a black person. I have never been graded by a person of color. And, until 2018, no person of color had ever written me a letter of reference. Sidebar over.

Within the logic of the Five Ws, it is important to note that Glenn Ligon, as white liberal parlance would have it, "happens to be black," a concept he has meditated upon at length both in his work and in his writing. There is no answer to the "why" of this. Or rather, the answer is so long and so burdensome, and so horrendous and so farcical, that Ligon, when writing about it, resorts to a kind of factual enumeration. Upon reading a news account that then presidential candidate Barack Obama "happens to be black," Ligon mused: "Because I never felt in a position to choose my racial identity, it never occurred to me that blackness was something that could happen to you, like being mugged, or winning the lottery. I thought one was just black and that was that."[1]

Negotiating the capriciousness of life is something Ligon's paintings and neon signs have been doing for over two decades. When Hurston notes that she feels most black when confronted with whiteness, she presages what James Baldwin (another major interlocutor for Ligon) will later understand in "Stranger in the Village" when he finds himself feeling both American and black, identities newly sutured together in the context of a small mountain hamlet in Switzerland. In other words, many of the texts that Ligon has used as the engine to make his paintings have trafficked in the nettlesome problem of what exactly it means when one "happens to be black," and have proffered the intertwined spatial and psychic dimension of this knot of identity. Indeed, to answer the questions posed by Ligon's work is to make a productive recourse to the who, what, where, and when of childhood knowledge apprehension. And I suppose this is the moment when I should come clean about how literally—instrumentally, even—I've been "using" art for the past thirty years. I can safely say, at the midpoint of my life, that my interest in and knowledge of American history has stemmed largely from my encounters with contemporary art. If the first four Ws have continually sent me to the library, then the "why" has been the engine through which I have tried to understand myself in relation to the epic scale of history.

I was pretty good at placing Ligon within a white, Anglo-European painterly tradition: the stencils lifted from Johns, the silkscreen a nod to Warhol, the use of language borrowed from Bruce Nauman. One of the things I typically loved about Ligon's previous work was the way his paintings triangulated a largely white art historical field with the literary and performative canon of black authors, leaving the viewer (aka me) to toggle back and forth, as if trying to avoid getting thrown out at second base in a double play.[2] So when I saw Ligon's most recent body of work, collectively titled *Debris Field*, I was brought up short by their demonstrable lack of an archival reference—there was nothing to read (figure 9.1). Staggering paintings of soaring scale (they are slightly over nine-by-seven feet), each is composed with a perfectly flat ground of cardinal red paint upon which are scattered black shapes that vaguely resemble letters, or, more precisely, parts of letters. Making literally no recourse to any text or image—real or imagined, appropriated or self-made—through which I could anchor my initial responses, these pictures, it seemed, "happen" to be abstract.[3]

My art historical cast of mind immediately produced a field of mid-twentieth-century affinities: the hieroglyphics of Emerson Woelffer, the audacity of flatness and its relation to the pavement beneath our feet in Jean Dubuffet, the use of flat red planes as a punchy trick in Alberto Burri, and the knotted-up mechanics of Melvin Edwards's welded wall reliefs. All of those artists were caught up in the post–World War II challenge to invent new languages that could carry culture over the abyss created by the Holocaust, the dropping of the nuclear bomb, and the return of black servicemen and women to the racially segregated United States whose freedom they had just given their lives to protect. What kind of utopian thinking must have been at play for folks to think that a new language, a pictographic one at that, might help repair such enormous rents and gashes in the fabric of humanity? What possessed those with creative imagination to think that they could continue to produce culture in the face of such an enormous "why"? One of the things Ligon's new paintings seemed to announce is that the historical travails of the midcentury, complete with attempts to imagine a broken world anew, were not exclusively utopian. For, no matter how much these new red and black canvases evoked the constructivist color palette of Russian revolutionary painting, the tension in this work—between the continuation of their silkscreened method on the one hand and their refusal to cohere into any kind of readerly syntax on the other—was so pronounced that it made me feel a simultaneous visual awe and a twisting of my insides that typically signals the beginning of an anxiety attack.

Because I live with an art historian whose specialty is the development of print culture in Northern Europe in the late fifteenth century, I am fortunate to be aware of how the rise of printed information was essential to the development of the public sphere that would ultimately cohere into something we once blithely called democracy. Hence, when artists use printing matrices in their work, I see them as experimenting with postmodern ideas about uniqueness and reproducibility, and I also see them as working in and around the ethics of uniqueness and reproducibility, which, when it comes to matters of race, tend to smuggle in the role print culture had in arresting uniqueness in favor of reproducibility, because when uniqueness gives way to mass reproduction, we find ourselves in the realm of the stereotype. This means that print culture was both essential to the democratic project and part of its undoing, because the deployment of the stereotype is one of the most insidious and effective ways of corroding the difficult work of parity and difference essential to democracy. Ligon has been exploiting this twinned aspect of printing technology for decades. Within the language of printing, Ligon's paintings are technically monotypes, and their uniqueness—of the text, its writer, its transcriber, and its reader—was always at issue in how one makes meaning of a Ligon picture. So, too, their legibility, the viewer's ability to read the text—which was sometimes a terrifically difficult feat—was essential to Ligon's project. Given this history, Ligon's new paintings' refusal to make sense, his refusal to be citational, his refusal to offer any kind of narrative, his refusal to even produce a field of letters akin to a game of Scrabble, felt like an indictment of the highest order, so much so that on opening night I found myself thinking, "Oh shit, even Glenn is losing hope."

To be sure, Ligon's work was always trafficking in the abstract: we need only think of the illegibility and accrued blackness at the bottom of his canvases, or how his monochromatic black-and-white canvases are filled with exquisite flights of painterly fancy, nods to Robert Ryman. But the deep structure of language and legibility remained, a kind of lighthouse of meaning making, a slow revolution of light, dark, light, dark, a metronomic play with the unconscious of America. When the canvases exploded with color, as Ligon moved from Hurston and Baldwin to Richard Pryor, it was like *The Wizard of Oz*, where fantasies of liberation and beating back one's internal demons carried the day. This was certainly how I read Ligon's magisterial show at Regen Projects from 2007, which included thirty-six black-on-gold paintings of which thirty-three were titled *No Room (Gold)*, each repeating the same Pryor joke on every canvas (figures 9.2, 9.3). The joke, lifted from Pryor's 1971 stand-up film *Live &*

Figure 9.2 Glenn Ligon, *No Room (Gold) #12*, 2007. Oil and acrylic on canvas, 32 × 32 inches. © Glenn Ligon; Courtesy of the artist, Hauser & Wirth, and Thomas Dane Gallery.

Smokin', read, "I was a nigger for twenty-three years. I gave that shit up. No room for advancement." Painted before President Obama was elected, this remarkable room of pictures registered the profundity of the abstraction that is race itself. The bald repetition of the joke should have lessened the effect of the punch line, but it didn't. The problem was intractable, sticky, and ludicrous. There was no way up or out. But the recent paintings, in which language refused to cohere, and even the letters themselves appeared like so much litter on a windy day, made it seem that Ligon had left the philosophical terrain of language—one of our most elevated forms of abstraction—for Babel itself. And now that we live in Donald Trump's America (though for sure we were all living in it before the Russians helped him "win" an election he lost by over three million actual votes), one of Ligon's primary interlocutors appears to be Jean-Michel

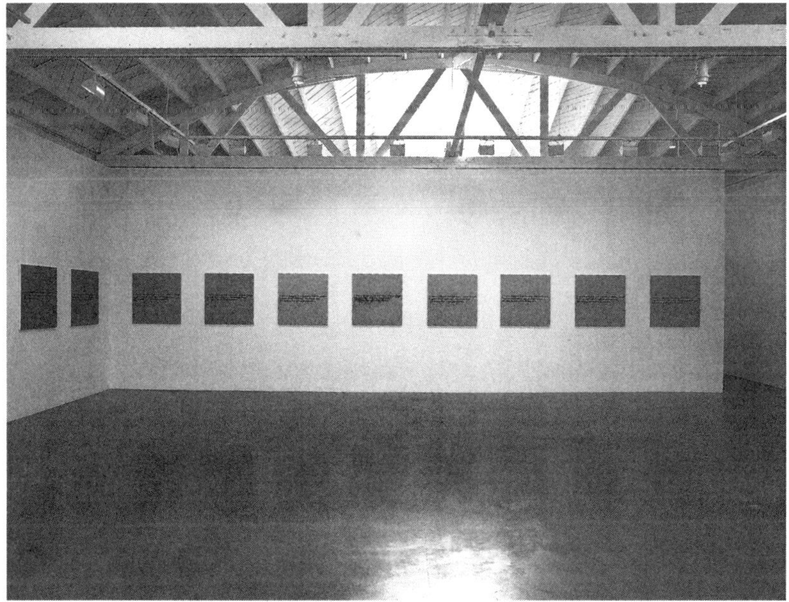

Figure 9.3 Glenn Ligon, installation view of *Glenn Ligon*, Regen Projects, Los Angeles, October 27–December 8, 2007. © Glenn Ligon; Courtesy of the artist, Hauser & Wirth, and Thomas Dane Gallery. Photo Credit: Joshua White.

Basquiat. Basquiat's use of text is, ironically, under sung in the assessment of his oeuvre; so, too, Basquiat's range as a colorist is typically overlooked in the market frenzy and general hagiography that attends his work. But Ligon took notice, and using the epistolary form as a narrative device, he penned a letter to the dead artist: "When I saw your work for the first time I knew it was important too, even though I wouldn't start making text paintings for many years. No one looking at my work would think of yours, but the space you opened up with your repeating text and phenomenal color (my Richard Pryor joke paintings owe both you and Warhol a great debt) continues to reverberate in my work."[4] In the *Debris Field* paintings, Ligon's repetition of broken letter forms, his ersatz scattering of them across the canvas as his compositional method, and his refusal to have the pieces of language cohere, hums with the vibration of one of Basquiat's central dilemmas: Is it possible to *not* make sense? Is it possible to render the components of the world in a disconnected manner on a single plane?

Is it possible to interrupt the drive toward narrative, toward explication, toward interpretation, toward cause and effect? And if you could escape sense-making, then might a new language be possible? For me, these are Basquiat's most trenchant questions, and Ligon's *Debris Field* paintings take them up.

A debris field is any location or site that contains the wreckage of what was once a whole object. If for Basquiat the debris field was the over four-century-long appearance of the African Diaspora in the hallowed ground of Western painting, almost always registered as a disruption—both ethical and aesthetic—then for Ligon the debris field is the fate of language under the pressures of unresolved and conventionally unspoken racism, which undergirds the American project. These debris fields of language politely perform the profundity of not being able to make sense of the senseless. (Their decorum is pointed. It's as if Ligon is saying, "Just because these fools have lost their damn minds doesn't mean I too must behave badly." And knowing, as he does, as we all do, that these paintings will end up in well-appointed living rooms with double-height ceilings and white-cube galleries with polished concrete floors, he is delivering his message with the brutal efficiency of a falconer.)

The Five Ws feel like a faraway relic, as lost to history as good penmanship, handwritten thank-you notes, and a general belief in the authority of the newspaper. The loss of language, and with it the lapsed ability to make sense of our current conditions, produces a condition akin to an Alzheimer's of the soul. It's no mistake that the only straightforward text that appears in the entire exhibition is a neon with the date of the next presidential election, November 3, 2020 (figure 9.4). Plugged in but not illuminated, the work will only be turned on during election day, the day we'll know how permanent our current conditions plan on being. The neon tubes are red; hence, I assume, when illuminated, the work will feel not unlike a FIRE EXIT sign, serving as both a warning and a potential solution. Titled *Synecdoche (For Byron Kim)*, the work is a gift offering to an artist friend who, similarly to Ligon, has spent a lifetime dedicated to unraveling the spurious category of race and its effect on the everyday. A synecdoche is a form of speech wherein a part is meant to stand in for the whole, which is another way of describing one of democracy's fundamental beliefs and virtues—that each of us is a microcosm of the nation, that citizenship is born of our responsibility for others, that our parts are always standing in for the greater whole. Both epigraph and coda, the neon was

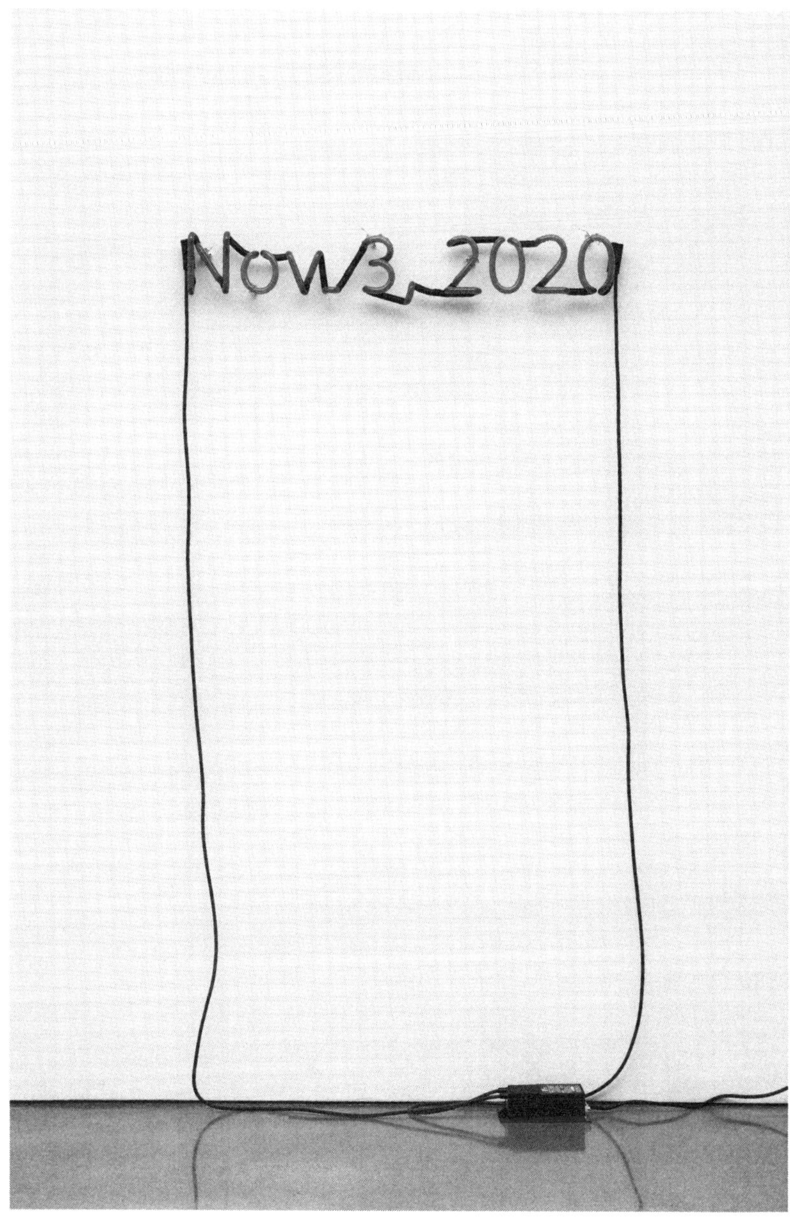

Figure 9.4 Glenn Ligon, *Synecdoche (For Byron Kim)*, 2018. Neon, $5 \times 30\frac{3}{4} \times 2\frac{3}{8}$ inches, edition of 1 and 1 artist's proof. © Glenn Ligon; Courtesy of the artist, Hauser & Wirth, and Thomas Dane Gallery. Photo Credit: Brian Forrest.

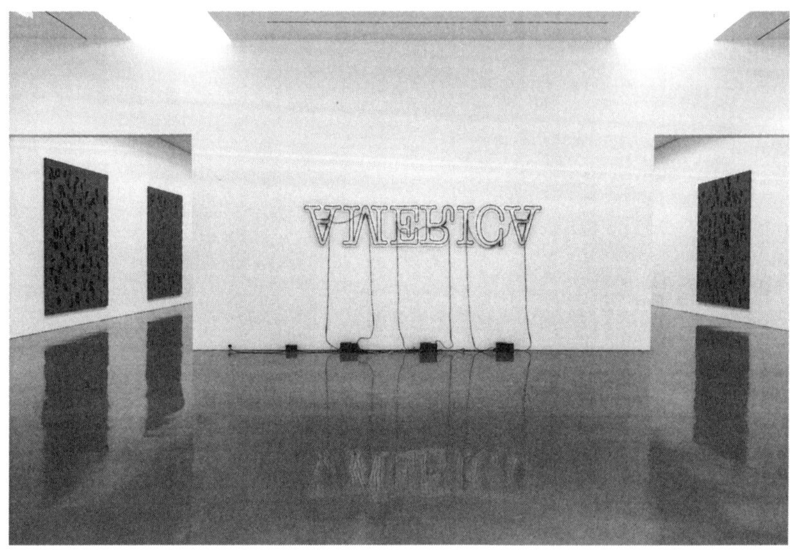

Figure 9.5 Glenn Ligon, installation view of *Untitled (America)/Debris Field/Synecdoche/ Notes for a Poem on the Third World*, Regen Projects, Los Angeles, January 12–February 17, 2019. © Glenn Ligon; Courtesy of the artist, Hauser & Wirth, and Thomas Dane Gallery. Photo Credit: Fredrik Nilsen.

installed in the entryway of the gallery and acted as a frame for the problems in sense-making that were to follow (figure 9.5).

It's not lost on me that what has also dropped out of Ligon's new pictures is the color white. White is the color of a newspaper's ground; it is the field that allows the black type to exist as figure. Without this structural and pictorial antimony, sense making, narrative production, and storytelling became exceedingly difficult. And the white dropping out also feels a bit like an affective experiment as well: what would it mean to displace whiteness, to erase it, or at the very least to temporarily suspend it, to ask it to sit on the sidelines? I suspect white has not been banished forever. I suspect Ligon is too invested in the problem-idea of America and the painterly problems of abstraction and language to give it up entirely. Nevertheless, the thought is there for the thinking, and pondering whiteness and its absence is certain to be crucial to whatever we might be able to know collectively about what happens on November 3, 2020, and will certainly be at issue for understanding the "why" of it on November 4.

Notes

1. In an untitled text that riffs on the alphabet for its structure, Ligon writes, "H is for Happens to Be Black." Glenn Ligon, *Yourself in the World: Selected Writings and Interviews*, ed. Scott Rothkopf (New Haven: Yale University Press, 2011), 27.

2. When Glenn read this essay he wrote, "Yes, true, but there is Gertrude Stein, Mary Shelley, Walt Whitman, Richard Dyer, Genet . . . ," and of course this is true. But I knew those authors, and what was shaming for me was that I didn't know Hurston. In this regard, Ligon was a teacher who helped break open the canon for me.

3. In a public discussion between Ligon and Hamza Walker held at Regen Projects on February 13, 2019, Ligon stressed his battle with a copyeditor of his aforementioned text about his insistence on placing the "s" at the end of happens to give it the inflection of black vernacular. The video can be accessed at Glenn Ligon, in conversation with Hamza Walker, Regen Projects, Los Angeles, February 13, 2019, https://www.regenprojects.com/exhibitions/glenn-ligon5/video?view=slider.

4. *Glenn Ligon: Encounters and Collisions*, ed. Glenn Ligon with Alex Farquharson and Francisco Manacorda (London: Nottingham Contemporary and Tate, 2015), 243. The letter is written to Basquiat posthumously as part of a curatorial project of Ligon's in which he asks artists if he can show their work and often does so by telling them the "why" of how their work is important to him.

10 The Race for Appropriation: Blackness, Authorship, and Ligon on Mapplethorpe

Hamed Yousefi

> At heart Tossy was a nomad, although he had lived in that basement for twenty years, worked at the Bureau of Printing and Engraving for even longer, and essentially had never left his parents' house. He fascinated me because he took what he had, which was almost nothing, and made something fabulous out of it, made it seem to encompass the whole world.
>
> —Glenn Ligon, "Black Light"[1]

Between 1991 and 1993, Glenn Ligon worked on an installation based on Robert Mapplethorpe's *Black Book* (1986). Using two copies of the book, he framed individual pages, which were originally printed with photographs on both sides. Depending on the site, the photographs were placed on two or three intersecting gallery walls, accompanied by two rows of individually framed printed quotations between them (figure 10.1). The quotations represented a range of views on the state of Blackness and homoerotic desire in the United States as well as divergent responses to Mapplethorpe's photographs of (mostly nude) Black men. What's more, the texts complicated Mapplethorpe's investment in the power of the image alone by introducing a conceptual and discursive aspect to his work. The installation, titled *Notes on the Margin of the Black Book* (1991–1993), pulled viewers back from the photographs to the streets of New York City, to intellectual reflections on race and desire in America, to Ligon's conversations with fellow Black queer artists, and to real spaces of Black

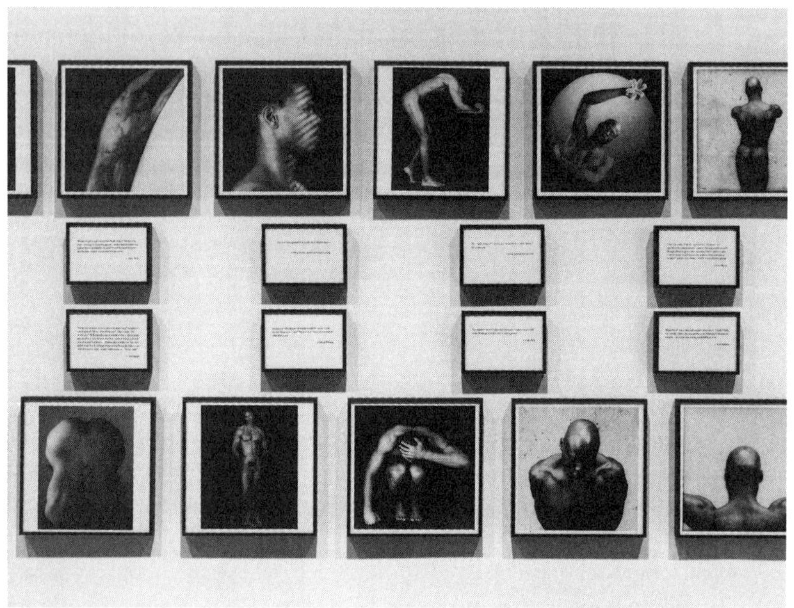

Figure 10.1 Glenn Ligon, *Notes on the Margin of the Black Book* (detail), 1991–1993. 91 offset prints, 78 text pages; each framed: prints 11½ × 11½ inches; text pages 5¼ × 7¼ inches. Collection of the Solomon R. Guggenheim Museum, New York. © Glenn Ligon; Courtesy of the artist, Hauser & Wirth, and Thomas Dane Gallery. Photography credit: Ronald Amstutz.

queer sociality. While the *Black Book*'s individualized, one-to-one mode of address encouraged private viewing and was suitable for moving across places and contexts—the volume is a hardcover coffee-table book with large, glossy pages—*Notes on the Margin* invited viewers to engage in a semi-choreographed public activity.[2] Here, gallerygoers physically walked through a monumental installation and collectively rethought the photographs in a specific sociohistorical context (figure 10.2). Kobena Mercer has argued that the substitution in Mapplethorpe's photographs of the Black male subject for "the archetypical white female nude" charged these pictures with a "potentially subversive aspect" in the history of Western art.[3] It follows, then, that Ligon's installation moved toward activating this potentiality by opening Mapplethorpe's ocular-centric work to the contingencies of a social dynamic—one that was simultaneously textual-discursive and corporeal. As such, *Notes* transcends mere commentary on

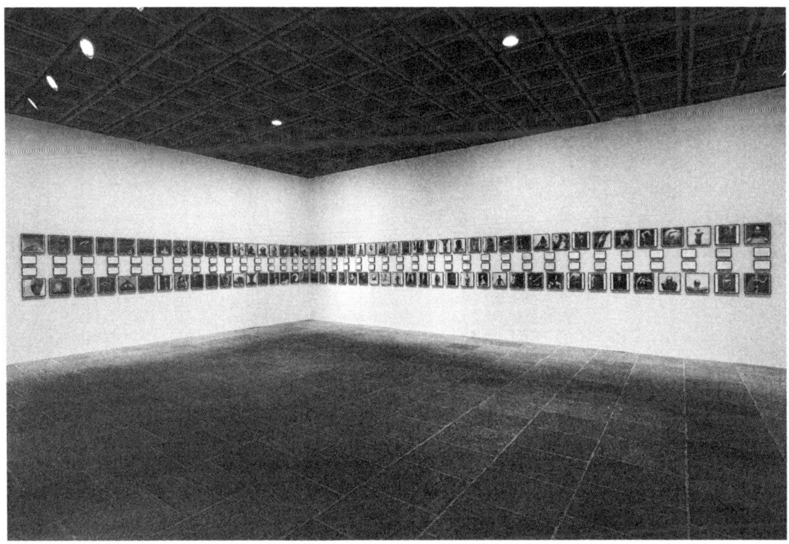

Figure 10.2 Glenn Ligon, *Notes on the Margin of the Black Book*, 1991–1993. 91 offset prints, 78 text pages; each framed: prints 11½ × 11½ inches; text pages 5¼ × 7¼ inches. Collection of the Solomon R. Guggenheim Museum, New York. © Glenn Ligon; Courtesy of the artist, Hauser & Wirth, and Thomas Dane Gallery. Photography credit: Ronald Amstutz.

Mapplethorpe. It interrogates the photographic image as such and the violence inherent in aesthetic formalism's claim to self-sufficiency.

In this inquiry into *Notes on the Margin of the Black Book*, I foreground the specific perspective of a Black gay male artist, prefacing my arguments with epigraphs from Ligon's interviews and theoretical writings about art and race. This approach is motivated by the work itself, especially as quotations from Ligon's personal diary and from conversations he had with fellow queer friends and artists punctuate the installation. Through its emphasis on positionality, *Notes* critiques a contemporaneous euphoria about the arrival of a homogeneous, post-identity art world. Putting the lie to such triumphalist narratives, the work's text panels confront viewers with the heterogeneities of New York City's metropolitan culture and the racism embedded in its art scene. Meanwhile, the incorporation of another artist's work in the installation evokes then-burning debates concerning artistic authorship and the rights and authority of an artist over other people's material. Like many other artworks of the previous two decades,

Ligon's *Notes* returns us to the classic Foucauldian question of avant-garde theory: "What is an Author?" Only this time, we are compelled to think of the answer in terms of Black authorship and its specific historical interpellation in the United States, where the law has consistently pushed Black people to the margins of personhood.

"Freedom in unfreedom is flight"

> RAN AWAY, a man named Glenn, five feet eight inches high, medium-brown skin, black-framed semi-cat-eyed glasses, close-cropped hair. Grey shirt, watch on left hand. Black shorts, black socks and black shoes. Distinguished-looking.
>
> —Glenn Ligon, text from one of the prints in *Runaways* (1993)

Ligon showed an early iteration of *Notes on the Margin of the Black Book* in 1991 at Art in General in New York; its final version became his contribution to the 1993 Whitney Biennial. As an alumnus of the Whitney's theory-oriented Independent Study Program, the young Ligon was conversant with the ways that the critical discourse of postmodernism had come to shape contemporaneous debates about art, subjectivity, and authorship. Under the rubric of postmodernism, American critics brought the legacy of Continental art theory and the early twentieth-century European avant-garde to the United States. This facilitated a transition in the New York art scene away from the image-based works of abstract expressionism and toward more expansive, radical, and less medium-specific modes of artistic practice.[4] In retrospect, of course, we can say that, despite the rhetorical function of the prefix "post-" as a marker of breakage, a key achievement of postmodernism was to reposition contemporary American art in a lineage of historical development, a trajectory that starts with the European avant-garde, goes through the neo-avant-garde of the post–World War II period, and culminates in the postmodernism of the 1980s and 1990s. In this context, when Ligon produced his installation, which centrally featured the work of another artist, postmodern discourse already had a name for such an intervention: "artistic appropriation."

Nearly a decade before Ligon's *Notes*, in a series of influential articles that contributed to the early-1980s discourse of postmodernism, Douglas Crimp and Benjamin Buchloh conceptualized appropriation as both a generic *and* a proper name. As a generic name, "appropriation" identified a technique shared by the historical and the new avant-garde alike. As a proper name, it described a particular group of younger white American artists who were otherwise known as the Pictures generation. Tracing the genealogy of appropriation back to the Duchampian readymade and Soviet photomontage, Buchloh argued that contemporary artists inherited appropriation from Duchamp's American disciples Robert Rauschenberg and Jasper Johns.[5] For them, appropriation signified a revolt against the cult of artist-as-author (typically exemplified in action painting's gestural expression and its afterlife in the neo-expressionism of the 1980s). Figures like Cindy Sherman, Richard Prince, and Sherrie Levine—artists whose work retroactively inspired the theorization of appropriation as a general avant-garde strategy—questioned the originality of "artistic expression" by turning to what Crimp called a "plurality of copies."[6] These artists' appropriated and mechanically produced works were meant to challenge bourgeois assumptions about a subject's self-possession and the autonomy attributed to that subject's expression. As such, appropriation was theorized in the United States as an exploration of self and subjectivity ("They use art not to reveal the artist's true self," Crimp wrote, "but to show the self as an imaginary construct")[7] through a new ontology of the art object as mechanical and appropriated (rather than as emerging from the interiority of the artistic subject).

For Buchloh, this meant that young artists were protesting capitalism. By devaluing the object "a second time," they rejected commodification's reduction of objects to exchange value. Levine, for example, depleted "the current commodity status of photographs by Walker Evans, Edward Weston, Eliot Porter, and Andreas Feininger for the second time by her willful act of rephotography, by restating their essential status as multiplied, technically reproduced imagery." Yet the theorists were also alarmed by the art's shortcomings. Buchloh warned that, instead of retrieving appropriated objects' "historical authenticity" and "social truth," Levine's strategy of rephotographing "subjects historical objects to an act of confiscation where their innate authenticity, historical function, and meaning is robbed." Finding this confiscation and robbery to be politically ambiguous, Buchloh specifically questioned Levine for "exerting a certain fascination over those contemporary critics, including myself, who are equally ambivalent toward their affiliations with the powers and privileges that the white middle class provides."[8]

Like Buchloh, Crimp's theorization of appropriation also utilized a terminology of theft and robbery to explain the work of postmodern artists, although he demonstrated less skepticism than Buchloh regarding the politics of this practice. For Crimp, artists' "purloined, confiscated, appropriated, *stolen*" images (emphasis in original) questioned the myth of originality in art. Equally important, by being stolen, these works demonstrated the absence of an original self behind the art: "the original cannot be located, is always deferred; even the self which might have generated an original is shown to be itself a copy."[9] Reading Buchloh and Crimp together, we can say that by the time of Ligon's work, the theoretical discourse on appropriation had already recognized two critical problems with this strategy: first, appropriation disregards the historical truth of the object; second, it presupposes a kind of subject-artist who is entitled to take, appropriate, and steal objects. The first problem concerns the status of the object in avant-garde art; the second involves the position/authority of the avant-garde artist as author. These tensions accompany us through Ligon's installation of Mapplethorpe's photographs. They also shape our analysis of his relationship with postmodernism and, by extension, the history of avant-garde thought and practice in general.

At first glance, *Notes on the Margin of the Black Book* seems to be a typical work of appropriation: Ligon takes other people's materials—images and writings that are essentially mechanically reproducible—and reuses them for his own work, ceding authorship in the course of ideological critique (the politics of race and homoerotic desire) and self-reflection (Ligon himself is implicated in several text panels). But Ligon's is not a typical engagement with appropriation. As his critical and theoretical writings demonstrate, he understands the postmodern condition in relation to the irreducible specificity of Black subjects' experience. For example, reflecting on the work of composer Sun Ra and conceptual artist David Hammons, he writes: "Their genius was to employ a postmodern concern with the emptying out of the self as a critical strategy, one that might have particular resonance with a people historically positioned at the margin of what was considered human."[10] Ligon and some other Black thinkers of his generation articulate this critical strategy through the concept of "fugitivity"—the state of a runaway slave.[11] Works such as *Narratives* and *Runaways* (the latter is cited in the epigraph to this section), both from 1993, underscore Ligon's investigation of fugitivity as a ground for reflection on self and subjectivity around the same time that he worked on the Mapplethorpe installation.[12]

In contradistinction to mainstream practices of appropriation, in which race seemingly does not exist in the work of white artists or is dismissed as irrelevant, Ligon's approach to postmodernism in these works brings race to the foreground. And not only that: it is my contention that his work exposes race as a neglected unconscious of appropriation art and theory. This argument will emerge more clearly when I turn to the treatment of objects in *Notes* (the "historical authenticity" and "social truth" of the quoted text panels and Mapplethorpe's photographs) and to the historical position of Black authorship. But for now, to qualify the scope of fugitivity as avant-garde practice, Fred Moten's reflections on Black avant-garde music provide a helpful entry point.

Like Ligon, Moten relates Black avant-garde explorations of subjectivity to the flight of a fugitive. A fugitive's flight, in his words, is "freedom in unfreedom";[13] it does not focus on the self as the site of subjectivity but rather contemplates the stealing away of "subjectivity" from and by the self: "Born not in bondage but in fugitivity, in stolen breath and stolen life."[14] As such, fugitivity interrogates modes of domination that collapse subjectivity and subjugation into one another. What this means for our understanding of appropriation is that it estranges the key terms of the debate—subject and object—from their usage in mainstream academic parlance. In the field of art history, "subjective" and "objective" commonly function as primary terms to distinguish between expression and mechanical (re)production. This is how theories of appropriation contrast the authorial gestures of abstract expressionism with what Crimp called "the photographic activity of postmodernism."

But if Blackness is the experience of "a people historically positioned at the margin of what was considered human"—those produced as objects whose fugitivity registered their resistance—then Blackness already suspends the assumption that personhood and subjectivity come together.[15] The work of the Black artist, therefore, is not to *arrive* at such a conclusion; it is to *depart* from it. Here, fugitivity has a distinction between subject and object written into it as what theorist Peter Osborne would call "the poles of determinations of forms of freedom and domination."[16] In art, fugitivity suspends the contrast between the possession of one's own expression and the possessive mastery and dominion of artists over objects (stolen or produced) and instead moves toward recognizing the objects' social truth. Yet the question remains: How can we see fugitivity manifested in *Notes*? What kind of authorial position does the fugitive subject occupy as an artist? And what would all of this mean for the postmodern discourse of appropriation and for the *longue durée* of avant-garde history, in which theories of artistic authorship have been and continue to be generated from the standpoint of white subjectivity?

Looking at the White Man, Looking at the Black Man

> [In Isaac Julien's film] on Langston Hughes . . . there is this incredible scene where a man, a white man, is flipping through the *Black Book* as if it were a catalogue. Pick the image . . . pick the fantasy.[17]
>
> —Glenn Ligon, 1991

It took Ligon more than one attempt to arrive at the final form of *Notes on the Margin of the Black Book*. When he first began working on Mapplethorpe's photographs, his initial motivation was to navigate the contradictions of Mapplethorpe's work: "There are some photographs that really speak to something about my own experience and there are some photographs which could be viewed as racist."[18] Ligon started out by writing on them, "literally taking the book and just writing whatever came to mind directly on the photographs."[19] In *Black Book*, Mapplethorpe's painstakingly composed and dramatically lit images combine the iconography of classical art with the market- and gallery-oriented medium of art photography. His frequent use of abstract composition and cropping can turn his photographic subjects into disembodied organs effectively detached from the actual personhood of the pictured individuals. In addition, the format of the coffee-table book amplifies the objectification of Black bodies as both sexual and commodity fetishes.

Ligon used a felt pen to scrawl his dissenting remarks on the pictures' glossy surfaces (figure 10.3). One of his study sketches from 1991 shows that he wrote two questions on a photograph that depicts the bust of Terrence Mason. In it, Mason's head is turned sideways and his chin is aligned over his left shoulder. His fixed sidelong eye is a final touch that completes the photograph's referencing of ancient Egyptian iconography. For Mapplethorpe, an auteur photographer, photographing Black men in a pose like this was a formal inquiry into "an area that hadn't been explored intensively." In a quotation cited in Ligon's installation, Mapplethorpe goes on to say, "If you went through the history of nude male photography, there

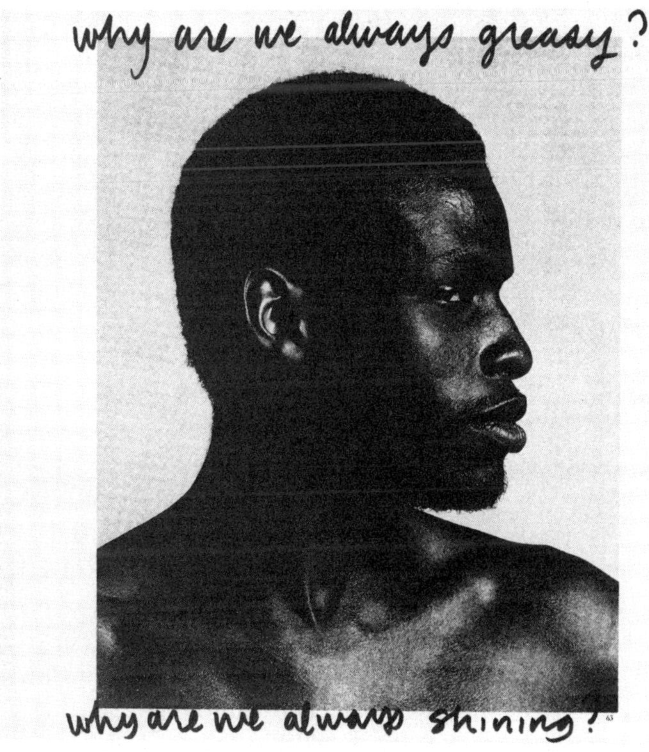

Figure 10.3 Glenn Ligon, *Study for Notes on the Margin of the "Black Book,"* 1991. Ink on book page, 11½ × 11½ inches. © Glenn Ligon; Courtesy of the artist, Hauser & Wirth, and Thomas Dane Gallery.

were very few black subjects. I found that I could take pictures of black men that were so subtle, and the form was so photographical." Referring to the picture of Mason, Ligon expresses unease with the way racist stereotypes get reproduced in Mapplethorpe's work: "Why are we always greasy? Why are we always shining?"

Although Ligon's concerns are phrased in terms pertinent to visual form (shine), the strategy of direct linguistic intervention was still too personal for the artist, so he never exhibited these early sketches: "It didn't seem interesting for me to go around with my little stamp saying 'racist' and 'not racist.'" The handwriting was "too autobiographical and confessional," and the accusatory tone of the questions conveyed a finality of judgment that Ligon did not seek. "There were other points of view that I wanted to get in which I wasn't getting by doing that."[20] This aim moved Ligon toward the large-scale installation format, which allowed him to include a multiplicity of positions through quoted texts. One way that Black positionality registers itself in the work is when Ligon no longer speaks as or for himself (regardless of the fixity or fluidity of that self). Rather, through existing images and words, he speaks in what Richard Meyer has aptly described as "a first-person voice of black subjectivity while registering the denial and relentless silencing of that same voice."[21]

But what role does Mapplethorpe play in this dynamic of registering Blackness? During the 1980s, few works of art stirred as much public controversy as Mapplethorpe's photographs. Numerous observers did indeed find his images of Black men to be racist. Mapplethorpe's insistence on a genitalized depiction of Black male sexuality was a key problem, even in some of his most formally "successful" pictures, such as the infamous *Man in Polyester Suit* (1980). In it, we see a fully clothed Black man with his penis hanging out of his unzipped trousers. The man's head and face (i.e., the markers of his individuality) are cropped out of the frame. His creased, cheaply made three-piece suit suggests impoverishment. His slightly bent left arm seems to be signaling something akin to distress, while a tiny thread of white fabric dangling from his shirt ensures that the viewer's gaze is directed toward his penis. A quotation from Frantz Fanon, cited in Ligon's installation, reads as a perfect caption for such an image: "One is no longer aware of the Negro, but of a penis: the Negro is eclipsed. He is turned into a penis. He *is* a penis." Yet, for Ligon and many other queer Black people, passing judgment on Mapplethorpe was complicated because of the place his photographs occupied in the culture wars of the Reagan-Bush era.[22] At the time, right-wing politicians and pundits found in this work a perfect target for their attacks on public funding for the arts. These attacks were every bit as homophobic as they were mired in a white-supremacist fear of miscegenation. How, then, to walk the fine line between defending artistic institutions against homophobic white supremacy and criticizing an art scene that itself perpetuated racism?

Two articles by Kobena Mercer, at the time a young but significant Black gay voice in art criticism, exemplify the difficulties of making conclusive judgments about Mapplethorpe. Quotations from both articles are included in Ligon's installation. In the first article, published in 1986 in the UK, Mercer attacks Mapplethorpe for the white, colonial position of power he assumes in making the photographs: "As an artist, Mapplethorpe engineers a fantasy of absolute authority over the image of the black male body by appropriating the function of the stereotype to stabilize the erotic objectification of racial otherness and thereby affirm his own identity as the sovereign I/eye empowered with mastery over the abject thinghood of the Other: as if the picture implied, Eye have the power to turn you, base and worthless creature, into a work of art."[23]

In a 1982 essay dedicated to evaluating the politics of appropriation art, Douglas Crimp had criticized Mapplethorpe for his "retrograde" mode of appropriation. While progressive appropriation challenged "conventional notions of artistic creativity," for Crimp, Mapplethorpe was an example of bad appropriation because he constructed "from his historical sources a synthetic 'personal' vision" that eventually established him as an *auteur*.[24] Mercer's point, however, is different. He is interested in the power dynamic internal to the process of production between the artist and his Black sitters. Through such an analysis of exploitation and privilege, Mercer considers Mapplethorpe's authorship of the photographs not merely as a personal vision but also in relation to the historically constructed authority of whiteness. Here, Mercer's argument follows a typical line of British cultural Marxism in which critics underscore power dynamics and class relationships to understand the political significance of race and gender.

Then, three years after his first article, Mercer wrote a second one on Mapplethorpe, this time in the United States. By then, Mapplethorpe's death from AIDS in 1989 and the disturbance that the photographs caused among right-wing Americans made it possible for Mercer to see the same set of photographs from a completely different angle. Instead of situating them in the context of the heterosexual, white, colonial gaze, he now had the context of the United States in his field of vision and understood Mapplethorpe's pictures as part of New York City's metropolitan queer stage. Mercer's new perspective brought to the fore a homosexual, intersubjective dynamic in the relationships between Mapplethorpe and his sitters. He now read the photographs as "a highly stylized form of reportage which documented aspects of the urban gay cultural milieu of the post-Stonewall era of the 1970s."[25] The unsettling "shock effect" in Mapplethorpe's photographs—the challenge they pose to structural formations of Western, white, heterosexual thought—is seen here as the result of gay Black men's sharing an alternative, queer stage with the artist in New York City. If privilege did not unite Black and white members of this community, precarity did: many of Mapplethorpe's sitters also died of AIDS. Eventually, Mercer resolved the Mapplethorpe dilemma for himself by publishing both articles together as one chapter of his book *Welcome to the Jungle*. He stands by his seemingly contradictory interpretations because each of these two positions contains an element of truth. Together, they argue that Mapplethorpe's photographs have a radical and subversive dimension, but also that, in his critique of white European heteronormativity, value still travels in one direction—establishing the authority and authorship of the white artist at the expense of objectified Black bodies.

For Ligon, however, the resolution was harder to achieve.[26] To the extent that *Notes* is a commentary on Mapplethorpe, it is a collective commentary that only comes together through the active engagement of its viewers. After subtracting his own hand from the work, Ligon inserted various potential interpretations on the gallery walls, including those of right-wing pundits, Mercer, Crimp, and numerous other commentators, some of whom Ligon interviewed specifically for the installation. If in the photographs Mapplethorpe was looking at Black men through his camera, now, with the assistance of the texts, we can look back at Mapplethorpe. But is it possible for the installation to reverse the relations of objectification internal to the photographs? Is it even reasonable to expect the work to reverse something that has been in the making for centuries? What Ligon offers by way of answer is an artistic inquiry that turns us toward an alternative economy of critique, an economy less complicit in exploitation and ownership and more explicitly based on collaboration, *bricolage*, and auto-critique. The challenge facing Ligon, however, was how to activate an engagement with Mapplethorpe that would also be an alternative to the racist logic that continued to animate the art scene, in which, as philosopher Étienne Balibar once put it, "the principal form of exclusion is *differential* inclusion."[27] The difficulty in challenging differential inclusion is that it operates in a more complicated manner than old-fashioned segregation: Black people are included, but only as vehicles of white self-exploration. Had he merely marginalized his own authorial voice, Ligon would not have been able to adequately respond to this particular dynamic of exploitation that is at work both in Mapplethorpe's practice and the larger social ecology from which it emerged.

Ken Moody, one of the *Black Book*'s models, offers insights that help us find better language for this dynamic. In a 1988 BBC documentary about Mapplethorpe, filmmaker Nigel Finch presses Moody about the question of the power imbalance between the artist and his sitters. Moody iterates the words of his answer carefully, one at a time: "I don't honestly think of it as exploitation. It's almost as if, and this is the conclusion I've come to now, because I really haven't thought about it up to now—it's almost as if he wants to give a gift to this particular group. He wants to create something very beautiful and give it to them. And he is actually very giving."[28]

If appropriation involves a similar economic system as exploitation, Moody's suggestion to see Mapplethorpe through an economy of the gift complicates the picture. "Taking" (appropriation) is now alternated with "giving." Compared to appropriation's colonialist assumptions, a more complicated analysis is required to break down the position from which a gift is given. What conditions make generosity possible? Is the gift a renunciation of the self or an affirmation of the sovereignty of the giving subject, an economy of exchange in which that which is given (the gift) is in fact kept, precisely by virtue of the generosity involved in the act of giving it?[29] It is fair to say that Mapplethorpe's photographs remain Mapplethorpe's, even though "he is actually very giving." Ligon includes this quotation from Moody in his installation, followed immediately by a second quotation from him: "When I look at it as me, and not just a piece of art, I think I look like a freak. I don't find that person in the photograph necessarily attractive, and it's not something I would like to own."

That Moody does not want to own his own image, an image that he can see only as "a piece of art" and not "as me," a gift that is given to him but that he does not want, is the complicated dynamic of differential inclusion that in Mapplethorpe produces a semblance of intersubjective collaboration between the artist and his models yet finds no reflection in the final outcome of the project. The photographs are so concerned with aesthetic perfection that they erase racial and economic tensions in the queer scene and cover over material gaps between the artist and his subjects. They also fail to account in any meaningful way for the *significance* of the mutuality of the relationship between the white gay artist and his Black queer models. The photographs appear to take this mutuality for granted, as if the material world outside the picture were as seamless as one of Mapplethorpe's staged and edited photographs.

The Photograph's Broken Speech

> [A]lthough race is a biological fiction, it remains an entrenched social and political fact.
>
> —Glenn Ligon, "Kelley Walker's Negro Problem"[30]

> If blackness is a construct, then we are all construction workers.
>
> —Glenn Ligon, "Black Light"[31]

Even as documents of a particular sociohistorical moment, Mapplethorpe's photographs are uncomfortably silent. Their studio setup, cleansed of any contact with everyday life, makes them appear outside of time and place. If we listen to them, we find that "the sonic frequencies of photographs," those haptic vibrations that Tina Campt locates in the ordinary texture of the quotidian as recorded in certain photographic images, are muted in Mapplethorpe's work.[32] This erasure of sound is, according to Moten, "a suppression of difference in the name of (a false) universality,"[33] that is, the universality of the aesthetic image. He links "the necessary repression—rather than some naturalized absence—of phonic substance" in photography to "the semiotic desire for universality, which excludes the difference of accent by excluding sound in the search for a universal language."[34] One of Ligon's goals in his installation is to interrupt this silence through voices that represent the actual experience of Black queer life, thereby providing, in Moten's terms, "distinguishable stances toward universality."[35] For his part, Ligon wants "to let the photographs be seen within the context."[36] But the "context" in Ligon's installation contains multitudes. Here the context is the conditions of representation and experience and the dynamic that determines the making and reception of Mapplethorpe's work: his celebration of Black queer magnificence, on the one hand, and the reproduction of racist tropes in his art, on the other. The context is also the structural racism surrounding representation and signification in general; the conservatives who attack the arts; the arts that must be defended against the attacks; homophobia among communities of color; racism in queer and artistic communities. This context is, in Moten's language, "a moan or shout that animates the photograph with an intentionality of the outside . . . with a piercing historicality."[37] Ligon's installation allows

Mapplethorpe's photographs to be seen in *these* contexts even as it demonstrates the limitations of them from the critical standpoint of an artist who, like the models central to (but silenced in) Mapplethorpe's work, is a homosexual Black male.

Let's look at some of the text panels more closely. Opening with a passage by Stuart Hall, the installation rejects the binary of self and Other right from the beginning. Hall's quotation reads: "The way in which black people, black experiences, were positioned and subject-ed in the dominant regimes of representation were the effects of a critical exercise of cultural power and normalization. Not only, in Said's 'Orientalist' sense, were we constructed as different and other within the categories of knowledge of the West by those regimes. They had the power to make us see and experience ourselves as 'Other.'"

As the inaugural utterance of the installation, Hall's quotation breaks down the distinction between outside and inside, subject and social context. Instead of understanding the "dominant regimes of representation" as social structures imposed on Black subjects only from the outside, he points out that such Othering is also internal to the experience of Black people, making us see *ourselves* as Other.

Hall's turn to the first-person plural in the final sentence of the quotation above plays a key role in the installation's unfolding. At one level, this "we" reserves a space for Ligon's viewer to be Black, in contradistinction to Mapplethorpe's fantastical utopia in which the white man spins his metropolitan fantasy. At another level, the turn to self-reflection in Hall's "we" implicates "us" as viewers, regardless of racial positionality, in the analytics of Othering outside *and* inside the installation. Throughout the work, a number of texts reinforce our awareness of the fact that we are engaged in a politics of viewing. A quotation from Rita Burke, president of the Massachusetts branch of Morality in Media, claims, "People looking at these kind of pictures become addicts and spread AIDS." Another, from curator Tom Sokolowski (presumably speaking to Ligon), underscores that we are participating in an installation that is itself a construct of an art-world system: "Just explain to the Mapplethorpe foundation that you're doing a project that celebrates the photos in some way."

Several of the cited voices directly address Mapplethorpe's work, while others reflect more generally on Blackness and desire, particularly between men of differing races. That the quotations are drawn from heterogeneous sources—a James Baldwin essay, snippets of casual conversations at a bar, excerpts from the artist's personal diary, and homophobic right-wing political commentary all jostling together—reflects the messiness inherent in the multiplicity of Mapplethorpe's metropolitan context. Their disjointed nature further qualifies the photographs' unified seamlessness. Nonetheless, as Richard Meyer further notes, the multiplicity of voices within *Notes* does not create a "happy plurality of diverse perspectives."[38] Rather, it reinforces the many antagonisms at play in claims of homogeneous, metropolitan multiculturalism. One particularly personal quotation from a conversation Ligon had with his (white) boyfriend is representative in this regard:

CLIFF: After they met you some people asked me if I was a "dinge queen," or if I was "into dark meat."

GLENN: After they met me? You mean people I talked to, had lunch with?

CLIFF: Yes, it happened several times.

The duality of white behavior—what is said when Black people are present and when they are not—that this conversation underlines points to the differential experience of metropolitan multicultural spaces for white people and for people of color.[39] It also pushes the viewer to a greater self-awareness while encountering Mapplethorpe's photographs, pointing out that the experience will be dependent on who is watching and in whose presence.

Meyer, however, seems to reduce the tension between Ligon's work and Mapplethorpe's photographs when he argues that Ligon "directs our attention to the ways the *Black Book* functions as a symbolic battleground on which conflicting claims—about race, desire, disease, art, and freedom—are registered."[40] His reading reflects what Ligon himself said in 1991, at an early stage of working on the installation: "I guess this project is the most curatorial because there is very little intervention on my part. Most of my other work involves some sort of change of medium—from the printed word to the painting or to the drawing. But this project is really just the photos and the text without any sort of handiwork. I think that's why initially the project involved handwriting because there was some anxiety about not having any handiwork there. But I got over it."[41]

Despite Ligon's removal of the traces of his own hand, *pace* his own account about his early study sketch, *Notes* did change the medium of

Mapplethorpe's *Black Book*: from the individualized, temporally flexible interface of a coffee-table book to the public, spatially defined registers of a gallery installation. In contrast to the one-to-one dynamic that defines the viewer's encounter with Mapplethorpe's photobook—ideally, they would have the book in their hands, in private, and flick through the pages at their own pace, one picture at a time—the spatial and temporal experience of Ligon's installation tips the balance of agency toward the Black male figures in the photographs. Individuals separated in the book gain a collective presence in the room that holds the viewers in space and subverts the kind of control on which the erotic phenomenology of viewing Mapplethorpe's book of Black nude males depends. Meanwhile, the polyphony of metropolitan voices in the text panels resituates the photographs within their material context, juxtaposing the coevalities at play in the social scene with racial and class tensions. That is how the work also acquires the quality of a performance.

The performative aspect of *Notes* unfolds through the act of reading the texts on the wall, which become sound in the viewer's mind. There are multiple layers to this experience. First, the totality of text panels operates as a temporally irreducible sequence. Each text demands to be given its own time; they cannot be captured simultaneously. This temporality conditions the duration of experiencing Mapplethorpe's photographs. Second, the texts dictate a choreography: the viewer reads about the pictures, then steps back to look around and (re)view them. Doing this makes one doubly aware of one's bodily interaction with other viewers and with the (fragmented) bodies of Mapplethorpe's sitters. As one (white) viewer observed, "To read the text panels in Ligon's work, you had to draw uncomfortably near to the images, almost poking your nose in a muscular ass or big cock," an experience "unrivaled in its charged significance at the time."[42] This adds a physical dynamic to the discursive nature of the text panels. Third, the text's temporality is phonic. The multiplicity of tones in the text panels introduces into Mapplethorpe's silent, frozen compositions a polyphony of urban soundtracks, rhythms, and spoken words, thus punctuating the work with added musicality. In text panels, coherent speech is mixed with noise, while the geometric organization and administrative aesthetics of the machine-typed text panels promise orderly discourse.[43] The social and power relations behind the production and performance of Blackness in New York during this era of "specious multiculturalism," to borrow art historian Huey Copeland's phrase, are thus dragged into

Mapplethorpe's photographs.[44] Consider the experience of reading the following text panels:

> I think white gay people feel cheated because they were born, in principle, into a society in which they were supposed to be safe. The anomaly of their sexuality puts them in danger, unexpectedly. Their reaction seems to me in direct proportion to the sense of feeling cheated of the advantages which accrue to white people in a white society.
>
> —James Baldwin

> When you're a man and a woman you can do anything. You can almost have sex on the street if you want to. The most anyone is going to say is "Hey, get a hump for me."
>
> —Unidentified voice in *Paris Is Burning*

> Isn't it interesting that the photographers always come just when the tribe is dying out? So too with the "celebration" in these Mapplethorpe pictures of black men. Better catch them before they die out.
>
> —bell hooks

> Wrong [—] to fuck with.
>
> —Photo backdrop, 125th Street

> Sometimes you feel like a nut . . . sometimes you don't.
>
> —jingle

> When I sat for the portrait I asked Robert why he was doing photographs exclusively of black men. He never really answered me: instead he gave me an essay Edmund White had written about him.
>
> —Bill T. Jones

> It's a black thing and I love it. Let me get back to work before I get a hard-on.
>
> —Greg, bartender at Keller's

These quotations relink the serenity of Mapplethorpe's fantastical world to the actual, tension-ridden context in which they operate. Borrowing from Moten's language, we can say that Mapplethorpe's photo-porno-graphic utopia, his imaged fantasy of a technologically advanced, compositionally harmonious, and homoerotically interracial world, erupts into a discourse-driven, phono-photo-pornographic reflection of and on the reality of experiencing metropolitan life, where coercion and positionality determine the scope of fluidity for certain subjects more than others.[45] The vocal temporality of the text panels, combined with the abrupt and unpredictable nature of the transitions between the texts themselves and between the texts and the photographs, adds to the choreographic experience of viewing the work. The result is a performance that demands conceptual engagement from the viewer but denies them final resolution.

By transubstantiating image and text into an orchestration of sound, noise, and performance, Ligon wants to, in Copeland's words, "take race out of the imaginary and make it a function of a larger symbolic system."[46] Like white appropriation artists, Ligon is also concerned with the constructed nature of subjectivity, but he is more successful in interrogating ideological structures in terms of their contingencies—their actual social, temporal, and intersubjective dynamics. The kind of performance that Ligon's work prompts is experienced in time and space as the work unfolds. His installation is socially determined but also open to human interaction. It challenges the authority of the fixed document (whether in the form of an image or a text) over live performance, but it does not attribute any romantic authenticity to art or to art's capacity for communicating bodily presence and corporeal immediacy: after all, the work is nothing more than a constellation of documents, and its performative aspect is only instigated if the viewers so activate it. Even then, the performance is continuously mediated and conditioned: here, "archive" (documents) and "repertoire" (embodied practice), the two key categories in Diana Taylor's critical theorization of performance, collapse into one another, as the work shows them to be mutually constitutive.[47] Moreover, Ligon's installation interrogates in equal measure the self (of the artist and of the viewer) and the general structural formations that have historically produced Black subjects as fugitives. It is through the open and contingent nature of this encounter with institutions of ideological interpellation that Ligon's work approximates a fugitive's flight, always refusing to be captured, and distances itself from the fantasy world of an authorial subject.

What Is a Black Author?

> [I]t seems that many museums and Kunsthalles find it easier to deal with images of blacks rather than with the people themselves.
>
> —Glenn Ligon, "Kelley Walker's Negro Problem"[48]

Ligon's turn to Black fugitivity positions him in a critical relationship not only with Mapplethorpe but also with the broader history of the avant-garde. While theories of the avant-garde adopted the vocabulary of theft and robbery to describe progressive art's opposition to private ownership and liberal subjectivity, the artistic practices they theorized remained, to a large extent, processes of making objects *one's own*. What the theories left unaddressed was the alliance between liberal subjectivity and possessive individualism: making anything one's own was a manifestation of liberal "bourgeois" subjectivity, not its subversion.[49] In reality, the postmodern discourse of appropriation ultimately affirmed the emergence of a new figure, the artist as author. This was a person with the special authority to transcend boundaries and make things their own. Here, theory was complicit in consolidating the entitlement of the artist. One pertinent case highlighted by Ligon is that of Kelley Walker, who has had a sustained interest in appropriating images of Black people. Walker seemingly considers the content of these images to be irrelevant and secondary to his appropriative strategy of montage and manipulation, but, more often than not, he chooses images that, as Ligon argues, "given our long, troubled history and current political reality, are so resistant to being made irrelevant."[50] While appropriation as a technique was supposed to demonstrate the death of the author (and of authorial expression), Walker's practice shows how it also facilitated the neutralization and annexation of the Other's history and the expansion of white supremacy.

Despite important warnings by Buchloh and Crimp, appropriationist theory, by and large, suffered from a blind spot related to the historical formations of the law and the law's concept of the author in Europe. Molly Nesbit has shown that when Roland Barthes and Michel Foucault, the two quintessential theorists of the author in the neo-avant-garde/postmodern context, conceptualized authorship, what they actually measured was a gap internal to French laws. In the French legal tradition, an authored work was defined as bearing the imprint of a unique personality. By contrast, the photographic apparatus was understood by the law as "a barrier that prevented the imprint of a human being on a certified, authorial material."[51] This meant that the law excluded mechanically produced and reproducible imagery from the category of "authored work." This legal gap conditioned the understanding of the mechanically reproducible image as a critique of authorship defined by the law. In the United States, however, the landscape was rather different: copyright debates over mechanical reproducibility in fact leaned on previous laws that governed those fugitive persons attempting to escape from slavery.

In his groundbreaking work on the dematerialization of copyright in the nineteenth-century United States, Stephen M. Best shows how slavery and intellectual property were brought into "an uneasy alliance."[52] New machines that reproduced the attributes of a person, such as one's voice, were deemed legally homologous to Black slaves. Unlike white individuals, whose subjectivity the law attributed to their personhood, when it came to Black individuals, as Moten would say, "the assumption of the equivalence of personhood and subjectivity" was suspended.[53] In other words, in the French context, mechanically produced art challenged the boundaries of authorship from a progressive standpoint, but in the United States, the law already defined Black authorship as homologous to the non-subjectivity of mechanical reproduction. Black authorship was therefore not an alternative to the mechanically produced image but its legal antecedent.

When Ligon uses Mapplethorpe's photographs in his work, or when he speaks through borrowed voices, turning to non-subjective and non-expressive modes of art making, his frame of reference is not European laws governing authorship. Rather, his work reflects an understanding of authorship that is rooted in and remains committed to historical struggles for (Black) liberation by fugitive authors whose interiority was denied by the law. For Ligon, the genius of Black authors who, like his Uncle Tossy, took whatever they had, "which was almost nothing and . . . made it seem to encompass the whole world," was not to possess but to cite and to annotate.[54] Ligon, I would argue, operationalizes this approach in *Notes* at the level of the art object. He does not confiscate or devalue Mapplethorpe but instead makes a specific attempt to respect the photographs' integrity as *quoted* objects, neatly framing each photograph and clearly disclosing its boundaries, as if putting it in visual quotation marks. Although the photograph has been removed from the book, there is no visible trace of rupture on its edge. They are carefully—one might even say respectfully—separated from the binding. The installation even honors their exhibitionist desire, their need to be seen.

As for the marginalia, if the initial idea of writing on the photographs amounted to making them his own, prioritizing his authorship over Mapplethorpe's, in *Notes* Ligon's strategy of citation qualifies and annotates the photographs without owning them. Indeed, while in Mapplethorpe's pictures the calculated elegance of the compositions is meant to convey his personal vision as an author, the neat, geometrically predetermined symmetry of Ligon's method further reduces the function of the author. His decision to quote from existing sources additionally shifts the nature of his artistic labor from aesthetic work in the photographs to artistic research in the installation. Of course, this strategy formally resonates with the critique of the self-sufficiency of the photograph launched by postmodernist artists such as Martha Rosler, particularly her *The Bowery in Two Inadequate Descriptive Systems* (1975). In Rosler's work, the classed experience of New York City in the mid-1970s—marked by homelessness, substance use, and the degeneration of neighborhoods—becomes the subject matter of a series of documentary photographs of Bowery storefronts and sidewalks, juxtaposed with text panels consisting of a series of vernacular terms related to drunkenness. As in *Notes*, in this work the texts work neither over nor against the photographs, but in a parallel sequence that reconnects the images to the contemporaneous social construction of downtown New York and its most Othered denizens. If we agree with artist and writer Allan Sekula that Rosler's project is a stance against elevating documentary photography to the status of high art—he argues that "documentary is thought to be art when it transcends its reference to the world, when the work can be regarded, first and foremost, as an act of self-expression on the part of the artist"—then Ligon's installation invites us to rethink high-art photographs beyond Mapplethorpe's emphasis on "the power of vision alone."[55] Ligon as author remains secondary to the "historical authenticity" and "social truth" of Mapplethorpe's photographs, that is, to the actual spaces of Black queer sociability and the social relations that the photographs can only register obliquely.

The difference here between the common economy of appropriation in the work of other artists and the economy of citation in Ligon's work corresponds to the gap between *un*qualified white "subjectivity" and Blackened being. Ligon's version of appropriation empties the technique of its exploitative aspect to such an extent that *appropriation* may no longer be a suitable word to describe it. In line with Black feminist scholars such as Tina M. Campt, who invite us to imagine the past's possible futures, one can argue that if avant-garde theory was written from the position of Blackness, the strategy of externalizing artistic expression through already existing material would be identified primarily in acts of citation and annotation rather than appropriation, although the two may formally seem homologous.[56] Citation and annotation, understood as such, are decolonizing methods that disarticulate art making from possessiveness.

Yet the most pressing challenge facing Ligon in *Notes* was not to reclaim appropriation as a historically fugitive strategy. The question that remains unresolved for Ligon is about the ultimate separation, the unbridgeable gap, between art and the actual experience of Black queer life—between the reality of social relations and their representation in art. Despite all his work to reconnect the photographs to actual places of Black queer sociality, at the close of the installation, Ligon gives up art for life. The final text reads: "Left Mapplethorpe on the bar at Sound Factory and danced for hours with Lyle [Ashton Harris]. (Diary, 1/24/93)."

With this conclusion, the installation is an invitation for all to join the Black queer artists on the dance floor. But that is not a place we can get to simply by looking at art.

Notes

This article emerged out of Huey Copeland's graduate seminar Appropriation at Northwestern University in the fall of 2017. I am grateful to the seminar's participants and particularly to Huey for his intellectual generosity and instructive feedback. I also thank Maya Dukmasova, Tristam Wolff, and Pamela Lee for their invaluable comments on earlier drafts.

1. Glenn Ligon, "Black Light: David Hammons and the Poetics of Emptiness," *Artforum* 43, no. 1 (September 2004): 243.

2. Although they have occasionally been displayed in exhibition spaces, Mapplethorpe's photographs of Black men have been disseminated as printed books since their very first showing at Amsterdam's Galerie Jurka in 1980. The catalog of that exhibition, called *Black Males*, included an introduction by the white author Edmund White, who had published *The Joy of Gay Sex* (written with Dr. Charles Silverstein) in 1977.

3. Kobena Mercer, *Welcome to the Jungle: New Positions in Black Cultural Studies* (New York: Routledge, 1994), 191.

4. For a representative example of how postmodernism transferred Continental philosophy to American art criticism, see Craig Owens, "Representation, Appropriation, and Power," in Owens, *Beyond Recognition: Representation, Power, and Culture* (Berkeley: University of California Press, 1992), 88–113. For a critique, from the standpoint of European philosophy, of

the limits of such transferring, see Hammam Aldouri, "A Critique of the 'Author Function' Concept in Art History," *Third Text* 35, no. 5 (November 2021): 591–604.

5. Benjamin H. D. Buchloh, "Allegorical Procedures: Appropriation and Montage in Contemporary Art," *Artforum* 21, no. 1 (September 1982): 43–56.

6. Douglas Crimp, "The Photographic Activity of Postmodernism," *October* 15 (Winter 1980): 91.

7. Crimp, "The Photographic Activity of Postmodernism," 100.

8. Buchloh, "Allegorical Procedures," 44.

9. Crimp, "The Photographic Activity of Postmodernism," 98.

10. Ligon, "Black Light," 249.

11. The list includes Saidiya Hartman, Fred Moten, and Stephen M. Best, among others. I am also thinking here of artists Fred Wilson, Lorna Simpson, and Renée Green, who are studied by Huey Copeland in *Bound to Appear: Art, Slavery, and the Site of Blackness in Multicultural America* (Chicago: University of Chicago Press, 2013).

12. *Runaways* presents a description of the artist in the visual and linguistic conventions of nineteenth-century advertisements that slave owners distributed to locate their runaway slaves.

13. Moten writes: "What Adorno says of Beethoven—that his is 'the most sublime music ever to aim at freedom under continued unfreedom'—is applicable to Miles [Davis]'s ascendant Jacobsean swerve in and out of the confinements of [George] Gershwin's composition and [Gil] Evans's arrangement. Freedom in unfreedom is flight and this music could be called the most sublime in the history of escape." Fred Moten, *Black and Blur* (Durham, NC: Duke University Press, 2017), 85.

14. Fred Moten, *In the Break: The Aesthetics of the Black Radical Tradition* (Minneapolis: University of Minnesota Press, 2003), 305.

15. In the opening chapter of *In the Break*, "Resistance of the Object: Aunt Hester's Scream," Moten writes: "The history of blackness is testament to the fact that objects can and do resist. Blackness—the extended movement of a specific upheaval, an ongoing irruption that rearranges every line—is a strain that pressures the assumption of the equivalence of personhood and subjectivity." Moten, *In the Break*, 1.

16. Peter Osborne, "Adorno's 'Aesthetic Theory,' 50 Years On," CRMEP podcasts, accessed February 19, 2021, https://soundcloud.com/user-455945207/adornos-aesthetic-theory-50-years-on.

17. Miwon Kwon, "Interview with Glenn Ligon," in *Positions of Authority: Leone & Macdonald, Glenn Ligon, Judith Weinperson*, exhibition brochure (Art in General, May 23–June 29, 1991), n.p.

18. Kwon, "Interview with Glenn Ligon."

19. Kwon, "Interview with Glenn Ligon."

20. Kwon, "Interview with Glenn Ligon."

21. Richard Meyer, "Borrowed Voices: Glenn Ligon and the Force of Language," in *Glenn Ligon: Unbecoming*, exh. cat., ed. Judith Tannenbaum (Philadelphia: Institute of Contemporary Art, 1997), 13 (reprinted in this volume).

22. For a general view of the debates around the culture wars of the time, see Brian Wallis et al., eds., *Art Matters: How the Culture Wars Changed America* (New York: New York University Press, 1999).

23. Mercer, *Welcome to the Jungle*, 176–177.

24. Douglas Crimp, "Appropriating Appropriation," in *Image Scavengers: Photography*, exh. cat., ed. Janet Kardon (Philadelphia: Institute of Contemporary Art, 1982), 30. Here Crimp distinguishes between two kinds of appropriation: appropriation of styles and appropriation of materials. While the first kind of appropriation (in Mapplethorpe or Michael Graves) results in the construction of "a synthetic 'personal' vision" that is merely yet another style, Crimp argues that by appropriating actual historical materials (not abstract styles), artists like Frank Gehry or Sherrie Levine respond to specific contextual questions.

25. Mercer, *Welcome to the Jungle*, 195–196.

26. Following his experiments with writing directly onto Mapplethorpe's photographs, Ligon worked between 1991 and 1993 toward developing an installation. The first installation, shown at Art in General's group exhibition *Positions of Authority* (curated by Miwon Kwon in 1991), included only thirty-eight of the *Black Book*'s ninety-one photographs, as well as fifty-two text panels. It occupied only a single wall, appearing as a portion of a much larger room, and shared the space with other artworks. It was not until 1993, at the Whitney Biennial, that Ligon's installation finally included all of the photographs, accompanied by seventy-eight text panels. The final work measured roughly fifty feet in length and was installed on its own in a contained space.

27. Étienne Balibar, *Citizen Subject: Foundations for Philosophical Anthropology* (New York: Fordham University Press, 2017), 298.

28. *Robert Mapplethorpe*, directed by Nigel Finch 1988; episode of the BBC television show *Arena*, https://vimeo.com/96609085.

29. For a deconstructive analysis of the economy of the gift (particularly in the context of European Christianity), see Jacques Derrida, *The Gift of Death* (Chicago: University of Chicago Press, 1992), 112.

30. Glenn Ligon, "Kelley Walker's Negro Problem," *Parkett* 87 (2010): 79.

31. Ligon, "Black Light," 249.

32. Tina M. Campt, *Listening to Images* (Durham, NC: Duke University Press, 2017), 8.

33. Moten, *In the Break*, 205.

34. Moten, *In the Break*, 205.

35. Moten, *In the Break*, 205.

36. Glenn Ligon, interview on the occasion of the opening of his show *America* at LACMA (2011), in *Glenn Ligon: AMERICA*, posted on YouTube by Los Angeles County Museum of Art, October 21, 2011, accessed July 5, 2021, https://www.youtube.com/watch?v=IrVH05Z8oHc.

37. Moten, *In the Break*, 208.

38. Meyer, "Borrowed Voices," 21.

39. Ligon further engages the racialized dynamics of urban experience—with Cliff and others—in *Picky*, also from 1993. As a passage from the work puts it, *Picky* is a reflection on the fact "that the spaces that white people move through with ease may be experienced differently by people of color." See Copeland, *Bound to Appear*, 118–119.

40. Meyer, "Borrowed Voices," 21.

41. Kwon, "Interview with Glenn Ligon."

42. Scott Rothkopf, "Glenn Ligon: America," *Glenn Ligon: America*, ed. Scott Rothkopf, exh. cat. (New York: Whitney Museum of American Art, 2011), 35.

43. On administrative aesthetics as an artistic strategy and a legacy of conceptual art, see Benjamin Buchloh, "Conceptual Art, 1962–1969: From the Aesthetic of Administration to the Critique of Institutions," *October* 55 (Winter 1990): 105–143.

44. Copeland, *Bound to Appear*, 71.

45. On the "phono-photo-porno-graphic" quality of Black performance as a disruptive force, see Moten, *In the Break*, 14.

46. Copeland, *Bound to Appear*, 129.

47. Diana Taylor, *The Archive and the Repertoire: Performing Cultural Memory in the Americas* (Durham, NC: Duke University Press, 2003). On collapsing the distinction between archive and repertoire as decolonial practice, see the second chapter in Jessica Horton, *Art for an Undivided Earth: The American Indian Movement Generation* (Durham, NC: Duke University Press, 2017).

48. Ligon, "Kelley Walker's Negro Problem," 80.

49. "Possessive individualism" is C. B. Macpherson's coinage in *The Political Theory of Possessive Individualism: Hobbes to Locke* (Oxford: Oxford University Press, 1962). For a discussion of the role played by appropriation (of land, labor, and property) in the historical development of liberal political theory, particularly the work of John Locke and his engagement with colonial appropriation of Native American land, see Domenico Losurdo, *Liberalism: A Counter-History* (London: Verso: 2011), 23–26 and chapter 2, "Liberalism and Racial Slavery: A Unique Twin Birth."

50. Ligon, "Kelly Walker's Negro Problem," 80.

51. Molly Nesbit, "What Was an Author?," *Yale French Studies* 73 (1987): 237. I am also indebted to Steve Edwards, whose brilliant work on the history of photography in the comparative context of French and British copyright laws guided and stimulated my thinking. Steve Edwards, "'Beard Patentee': Daguerreotype Property and Authorship," *Oxford Art Journal* 36, no. 3 (December 2013): 369–394.

52. Best's argument concerning the connection between intellectual-property rights and fugitive-from-labor laws can be summarized in his own words as follows: "Novel copyright appropriations reeked . . . of the commodification of attributes previously protected, by law, as inalienable and 'personal.' Mechanical reproduction, in short, returned civil law to the problem of expropriation and the injurious commodification of personhood. Yet . . . the ultimate goal of intellectual property law would ironically be to embrace something like enslavement, to make use of a cultural tradition that had been able to transform expropriation into legitimate exchange—property into something resembling contract." Stephen M. Best, *The Fugitive's Properties: Law and the Poetics of Possession* (Chicago: University of Chicago Press, 2004), 53.

53. Moten, *In the Break*, 1.

54. On the centrality of annotation to Ligon's practice, see Huey Copeland, "Feasting on Scraps," *Small Axe* 16, no. 38 (July 2012): 198–212.

55. Allan Sekula, "Dismantling Modernism, Reinventing Documentary (Notes on the Politics of Representation)," *Massachusetts Review* 19, no. 4 (Winter 1978): 864, 869.

56. "The grammar of black feminist futurity is a performance of a future that hasn't yet happened but must." Campt, *Listening to Images*, 17.

11 The Black Residuum, or That Which Remains

Rizvana Bradley

To be unaware of one's form is to live a death.

—Ralph Ellison, *Invisible Man*[1]

But what was to be done with Topsy?

—Harriet Beecher Stowe, *Uncle Tom's Cabin*[2]

Glenn Ligon's 2008 installation *The Death of Tom* (16mm black-and-white film/video transfer, 23 minutes) evades the sort of prefabricated description that is variously resuscitated through the reflexes of medium-specific interpretive schemas. *The Death of Tom* emerges recursively from the tremulous borders between art installation, film, theatrical performance, and sentimentalist literature, recalling the deconstructionist impulse of Ligon's earlier text-based artworks. Inside the black box that does not merely mimic the cinematic but troubles the distinction between exhibition and spectatorship,[3] the viewer is confronted with a phantasmagoria of black-and-white frames, their procession of stretched and sputtering images wavering within an eerie atmospherics.[4] Caught between sharp flashes of light, the dimensionless dark, and the oscillating fade of luminosity, it is as if the viewer is made to perpetually search for a specter's shadow, to no avail (figure 11.1).

Ligon had initially set out to restage the final scene from the 1903 film *Uncle Tom's Cabin, or, Slavery Days*, produced by Thomas Edison and directed by Edwin S. Porter, the first of the many cinematic adaptations over the course of the twentieth century of Harriet Beecher Stowe's

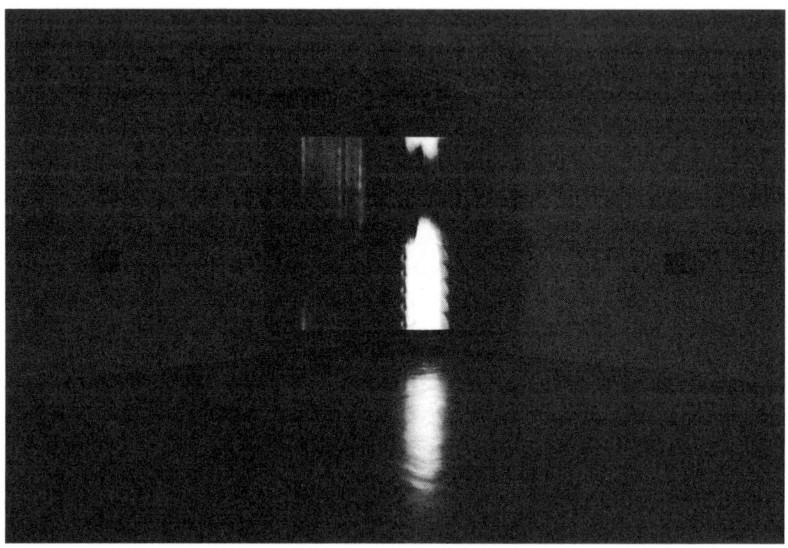

Figure 11.1 Glenn Ligon, installation view of *The Death of Tom* (2008), in *Off Book*, Regen Projects, CA, December 12, 2009–January 23, 2010. 16mm black-and-white film / video transfer, 23 min., edition of 3 and 1 artist's proof. © Glenn Ligon; Courtesy of the artist, Hauser & Wirth, and Thomas Dane Gallery.

singularly influential 1852 novel *Uncle Tom's Cabin; or Life among the Lowly*.[5] In this scene, dubbed "Tableau: Death of Uncle Tom" in the associated Edison Studios catalog,[6] Tom, "the gentle, childlike, self-sacrificing, essentially *aesthetic* slave,"[7] becomes fully sainted in death[8] amid heavenly visions of his master's prematurely departed, angelic daughter, Little Eva, and the grand patriarchs of white sacrifice and beneficence Abraham Lincoln and John Brown.[9] Implicitly referring to a complex and often subversive tradition of "black-on-black minstrelsy," which Louis Chude-Sokei has importantly theorized,[10] Ligon himself played Tom alongside several student collaborators, while Deco Dawson filmed the scene on 16mm film. Working closely with Dawson, Ligon endeavored "to shoot . . . [the film] exactly the way Edison's cinematographer did—on a hand-cranked camera, black-and-white, 16 millimeter, with a double exposure."[11]

Despite his precise attention to the minutiae of reenactment and reproduction, however, after processing the film, Ligon discovered that it had not been properly threaded in the camera, such that the work appeared as a series of "blurry, fluttery, burnt-out black-and-white images, all light and shadows."[12] Nevertheless, he opted to retain the nominally ruined film, transferring it to tape and later to DVD for exhibition purposes, because, in his words, "that failure of representation was in line with my larger artistic project, which has always been about turning something legible like a text into an abstraction."[13] That is, Ligon recognized the glitch—what Lauren Berlant defines as "an interruption amid a transition"[14]—as a fitting stroke of chance. Indeed, this technical failure aptly mimicked the disfigurement that necessarily constitutes every effort to reduce the opacity of blackness, which is always already anterior to representation, to a substantially enclosed, transparent phenomenon. As with the anteaesthetic practice in which Nina Simone improvisationally exploits the contingent and structural impositions of racially gendered spectatorship to disclose and refuse the anteriority her performance was made to bear, Ligon unmakes the very law his filmic performance is called to renew: the death-work of cinema.[15] Precisely through his return to that law in and through a recursive deconstruction of it, Ligon refashions the glitch as an instrument of nonperformance,[16] one whose deconstructive impetus hinges upon the form that is medium. In short, Ligon mobilizes the glitch toward an anteaesthetic interrogation of the formal technics of the cinematic.

But the glitch would not be the only instrument within Ligon's ensemble, for it was at this stage in the development of the work that it occurred to Ligon that the screening of Porter's 1903 film might well have had a piano accompaniment, as was indeed common for early cinema's "silent" films.[17] Ligon thus invited the jazz pianist Jason Moran to create a soundtrack for the film. Improvising upon Bert Williams's famous vaudeville song, "Nobody," first performed only two years after the release of Porter's 1903 film, Moran watched Ligon's film and, as the musician evocatively puts it, "played to the shadows."[18] The installation's first exhibition at the Museum of Modern Art assumed the form of their collaborative, visual-sonic assemblage. We will return to the significance of Ligon and Moran's improvisatory ensemble for an anteaesthetic reading of *The Death of Tom* shortly. But first we must take a deeper look at the literary, cinematic, and theatrical histories Ligon and Moran's (non)performance invoke and unsettle.

The historical significance of Harriet Beecher Stowe's *Uncle Tom's Cabin* has been widely discussed and debated since it was published in 1852; here I will only scratch the surface of the expansive critical literature the novel has occasioned. In literary scholar Jane P. Tompkins's view, Stowe's novel "was, in almost any terms one can think of, the most important book of the century."[19] It is most commonly known as the first abolitionist novel to attain mass popularity, with the first edition selling some 300,000 copies in the United States and 150,000 in Britain within the very first year following its publication, setting a record at the time for the most purchased book ever, second only to the Christian Bible.[20] Immediately propelled to a place of prominence among other leading antislavery figures, Stowe is said to have been welcomed by Abraham Lincoln during her 1862 visit to the White House with the exclamation: "So this is the little lady who started this great big war."[21] While it would, of course, be facile to construe Stowe's novel as an ideological catalyst for the Civil War (which, after all, had nothing to do with a genuine investment on the part of either the Union or Northern civil society in black emancipation or dismantling the world forged by racial slavery, as such a project would require nothing less than the abolition of the reigning social formation), this anecdote neatly illustrates the discursive purchase the novel attained in the romance of nationhood.

Initially published in serial form in the *National Era* and borrowing heavily from the slave narratives of Frederick Douglass, Josiah Henson, and Solomon Northup, as well as Theodore Weld's *American Slavery As It Is*,[22] Stowe's novel is a paragon of the sentimentalist tradition in which politics are deployed and displaced through universalist genres of feeling. As Berlant observes, "Sentimental politics are being performed whenever putatively suprapolitical affects or affect-saturated institutions (like the nation and the family) are proposed as universalist solutions to structural racial, sexual, or intercultural antagonism."[23] More pointedly, following Saidiya Hartman, *Uncle Tom's Cabin* marked a signal literary instantiation of a more general enterprise which was embedded in "abolitionism's sentimental structure of feeling":[24] namely, the aesthetic recuperation of the material, discursive, and libidinal economies that reproduce the world as an antiblack metaphysics, which would ultimately be registered historically as "the nonevent of emancipation."[25] The character of Tom, who has come to most prominently figure "the nexus between minstrelsy and melodrama,"[26] was and remains a salient instrument of this enduring recuperative project. In the novel, Tom's aesthetic function is tethered to Little Eva, "the emblematic child-angel of the nineteenth century" who so powerfully illustrates the centrality of performances of white girlhood in the ongoing reproduction of the subterfuge of "racial innocence."[27]

Tom and Little Eva have a twinned role in the "family romance" of the plantation through which Stowe advances her sentimental abolitionism, a modality of seduction "in which domination is transposed into the bonds of mutual affection, subjection idealized as the pathway to equality, and perfect subordination the means of ensuring great happiness and harmony."[28] Tom and Little Eva's part in Stowe's romance begins with their mutual befriendment onboard the ship transporting Tom down the Mississippi to be sold, and is diegetically consolidated when Tom dives into the river to save Little Eva, who has fallen off the boat. Their friendship is ultimately rendered sacrosanct at the scene of Tom's death, which follows his being brutally beaten by an overseer for refusing to give up the location of two escaped fellow slaves, Cassy and Emmeline. As Hortense Spillers argues, in their coupled figuration, Tom and Little Eva serve as "the sacrificial lamb of *Uncle Tom's Cabin*," though it is, of course, Tom's tortured "body" which bears the burdens of "the *requirements of sacrifice*," or the diegetic reflex that in fact "galvanize[s] the murderous instincts of . . . [the antiblack world] rather than . . . [challenging] them."[29]

Tom's corporeal brutalization and saintly death serve as the diegetic instruments for the realization of the redemptive arc of Stowe's sentimentalist abolitionism, as well as the extra-diegetic instruments for the realization of the libidinal abundance and metaphysical suture that every instantiation of black death affords civil society. As David Marriott shrewdly observes, black death always evinces a "dual property of zero and surplus," which is precisely how it "acquires its beautiful perfection: as *ante legum*, its being is always already dead and so cannot be killed; and as property, it can be punished according to the forensic rules and pronouncements of the forum, a law that can be re-enacted each time white desire needs to defend or affirm itself *as the rightful law of the living*."[30] Black death must be endlessly repeated, because it is an indispensable means of sustaining the expropriative displacements required for the metaphysical distinction between life and death upon which the world (of the living) depends.[31] Tom's death constitutes a singularity only in that it poses a reflexive exhibition of its own illimitable repetition. His endlessly repeated death marks the burial grounds, or rather buried ground, of the cinematic—the black death that cinema's formal technics both require and extend.

Indeed, the scene of Uncle Tom's death would find no shortage of opportunities for repetition, both directly and indirectly, as the unprecedented novelistic success of *Uncle Tom's Cabin* spawned a host of theatrical adaptations and spin-offs, which were performed not only in the metropoles but also by traveling companies known as "Tom Shows" or "Tommer Shows," which brought Stowe's novel and its derivatives into a vast number of small towns and villages.[32] The minstrel show—as the quintessential formal genre of the "orchestrated amusements" through which the abomination of slavery was performatively diffused,[33] a reproductive transmission that was also a reproductive sublimation—was at once the condition of possibility for *Uncle Tom's Cabin* and a crucial means by which its signal tropes became culturally ubiquitous.[34]

As *Uncle Tom's Cabin* worked its way through various forms of theatrical performance, its melodramatic sentimentality was increasingly supplanted by the sadistic humor characteristic of blackface minstrelsy, though certainly both of these affective genres were in evidence in the slew of Uncle Tom memorabilia that emerged throughout the nineteenth century, including figurines, engravings, dioramas, needlepoint, card games, gift books, plates, and silverware.[35] Familiarity with the minstrel form was inextricable from the general reception of the theatrical iterations of *Uncle Tom's Cabin*,[36] a fact which is unsurprising when one comes to recognize the racial melodrama of sentimentalism and the racial comedy of minstrelsy as complementary rather than antagonistic genres, with each affording its own unique mechanisms for the spectator's (dis)possessive catharsis. "Whippings were to minstrelsy what tears were to melodrama," Hartman writes.[37] Tom's death, the vision of which Stowe herself suggested was both the catalyst for and telos of the novel,[38] serves as a crucial means for sustaining the complementarity of these genres of affect, and thus its endless, morbid repetition becomes instrumental in the extensive and variegated transits of *Uncle Tom's Cabin* across mediums, geographies, and forms.[39] If the image of Tom's death may be said to acquire its perfection only in the fact of its differential repetition of the same, then what is its relationship to the moving image?

Edwin S. Porter not only holds the dubious distinction of directing the first filmic adaptation of Stowe's novel in 1903,[40] but he is also among the signal progenitors of modern cinema, particularly in his associations with the Edison Manufacturing Company between 1896 and 1909. According to film historian Charles Musser, during these pioneering years of commercial motion picture making, "Edwin S. Porter emerged as America's foremost filmmaker" and was crucially implicated in the "production and representational practices, . . . subject matter and ideology, and . . . commercial methods" which together shaped this pivotal epoch in the emergence of modern cinema.[41] A rigorous media archaeology of early cinema would be beyond the scope of this chapter (even as Ligon's *The Death of Tom* is itself a rigorous experiment in black media archaeology). Needless to say, the emergence of the cinematic medium constituted a major historical transformation in the spatial and temporal operations of modernity's regime of representation.

As Mary Ann Doane famously argued in *The Emergence of Cinematic Time*, the cinematic medium sustains a complex and often contradictory interdependence between, on the one hand, the abstract, rationalized time that correlates with the rise of the commodity form and the capitalist law of value, and, on the other, the contradictory figure of contingency, which "proffers to the subject the appearance of absolute freedom, immediacy, directness . . . [extending] the possibility of perpetual newness, difference, the marks of modernity itself."[42] Moreover, cinema, in its "technological assurance of indexicality," promised the representability of the contingent, a "pure record of time," an unrivaled archive of presence.[43] It was precisely "its ability to inscribe movement through time" which marked "cinema's decisive difference from photography."[44] With Doane's exemplary study in mind, it becomes clear that Ligon's planned filmic reenactment of Porter's *Uncle Tom's Cabin* and subsequent exploitation of the glitch as an instrument of nonperformance are no less than deconstructive interrogations of the anterior remains of blackness—not only with respect to the cinematic medium but with respect to this medium's historic modulation of temporality and the modern metaphysics of presence.

Without reprising the more nuanced debates regarding the specific dynamics, chronology, or inevitability of the historical change, there is at least broad agreement among contemporary film historians that by at least 1907/08 the narrative form with which classical cinema is associated had definitively triumphed. In Tom Gunning's well-known argument, this era witnessed a transition from a "cinema of attractions," principally "dedicated to presenting discontinuous visual attractions, moments of spectacle rather than narrative," to what he and André Gaudreault term a period of "narrative integration."[45] Porter's *Uncle Tom's Cabin* occupies an unusual place in this formal typology. Musser has argued that the narrative form

Gunning associates with the work of D. W. Griffith and the attendant transformations of the film industry after 1908 are, in fact, anticipated by the work of Porter, particularly "after the pivotal year of 1902/03" and most notably exemplified in Porter's *Life of an American Fireman* (1902/03).[46] However, while *Uncle Tom's Cabin* was not without technical innovations that evinced the emerging impetus to narrative form—for example, its direct integration of the intertitle into the production process, which had hitherto been the responsibility of exhibitors[47]—the film has often been regarded as little more than a filmed theatrical production and hence as something of an anachronism within Porter's oeuvre. Indeed, Porter utilized an existing Tom troupe and relied heavily on the formal trappings of blackface minstrelsy to such a degree that the film is regarded as "perhaps the best extant documentation of a Tom Show available to historians."[48] In this respect, Porter's film would seem to possess more of the spectacular quality characteristic of Gunning's cinema of attractions than the hegemony of narrativity that would come to define classical cinema.

Yet, as Noël Burch argues, Porter's *Uncle Tom's Cabin* was significant precisely because it was called upon to reproduce a story that was so widely known and among the most significant instances of popular (rather than bourgeois) theater, such that Stowe's lengthy novel could be fragmented and compressed into fourteen tableaux spanning roughly twelve minutes at the standard silent film speed and nevertheless retain its narrative force and coherence.[49] The diegesis of the film "was predicated upon the [prior] knowledge of the audience, who were left to fill in enormous narrative gaps for themselves," a linearizing inhabitation which proceeded, in no small part, through "the establishment of a thoroughly haptic screen space."[50] I am less concerned with making a formalist case for the place of *Uncle Tom's Cabin* in the taxonomies of film history than I am with interrogating the manner in which it functionally serves as a bridge between forms, retrospectively figured teleologically as developmental stages, at the scene of cinema's emergence. *Pace* Burch, I would suggest that, to the extent that *Uncle Tom's Cabin* established a "haptic screen space," which in this instance effectuates a form that straddles the cinema of attraction and narrative integration, it is a hapticity principally achieved not through technical innovation but through the morbid (im)mediations afforded by Tom's brutalized "body" and the fleshly labors which sustain its endless dissimulation. The fact that the Tom of Porter's film is played by a white actor in blackface does not temper the fact that the cinematic cathexis is effectuated through fulfillment of a black death always already anticipated. That the (moving) image of black death given to the emergent cinematic subject arrives in the form of blackface minstrelsy only accentuates the dissimulative character of every phenomenalization of black death.

It has been suggested that the definitive ascendance of narrative after 1907 effectively disciplines, without eliminating, contingency within the operations of cinematic time. Significantly, Doane observes, "If cinematic narration develops, in part, as a structuring of contingency (and hence its reduction as such), the most intractable contingencies would seem to be those having to do with the body and death. . . . With death we are suddenly confronted with pure event, pure contingency, what ought to be inaccessible to representation."[51] Doane's indispensable work helps us in confronting the question of how we might square either the lineaments of narrative or the shudder of contingency with the phenomenological feint that is Tom's "body," which is conjured only to die again and again as narrative's impetus and detritus. The absolute noncontingency of Tom's death, its predestination before the event, marks the metonymic trace of the gratuitous violence and necrogenic expropriations that subtend both the figure of contingency and its disciplinary structuration in the figure of narrativity. Tom's death repeatedly binds the sentimental and the spectacular, the empathetic and the sadistic, the sodden weight of the past, the ephemeral plentitude of presence, and the glimmering horizon of the future, so that the properly historical beings of civil society might fret over or luxuriate within the dialectical plays and strains of the structural and the contingent which define the experience of modernity. Black death is at once the prerequisite to and outcome of both narrative and event in cinema as in the world.[52] Or as David Marriott plainly states the case, "For Afro-pessimism, . . . the white film-work is always a *death-work*."[53]

I want to suggest that Ligon's *The Death of Tom*, far from simply exposing or indicting the racist origins of American cinema, recursively deconstructs the cinematic itself, disclosing black mediality—in its absolute inseparability from the orchestrated amusements and gratuitous violence of racial terror, from mutilation and black death—as the condition of possibility for the medium's emergence. Blackness is anterior to the cinematic. At the same time, Ligon's piece gestures to the manner in which blackness marks the immanent failure of cinema's ambitions to function as a totalizing archive of presence or as an apparatus which can effectively "make the contingent legible."[54] In this respect, Ligon's deployment of an anteaesthetic modality of experimentation that could be thought through the rubric of the post-cinematic (which some scholars have associated with a revival of formal dimensions characteristic of Gunning's cinema of attractions or of early cinema more broadly)[55]—does not so much exhibit a similitude between the proto- and post-cinematic as it theorizes the blackness which remains before the cinematic, then as now. To put what film studies would generally regard as too fine of a point on it, we might recall the rhetorical questions posed by Gunning, after his recounting of an episode in which he was asked incredulously by a young scholar how it was that he had managed to write an entire book on the films of D. W. Griffith without substantively theorizing race in any way: "Was his claim that race was essential to the evolution of cinema's narrative style? Or was it that race was such an essential topic that every book must devote some time to it?"[56] To both of Gunning's rhetorical questions, *Anteaesthetics* would answer, with considerably less analytic prevarication, unequivocally, yes, before proceeding with more serious inquiries into cinema's black anterior.

I contend that the anteriority of blackness to cinema is the condition of (im)possibility for the phenomenology of filmic experience that is celebrated and mourned by scholars such as Vivian Sobchack. For Sobchack, "cinema is an objective technology of perception and expression that comes—and becomes—before us in a structure that implicates both a sensible body and a sensual and sense-making subject . . . [affirming and showing] that, sharing materiality and the world through vision and action, we are intersubjective beings."[57] If the anteriority of blackness makes possible the pretense of a universal body-subject for whom cinema would mediate an unbroken relay of phenomenological experience, it is only because those who are made to bear the (im)mediations of the flesh are always already barred from subjectivity, intersubjectivity, and the corporeal division of the world upon which each are predicated. Sobchack's disquietude over the "crisis of the lived body"—which she regards as both constitutive and symptomatic of the supersession of the cinematic by the "techno-logic of the electronic," with its "spatially decentered, weakly temporalized and quasi-disembodied" mode of experience[58]—takes on the quality of the grotesque when one considers the figure of Tom, the no-body, whose dissimulated corpus becomes an inexhaustible site for the ritual execution that serially inaugurates the lived body and Sobchack's self-affirming cinematic world. But as we know, the expropriative displacement of exorbitant

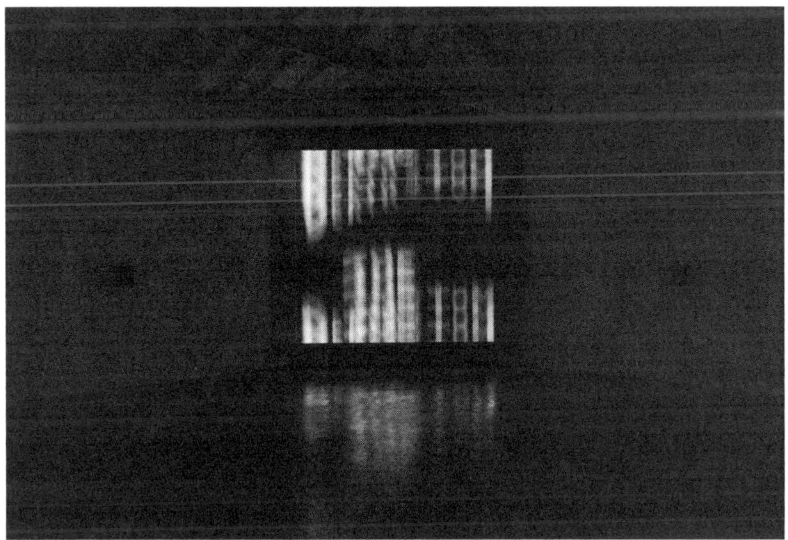

Figure 11.2 Glenn Ligon, installation view of *The Death of Tom* (2008), in *Off Book*, Regen Projects, CA, December 12, 2009–January 23, 2010. 16mm black-and-white film / video transfer, 23 min., edition of 3 and 1 artist's proof. © Glenn Ligon; Courtesy of the artist, Hauser & Wirth, and Thomas Dane Gallery.

materiality this black mediality requires is necessarily incomplete and thus remains a problem for both the phenomenology of the cinema and historicist lamentations of its passing.[59]

Returning to *The Death of Tom*'s phantasmagoric play of light and shadow, silence and song, let us observe that the only phenomenological anchor that would seem to be afforded the viewer is the work's successive return to an apparent opening title, or rather terminal intertitle, which reads again and again "The Death of Tom" (figure 11.2). And yet the repetition of this multiplied and distorted text (which reappears eight times over the twenty-three-minute duration of the work) that would seem to lend a regularity to time simultaneously interrupts spectatorial vision through its unfinished redoubling of the transcription across the space of the screen. The regularity the intertitle would appear to lend to time is simultaneously undone by the irregularity it announces in space. Tom's perpetually repeated yet perennially unfinished death becomes the indeterminate locus of a peculiar kind of hauntology.

The specter of Tom is not merely "a repressed or unresolved social violence . . . making itself known,"[60] or rather felt, no matter how opaquely, as the haptic trace of the unthought and unthinkable. That is, "what haunts is not so much the imago spun through with myths, anecdotes, stories, but the shadow or stain that is sensed behind it and that disturbs well-being."[61] It is the irreducible materiality of this disturbance which constitutes its hapticity—as the sensorial anterior that precedes and is subject to phenomenological experience and yet cannot appear as anything other than the dissimulation of a presence which is not one. An anteaesthetic iteration of what David Marriott, invoking a theatrical idiom, refers to as "corpsing," or "the violation of rules of prescribed performance under the command of social laws," Ligon's art of dissimulation produces "the knowledge and loss of the rules determining the subject."[62] In short, the serial nonevent of Tom's death is at once the catalyst and lysis for the cinematic medium and the phenomenological relay of cinematic communication: a black mediality through which the absence of form paradoxically gives form to the medium.

Playing to the Shadows

> The trace is not only the disappearance of origin—within the discourse that we sustain and according to the path we follow it means that the origin did not even disappear, that it was never constituted except reciprocally by a nonorigin, the trace, which thus becomes the origin of the origin.
>
> —Jacques Derrida[63]

Ligon's *The Death of Tom* recursively deconstructs the black mediality which is the constitutive anterior of the cinematic medium. The artwork also suggests that the secret of black mediality lies in the irreducibility, ineradicability, and absolute opacity of its remainder: the black residuum. What message is borne in, by, and as a medium whose communicative codes and strictures prohibit its own anterior—the formless death which perpetually gives life to and bedevils the life of the cinematic?

Insofar as we are concerned with the message of "the commodity who speaks,"[64] the answer is, of course, only a disfigured and disfiguring message. *The Death of Tom* is exemplary (an exemplar which is not simply one among others) of what Alexander R. Galloway, Eugene Thacker, and McKenzie Wark theorize as the "excommunication [which] seems to haunt every instance of communication."[65] Excommunication is not concurrent with but anterior to communication. As Galloway, Thacker, and Wark would have it, "Every communication harbors the dim awareness of an excommunication that is prior to it, that conditions it and makes it all the more natural,"[66] even if, as Ligon's work suggests, this naturalization is constantly threatened by the immanent contamination it relies upon for its reproduction. Specifically, Ligon's work epitomizes what Eugene Thacker terms "dark media," a form of media that betrays the very opacity which is its condition of (im)possibility. Dark media, in Thacker's view, effectuates something like "seeing something in nothing (e.g., the animate images appearing on the screen or alchemical glass), and finding nothing in each something (the paradoxical absence or presence of the 'demon' behind each thing)."[67] However, whereas Thacker conveniently displaces the matter of raciality from his inquiry into dark media, Ligon's work understands that the anteriority of opacity always already turns upon the matter of blackness, the exorbitant materiality which returns to us as the black residuum.[68] If Ligon's excommunicative experiment interrogates a black mediality that is conscripted in the reproduction of modernity's "communicational imperative" but that can only be "expressed as the impossibility of communication," then it also directs our attention to the paradoxical operations by which communication's "enigmatic residue" is disjunctively corporealized.[69]

Ligon discloses the dissimulative nonevent of Tom's perpetual death as the condition of possibility for every communicative medium, as the projection of "something . . . [onto] nothing" which sustains the animative "nothing in each something." As such, one cannot help but observe a terrible racial irony lurking beneath Sobchack's admonition that by "devaluing the physically lived body and the concrete materiality of the world, the dominant cultural and techno-logic informing our contemporary electronic 'presence' suggests that—if we do not take great care—we are all in danger of soon becoming merely ghosts in the machine."[70] Yet the ghost in the machine is not Tom's per se; it is the conscripted black mediality which necessitates his corpsing ad infinitum. Extending Saidiya Hartman's contention that "slavery is the ghost in the machine of kinship," film phenomenology must consider that some of us have always been spooks, bearers of a blackness whose anteriority to every apparatus is "made visible as a haunted technological medium."[71] Ligon's dark media suggests that the black has only ever approached the machine as its phantasmatic anterior, bound to the (im)mediations of the flesh and the ruse of presence, the ante-phenomenological specter cinema at once needs and abhors.

In the final chapter of *Anteaesthetics*, I further expound upon the inextricability of dark media from the hieroglyphics of flesh.[72] For now, however, let us note that the cinematic hauntology elliptically disclosed in and by *The Death of Tom* could be said to be subtended or borne by another, one which is, in this instance, granted the dissimulation neither of presence nor the absence of presence: a racially gendered enfleshment which becomes (displaced within) the apparatic body of the cinematic medium.[73] Among the litany of (mis)namings this black feminine vestibularity is generally made to assume within the particular context of the literary, cinematic, and theatrical histories with which the anteaesthetics of *The Death of Tom* are recursively entwined, we might say that one name stands out among others: Topsy.

While Topsy is denied the saintly trappings granted Tom at the moment of his death, she nevertheless figures centrally in the libidinal, symbolic, and material economies that subtend the diegesis in *Uncle Tom's Cabin* as well as the novel's aesthetic transits across theatrical performance, cinema, and visual culture more broadly. Generally regarded as the paradigmatic exemplar of the "pickaninny," Topsy's figure would prove to be a no less dynamic resource for racial troping over the next 170 years than that of Uncle Tom.[74] In the novel, Topsy, "a little Negro girl, about eight or nine years old," is purchased by St. Clare for Miss Ophelia as an "experiment"—an experiment meant to test whether this fallen "creature" could be wrested from her debasement and educated in the refinements of sentiment, the faculties of reason, and the decorum of civility that distinguish full-fledged human beings from the wretched.[75] Miss Ophelia, good sentimentalist that she is, objects, "It is your system makes such children," to which St. Clare responds, "I know it; but they are *made*,—they exist,—and what is to be done with them?"[76]

Like the Hottentot Venus, Topsy may be taken as one of several paradigmatic figurations of the black feminine—in this instance, that of the pickaninny, whose (un)gendering is distinguished, in part, by an incapacity to lay claim to either girlhood or womanhood. Also like the Hottentot Venus, the process of aesthetically rend(er)ing Topsy unfolds principally through the dissimulation of her "body" and the constellation of affects which adhere to it. Stowe wastes no opportunity to weave Topsy's exceptionally degraded, pathological, pitiable nature through her spectacularized corporeality, though the moment of her first appearance in the novel is a particularly prominent example:

> She was one of the blackest of her race; and her round, shining eyes, glittering as glass beads, moved with quick and restless glances over everything in the room. Her mouth, half open with astonishment at the wonders of the new Mas'r's parlor, displayed a white and brilliant set of teeth. Her woolly hair was braided in sundry little tails, which stuck out in every direction. The expression of her face was an odd mixture of shrewdness and cunning, over which was oddly drawn, like a kind of veil, an expression of the most doleful gravity and solemnity. She was dressed in a single filthy, ragged garment, made of bagging; and stood with her hands demurely folded before her. Altogether, there was something odd and goblin-like about her appearance—something, as Miss Ophelia afterwards said, "so heathenish," as to inspire that good lady with utter dismay; and, turning to St. Clare, she said,
>
> "Augustine, what in the world have you brought that thing here for?"
>
> "For you to educate, to be sure, and train in the way she should go. I thought she was rather a funny specimen in the Jim Crow line. Here, Topsy," he added, giving a whistle, as a man would to call the attention of a dog, "give us a song, now, and show us some of your dancing."
>
> The black, glassy eyes glittered with a kind of wicked drollery, and the thing struck up, in a clear shrill voice, an odd Negro melody, to which she kept time with her hands and feet, spinning round, clapping her hands, knocking her knees together, in a wild, fantastic sort of time, and producing in her throat all those odd guttural sounds which distinguish the native music of her race; and finally, turning a summerset or two, and giving a prolonged closing note, as odd and unearthly as that of a steam-whistle, she came suddenly down on the carpet, and stood with her hands folded, and a most sanctimonious expression of meekness and solemnity over her face, only broken by the cunning glances which she shot askance from the corners of her eyes.[77]

Topsy's character serves as not only the constitutive foil for all of the novel's main characters,[78] but also the principal figural means of effectuating the complementarity between the racial melodrama of sentimentalism and the racial comedy of minstrelsy. It is significant that both operations are accomplished by mobilizing Topsy's wayward corporeality, or in the terms of my argument, the singular quality of her (dis)placement before the corporeal division of the world, as well as the libidinal economy of gratuitous violence this anterior corporeality would appear to necessitate.[79] As Hartman observes, "Uncle Tom's tribulations were tempered by the slaps and punches delivered to Topsy."[80] Both Topsy and Uncle Tom, of course, were the objects of corporeal violence, but whereas the violence directed against Tom "caused the virtuous black body of melodrama to be esteemed," the violence directed against Topsy "humiliated the grotesque black body of minstrelsy."[81] Although the constitutive opposition of Topsy and Little Eva is not, strictly speaking, analogous to that of Topsy and Uncle Tom, it is aesthetically accomplished through a similar juxtaposition of corporeal and affective traits:

> There stood the two children, representatives of the two extremes of society. The fair, high-bred child, with her golden head, her deep eyes, her spiritual, noble brow, and prince-like movements; and her black, keen, subtle, cringing, yet acute neighbor. They stood the representatives of their races. The Saxon, born of ages of cultivation, command, education, physical and moral eminence; the Afric, born of ages of oppression, submission, ignorance, toil, and vice![82]

One of the most notable features assigned to Topsy's dissimulated "body" is animatedness. Following Sianne Ngai, I understand Topsy's animatedness not as an innocent curiosity or figurative idiosyncrasy but as the sign of a violent process by which the regime of aesthetics "visibly harnesses the affective qualities of liveliness, effusiveness, spontaneity, and zeal to a disturbing racial epistemology, and makes these variants of 'animatedness' function as bodily (hence self-evident) signs of the raced subject's naturalness or authenticity."[83] As a corporealized affect, animatedness suggests an intimate proximity to animation which is more than etymological; the declensions "between the organic-vitalistic and the technological-mechanical, and between the technological-mechanical and the emotional"[84] register racial taxonomies of affectability which are internal to modern affective categories. More pointedly, "the animation of the racialized body . . . involves likening it to an instrument, porous and pliable, for the vocalization of others."[85]

That said, although both Uncle Tom and Topsy are animated in Ngai's sense of the word, the racial ventriloquism to which they are both subject (whether that ventriloquism appears in embodiment or speech) assumes a markedly different form in each instance. Whereas Tom's animatedness functions as a sentimental mechanism of endearment, Topsy's is comical, degraded, grotesque, and immediately associated with ungovernability. Moreover, Tom's and Topsy's differential animations and the racially gendered taxonomic distinctions in affectability to which they correspond are also expressed as a formal divergence in the quality of the touch to which they are respectively subject, even if this representational bifurcation of the violence of (im)mediation ultimately serves a unitary aesthetic project. Whereas Tom's animatedness lends itself to an idiom of tenderness, a sensualized openness to and bestowal of touch that would assume overtly erotic overtones in the expansive aesthetic transits *Uncle Tom's Cabin* undertook in the wake of the original novel,[86] Topsy encounters touch principally through the brute force of terror, as the wildness of her dissimulated "body" "can only be governed by the lash" (and even this would appear to be insufficient to tame her unruly nature).[87] Topsy's presumptive embodiment of radical affectability produces no contradiction with the apparent insensateness that enables her endless "hurt-ability."[88] What mercy Topsy receives is not only therefore effectively redundant but furthermore serves to ennoble Little Eva. Topsy remains obstinate and unredeemable. In short, a racially gendered economy of animatedness sustains the violence of distinctive, if conjoined forms of (im)mediation.

Nevertheless, following a line of thought introduced in Fred Moten's analysis of Édouard Manet's *Olympia* (1865) and Thomas Eakins's "African-American girl nude, reclining on couch" (c. 1882), I want to suggest that what is concealed in the affective relay produced by Tom's and Topsy's contrapuntally gendered animations is, in fact, something on the order of a deanimation[89]—or more precisely, a petrification through animation which serves to displace the racially gendered bearing of an exorbitant materiality that cuts the difference modern hierarchies of animacy seek to still. In this instance, Moten's contention that early cinema's movement "from disruptive attraction to seamless arc . . . [is] a forced movement embedded in the stillness of the little girl"[90] can be partially inverted without altering its substance: with Topsy, we glimpse the emergence of the cinematic through a stillness embedded in the forced movement of the little (black) girl. But on this point we must be very clear: the black feminine anteriority or enfleshed black mediality which serves as the vestibule for and casualty of the emergence of the cinematic cannot be reduced to the figural, regardless of whether the figure in question can be said to have "really existed." After all, an existence without ontology fundamentally belies any neat distinction between (aesthetic) fantasy and (material) reality. That is, although Topsy, in this instance, becomes the figurative site, the dissimulated "body" which comes to mark a racially gendered, enfleshed mediality which is, in fact, absolutely unrepresentable: her figure both bears the trace of flesh and occasions its concealment.

This point helps us to understand the significance of Topsy's cameo appearance on the very first page of Mary Ann Doane's canonical work *The Emergence of Cinematic Time*. Referring to a story by James Brander Matthews entitled "The Kinetoscope of Time," published in the December 1895 issue of *Scribner's Magazine*, the very same month that the films of the Lumière Cinématographe were first publicly screened, Doane suggests that this particular "story conveys something of the uncanniness of the new technology's apparent ability to transcend time as corruption by paradoxically fixing life and movement, providing their immutable record. It condenses many of the fears, desires, anxieties, and pleasures attached to the idea of the mechanical representability of time."[91] To paraphrase Doane's recounting: in Matthews's story, an anonymous, first-person protagonist narrates a gothic encounter with an emergent technology that straddles the uncanny and the marvelous.[92] The midnight toll of a clock tower and a sudden gust of bitter wind announce this protagonist's wandering through the streets of an unknown city beneath a moonless sky. An uncertain yellow gleam and an unspoken voice beckon the protagonist to an obscure building, which he enters as if by necessity. In an unfurnished, dimly lit rotunda, its walls draped in velvet, he encounters a series of kinetoscopes, Edison's individual viewing machine that directly preceded the invention of cinema. Heeding the command of a message projected onto the velvet curtains, whose words are immediately forgotten but whose meaning is retained, he peers through the first of the eyepieces. In the pages that follow, the protagonist encounters "a succession of strange dances," including scenes from the tale of Salomé, *The Scarlet Letter*, and *Uncle Tom's Cabin* (specifically, the scene described earlier, in which Topsy is commanded to dance before her new masters), followed by glimpses of the *Iliad*, *Don Quixote*, *Faust*, and the Custer massacre.[93] When he withdraws from the apparatus, he encounters a strange man that he speculates is "Time himself," who offers him the chance to view his own past and future demise but at a cost: "The Vision of life must be paid for in life itself. For every ten years of the future which I may unroll before you here, you must assign me a year of your life—twelve months—to do with as I will."[94] Having refused the Faustian bargain, the protagonist is sent away and eventually works his way from this space of mysterious darkness and illumination back to the street, where the flood of electric street lamps and the roar of a nearby train confirm that he has come "back to the world of actuality."[95]

In Doane's reading, "the story conjoins many of the motifs associated with the emerging cinema and its technological promise to capture time: immortality, the denial of the radical finitude of the human body, access to other temporalities, and the issue of the archivability of time."[96] But what are we to make of the appearance of Topsy, in all of her "wicked drollery," in this literary anticipation of cinema's emergence, where the grand historical promises of the moving image enthrall the subject with a phantasmagoria that would seem to blur the distinction between the scientific and the fantastic? It is worth noting that this is also precisely the capacity in which Topsy appears in Porter's 1903 film, in which some two and a half minutes of the nearly twelve-minute film are taken up by the minstrel dancing of blackface slaves.[97] For Doane, Topsy's appearance in Matthews's gothic story bespeaks a literary reinscription of "recognizable tropes of orientalism, racism, and imperialism essential to the nineteenth-century colonialist imperative to conquer other times, other spaces. . . . These are the recorded times, the other temporalities, that allow the protagonist to disavow, for a while, his own temporality of clattering trains and clanging cable cars."[98]

Doane rightly observes that orientalist, racist, and imperialist imaginaries provide ample means for the normative subject to displace his or her own alienation through what Srinivas Aravamudan would call "eclectic relativism"[99] and brilliantly discerns the manner in which the rhetorical valences of Matthews's story "echo . . . that which accompanied the reception of early cinema" in its preoccupation with the possibilities and problematics this medium posed for "the representability of time."[100] Nevertheless, I would suggest that Topsy's appearance cannot be reduced to a supplementary spatiotemporal conquest or flight. For the temporality affixed to Topsy's animated skin is neither the enduring stasis ascribed to the orient,[101] nor the prehistoric quietus ascribed to the indigenous.[102] As I have elsewhere noted by way of Hegel's insistence, the African, the black, is utterly bereft of history. Blackness marks the derelict anterior of historicity, a singular, constitutive negation which, apropos Lindon Barrett, "organizes the linear progression of historical temporality."[103] The existence which Topsy's dissimulative figure simultaneously mimics, bears, and obscures emerges from a "*temporality without duration*" that Calvin Warren terms "*black time*."[104] Differentially extending Doane's inimitable intervention, I want to argue that Topsy's appearance evinces an unconscious knowledge of black feminine vestibularity to the fraught, contradictory valences of modernity's historical spatiotemporality as it is advanced, consolidated, and solipsistically projected and reflected in this proto-cinematic literary imagination.

Topsy's formal appearance in Matthews's proto-cinematic literary text marks an unconscious knowledge of black mediality in at least two respects: firstly, the reader's visual-textual recollection of the "wild, fantastic" rhythm and "odd guttural sounds which distinguish the native music of . . . [Topsy's] race" bespeaks more than a familiar racial exoticism by which the protagonist (and reader, by proxy) might briefly find reprieve from the temporal vicissitudes and enclosure of modernity. While the fungibility of the slave certainly lends itself to all manner of libidinal excitation and exotic fantasy, with respect to time, I would suggest that Topsy's primordial dancing primarily signals the spatial (dis)location of the black (feminine) before the scene of nature and thus beyond the geographic bounds of the social, which corresponds to a constitutive a(nte)temporality: the black time that lies before and without history. The Foucauldian analysis of the heterotopic and heterochronic falters in the face of the antetopic and antechronic.[105]

Secondly, the reader's visual-textual recollection of Topsy's animatedness marks the dissimulative appearance of the fleshly (im)mediation that enables the fantasy of the subject's mastery over time, whether that mastery is expressed as the historical will to brave the contingent (and thus the making of history) or the scientific will to abstraction and rationalization (and thus the recording of history). That is, the dancing commodity[106] (whose disfigured speech Marx required but could not imagine),[107] the anoriginary mediality which occasions the modern "extensions of Man," is made to bear the stilling of movement and the movement in stillness that accomplishes the synthesis of "time and space *as animation* in a completely new 'cinematic' mode."[108] In short, Topsy's appearance is not incidental but rather a dissimulative figure who in this instance comes to obliquely mark the fleshly (im)mediation which is anterior to the cinematic and its technologies of worlding.

In Ligon's *The Death of Tom*, Topsy's trace can be discerned neither in the figurative nor its absence; rather, she manifests as the artwork's haptic suffusion with a hauntology of the flesh, an antephenomenological feel that finds expression in the shudder of what Kathleen Stewart would call "atmospheric attunement."[109] Topsy is the ungovernable materiality of the glitch which subtends the warble of grayscale, the wild dance of opacity beneath the figments of harrowing darkness, gaunt shadow, incandescent light. The "negro girl meagre" who makes and breaks the ledger,[110] she is everywhere and nowhere, the exorbitance which remains before every calculus. Yet she is equally the anorigin of every experimental flight from the (cinematic) worlding which requires the serial nonevent of Tom's death, the perpetual corpsing which draws the proscenium's heavy curtains. The meagre must come before the minor as surely as the major.[111] In fact, in *The Death of Tom*, Topsy's trace is perhaps even more immediately palpable as the anterior remains of a singularly black tradition of improvisation.

Recall that Ligon's installation was ultimately (in)completed by the improvisatory accompaniment of jazz pianist Jason Moran, who "played to the shadows." Significantly, Moran chose Bert Williams's signature vaudeville song "Nobody" to occasion his improvisation. As Louis Chude-Sokei observes, "It is no mere coincidence that Bert Williams's most well-known song, first performed in 1905, was the great paean to self-negation 'Nobody.'" Williams's "black-on-black minstrelsy" was a mode of performance that doubled down on the imposition of "bodily" dissimulation, a fabrication of stage presence in, through, and as "hyperbolic absence."[112] Moran's choice to riff off of Williams's "Nobody" redoubles Uncle Tom's present absence and absent presence in the film. Furthermore, it alludes to the ways in which the ongoing nonevent of Tom's death perennially reiterates the marking of a body and personhood which is not, a no-body who stands only "before the horizon of death."[113] But beneath these thematic associations, there is an unstated formal question, which is serially and differentially rehearsed as a mode of experimentation across the black diaspora: whence a song that is sung by no-body, a music that comes from nowhere? That is, black improvisation is always already an anticipatory response to a question with no answer, a question of origins.

There is a moment in Stowe's novel that has become subsequently imbricated in black vernacular traditions as a trope for signifyin(g). Miss

Ophelia is interrogating Topsy about her origins, a rhetorical exercise in which humiliation is staged in the trappings of a question:

> "Who was your mother?"
>
> "Never had none!" said the child, with another grin.
>
> "Never had any mother? What do you mean? Where were you born?"
>
> "Never was born!" persisted Topsy, with another grin, that looked so goblin-like, that, if Miss Ophelia had been at all nervous, she might have fancied that she had got hold of some sooty gnome from the land of Diablerie. . . .
>
> "Have you ever heard anything about God, Topsy?"
>
> The child looked bewildered, but grinned as usual.
>
> "Do you know who made you?"
>
> "Nobody, as I knows on," said the child, with a short laugh.
>
> The idea appeared to amuse her considerably; for her eyes twinkled, and she added, "I spect I grow'd. Don't think nobody never made me."[114]

Taking the race-reproduction nexus as its central thematic—albeit while displacing the onto-epistemological significance of this nexus onto Topsy's moral and spiritual debasement—this well-known passage, in its synthesis of melodrama and minstrelsy, underlines the singular black displacement from origin that recursively discloses the general displacement of origin that Derrida would alert us to.[115] Moreover, the black mother, whose "only claim . . . [is] to transfer her dispossession to the child," is perpetually forced to become the medium of this "originary displacement."[116] Black music, as thinkers such as Fred Moten and Nathaniel Mackey have suggested, serially returns to this anoriginary displacement as a site of departure, of flight in and as a broken refrain.[117] Perhaps James Weldon Johnson had an affinitive thought in mind when he famously invoked Topsy, this dissimulative form without origin, as an analogue for black music: "The earliest Ragtime songs, like Topsy, 'jes' grew.' . . . The tune was irresistible, and belonged to nobody."[118] In other words, the conscription of black feminine mediality remains before not only the cinematic and its technologies of worlding but also those myriad improvisational flights from the world, which are animated by the harrowing tremolo of black femininity's lyrical surplus.[119] But the black residuum is a decidedly antelyrical materiality: an obstinate wrench(ing) within the machinery of reproduction, an aporetic remainder that cleaves to, even as it is cleaved from, the serially forced labor of making and breaking from the world.

Notes

1. Ralph Ellison, *Invisible Man* (1952; repr., New York: Vintage: 1995), 7.

2. Harriet Beecher Stowe, *The Annotated Uncle Tom's Cabin*, ed. Henry Louis Gates Jr. and Hollis Robbins (New York: W. W. Norton, 2007), 486.

3. Cf. Andrew V. Uroskie, *Between the Black Box and the White Cube: Expanded Cinema and Postwar Art* (Chicago: University of Chicago, 2014). For an influential analysis of phantasmagoria as a specific operation that has "pervaded the worlds of art and cinema, theater and spectacle," see Noam M. Elcott, "The Phantasmagoric Dispositif: An Assembly of Bodies and Images in Real Time and Space," *Grey Room*, no. 62 (Winter 2016): 47.

4. See Mark Fisher, *The Weird and the Eerie* (London: Repeater, 2017), 61.

5. For detailed accounts, see John W. Frick, *Uncle Tom's Cabin on the American Stage and Screen* (New York: Palgrave Macmillan, 2012); Ben Brewster and Lea Jacobs, *Theatre to Cinema: Stage Pictorialism and the Early Feature Film* (Oxford: Oxford University Press, 1997).

6. Quoted in Brewster and Jacobs, *Theatre to Cinema*, 54.

7. Eric Lott, *Love and Theft: Blackface Minstrelsy and the American Working Class* (Oxford: Oxford University Press, 1993), 34; emphasis in original.

8. Saidiya V. Hartman, *Scenes of Subjection: Terror, Slavery, and Self-Making in Nineteenth-Century America* (New York: Oxford University Press, 1997), 28.

9. In Ligon's exhibition, the viewer is greeted by a wall text with a synopsis of this scene before encountering the film itself: "The scene shows an old woodshed. Uncle Tom is lying on the floor, and Cassy is seen to steal in, raise Uncle Tom's head, give him a drink of water, and steal away again. George Shelby enters. Going over to Uncle Tom, he raises his head from the floor and asks him if he did not remember him, also saying that he had come to take Tom back home. Tom tells him that it is too late; he is dying, and pointing to the sky, says that he can see his Heavenly home; a vision of Eva in Heaven appears on the wall of the shed, and as it disappears, Tom drops back dead. Shelby kneels by his side, and in rapid succession[,] visions of John Brown being led to execution, a battle scene from the Civil War, and a cross with a vision of emancipation, showing Abraham Lincoln with the negro slave kneeling at his feet with broken manacles, appear." "Uncle Tom's Cabin: Edison Film," in Thomas A. Edison, *Film Catalogue* (1903), http://utc.iath.virginia.edu/onstage/films/ficattaeat.html.

10. Louis Chude-Sokei, *The Last Darky: Bert Williams, Black-on-Black Minstrelsy, and the African Diaspora* (Durham, NC: Duke University Press, 2006).

11. Glenn Ligon, quoted in Jason Moran, "Glenn Ligon," *Interview Magazine*, May 22, 2009, https://www.interviewmagazine.com/art/glenn-ligon.

12. Ligon, quoted in Moran, "Glenn Ligon."

13. Ligon, quoted in Moran, "Glenn Ligon."

14. Lauren Berlant, *Cruel Optimism* (Durham, NC: Duke University Press, 2011), 198.

15. See the discussion of Nina Simone in Rizvana Bradley, *Anteaesthetics: Black Aesthesis and the Critique of Form* (Stanford, CA: Stanford University Press, 2023), 3–10, 20–32, 50–51.

16. Cf. Legacy Russell, *Glitch Feminism: A Manifesto* (London: Verso Books, 2020).

17. Moran, "Glenn Ligon"; Rick Altman, "The Silence of the Silents," *Musical Quarterly* 80, no. 4 (1996): 648–718.

18. Moran, "Glenn Ligon"; Chude-Sokei, *The Last Darky*, 35.

19. Jane P. Tompkins, "Sentimental Power: Uncle Tom's Cabin and the Politics of Literary History," in Elaine Showalter, *The New Feminist Criticism: Essays on Women, Literature, and Theory* (New York: Pantheon Books, 1985), 82.

20. Michelle Wallace, "Uncle Tom's Cabin: Before and after the Jim Crow Era," *TDR* 44, no. 1 (Spring 2000): 141; Amanda Claybaugh, introduction to Stowe, *Annotated Uncle Tom's Cabin*, xliii.

21. Quoted in Wallace, "Uncle Tom's Cabin," 142.

22. Wallace, "Uncle Tom's Cabin," 142; Manisha Sinha, *The Slave's Cause: A History of Abolition* (New Haven, CT: Yale University Press, 2016), 440. Indeed, as Sinha notes, the black abolitionist Martin Delany decried Stowe for effectively stealing from the autobiographies of former slaves. Sinha, *The Slave's Cause*, 444.

23. Lauren Berlant, "Poor Eliza," *American Literature* 70, no. 3 (September 1998): 638.

24. Hartman, *Scenes of Subjection*, 28.

25. Hartman, *Scenes of Subjection*, 28.

26. Daphne A. Brooks, *Bodies in Dissent: Spectacular Performances of Race and Freedom, 1850–1910* (Durham, NC: Duke University Press, 2006), 30.

27. Robin Bernstein, *Racial Innocence: Performing Childhood from Slavery to Civil Rights* (New York: New York University Press, 2011), 4, passim.

28. Hartman, *Scenes of Subjection*, 89.

29. Hortense J. Spillers, *Black, White, and in Color: Essays on American Literature and Culture* (Chicago: University of Chicago Press, 2003), 188; emphasis in original. On the Black "body," see Bradley, *Anteaesthetics*, 87: "Black people do not properly have bodies, insofar as such 'having' is in fact a linguistic concealment of a terrible claim: both to the presumptive ontic status of normative personhood and to the regimes of property and propriety to which the metaphysics of individuation are inextricably bound. Rather, black people are no-bodies, given to an enfleshed existence, which the body as racial apparatus can neither escape nor completely subsume, as flesh constitutes the body's very condition of (im) possibility."

30. David Marriott, "Perfect Beauty of Black Death," *Los Angeles Review of Books*, Philosophical Salon, June 2017; emphasis in original.

31. For another inquiry that stresses the significance of repetition, see Yasmin Ibrahim, "The Dying Black Body in Repeat Mode: The Black 'Horrific' on a Loop," *Identities* 29, no. 6 (2022), 711–729.

32. Frick, *Uncle Tom's Cabin on the American Stage and Screen*, 133. See also Marc Robinson, *The American Play, 1787–2000* (New Haven, CT: Yale University Press, 2009).

33. Cf. Hartman, *Scenes of Subjection*.

34. Lott, *Love and Theft*.

35. Eric J. Sundquist, ed., *New Essays on Uncle Tom's Cabin* (Cambridge: Cambridge University Press, 1987), 4.

36. Frick, *Uncle Tom's Cabin on the American Stage and Screen*, 17.

37. Hartman, *Scenes of Subjection*, 30.

38. As Bernstein notes, "It was this vision of Tom's death that motivated . . . [Stowe] to write her novel . . . [and] she wrote the first forty chapters to build toward that climax." Bernstein, *Racial Innocence*, 135–136.

39. In this regard, it is telling that Stowe sometimes slipped between narrating Tom's death and Tom's whipping as the visionary impetus for the novel. See Thomas F. Gossett, *Uncle Tom's Cabin and American Culture* (Dallas: Southern Methodist University Press, 1985), 92–93, on this discrepancy.

40. While discussion of these subsequent adaptations is not immediately pertinent to the present argument, it is worth noting that there were numerous filmic and televisual adaptations of *Uncle Tom's Cabin*, in both the United States and internationally, over the course of the twentieth century. Indeed, Stephen Railton notes that were nine filmic adaptations during the 1903–1927 era of silent film alone. See Stephen Railton, "Readapting Uncle Tom's Cabin," in *Nineteenth-Century American Fiction on Screen*, ed. R. Barton Palmer (Cambridge: Cambridge University Press, 2007), 62–76.

41. Charles Musser, *Before the Nickelodeon: Edwin S. Porter and the Edison Manufacturing Company* (Berkeley: University of California Press, 1991), 1, 4. See also Charles Musser, *The Emergence of Cinema: The American Screen to 1907* (Berkeley: University of California Press, 1994).

42. Mary Ann Doane, *The Emergence of Cinematic Time: Modernity, Contingency, and the Archive* (Cambridge, MA: Harvard University Press, 2002), 11. I should stress that, for Doane, contingency is hardly axiomatic but rather a rich and complicated concept that assumes a "double function" due to "the tensions internal to its own definition"—expressing, on the one hand, "a resistance to systematicity" that nevertheless "partakes of systematicity, locked within the terms of its antagonist," and, on the other hand, a "reflexive concept" which compels reflection on "the history of its own impossible fate within modernity." Doane, *Emergence of Cinematic Time*, 231–232.

43. Doane, *Emergence of Cinematic Time*, 22, 22–23.

44. Doane, *Emergence of Cinematic Time*, 24.

45. Tom Gunning, "The Cinema of Attractions: Early Film, Its Spectator, and the Avant-Garde," in *Early Cinema: Space, Frame, Narrative*, ed. Thomas Elsaesser (London: British Film Institute, 1990), 56–62; Tom Gunning, "Cinema of Attractions," in *Encyclopedia of Early Cinema*, ed. Richard Abel (London/New York: Routledge, 2007), 124; André Gaudreault and Tom Gunning, "Le cinéma des premiers temps: Un défi à l'histoire du cinéma?," in *Histoire du cinéma: Nouvelles approches*, ed. Jacques Aumont, André Gaudreault, and Michel Marie (Paris: Sorbonne, 1989), 49–63. See also Tom Gunning, "An Aesthetic of Astonishment: Early Film and the (In)Credulous Spectator," *Art and Text*, no. 34 (Spring 1989): 31–45.

46. Charles Musser, introduction to "The Early Cinema of Edwin S. Porter," *Cinema Journal* 19, no. 1 (Fall 1979): 1–38, reprinted in *The Wiley-Blackwell History of American Film*, ed. Cynthia Lucia, Roy Grundmann, and Art Simon (Oxford: Wiley-Blackwell, 2011); Tom Gunning, *D. W. Griffith and the Origins of American Narrative Film: The Early Years at Biograph* (Urbana: University of Illinois Press, 1991).

47. Musser, *Emergence of Cinema*, 349.

48. Stephen Johnson, “Time and Uncle Tom: Familiarity and Shorthand in the Performance Traditions of Uncle Tom’s Cabin,” in *Performing Adaptations*, ed. Michelle MacArthur, Lydia Wilkinson, and Keren Zaiontz (Cambridge: Cambridge Scholars Press, 2009), 87; cited in Frick, *Uncle Tom’s Cabin on the American Stage and Screen*, 193.

49. Noël Burch, “Porter, or Ambivalence,” *Screen* 19, no. 4 (Winter 1978): 91–105.

50. Burch, “Porter, or Ambivalence,” 97, 98.

51. Doane, *Emergence of Cinematic Time*, 163, 164.

52. Frank B. Wilderson III, *Red, White, and Black: Cinema and the Structure of U.S. Antagonisms* (Durham, NC: Duke University Press, 2010).

53. David Marriott, *Lacan Noir: Lacan and Afro-pessimism* (Cham, Switzerland: Palgrave Macmillan, 2021), 160; emphasis in original.

54. Doane, *Emergence of Cinematic Time*, 230.

55. See, e.g., Steen Christiansen, “Metamorphosis and Modulation: Darren Aronofsky’s *Black Swan*,” in *Post-Cinema: Theorizing 21st-Century Film*, ed. Shane Denson and Julia Leyda (Falmer, UK: Reframe Books, 2016; https://shanedenson.com/post-cinema.pdf), 516; and Ruth Mayer, “Early/Post-Cinema: The Short Form, 1900/2000,” in Denson and Leyda, *Post-Cinema*, 616–646.

56. Tom Gunning, “A Little Light on a Dark Subject,” *Critical Quarterly* 25, no. 4 (2003): 50–51.

57. Vivian Sobchack, *Carnal Thoughts: Embodiment and Moving Image Culture* (Oakland: University of California Press, 2004), 160–161.

58. Sobchack, *Carnal Thoughts*, 161, 153.

59. See especially the chapter “Before the Nude, or Exorbitant Figuration,” in Bradley, *Anteaesthetics*, 147–220.

60. Avery F. Gordon, *Ghostly Matters: Haunting and the Sociological Imagination* (Minneapolis: University of Minnesota Press, 1997), xvi.

61. David Marriott, *Haunted Life: Visual Culture and Black Modernity* (New Brunswick, NJ: Rutgers University Press, 2007), 2.

62. David Marriott, “Corpsing; or, The Matter of Black Life,” *Cultural Critique* 94 (Fall 2016): 33, 35.

63. Jacques Derrida, *Of Grammatology* (Baltimore: Johns Hopkins University Press), 61.

64. Fred Moten, *In the Break: The Aesthetics of the Black Radical Tradition* (Minneapolis: University of Minnesota Press, 2003), 8.

65. Alexander R. Galloway, Eugene Thacker, and McKenzie Wark, *Excommunication: Three Inquiries in Media and Mediation* (Chicago: University of Chicago Press, 2014), 13.

66. Gallaway, Thacker, and Wark, *Excommunication*, 10.

67. Eugene Thacker, “Dark Media,” in Galloway, Thacker, and Wark, *Excommunication*, 85.

68. For more extended reflections on the racial entanglements of lightness and darkness, transparency and opacity, color and its absence, see Fred Moten, *The Universal Machine* (Durham, NC: Duke University Press, 2018), 140–246; Jared Sexton, “All Black Everything,” *e-flux*, no. 79 (February 2017), https://www.e-flux.com/journal/79/94158/all-black-everything/.

69. Thacker, "Dark Media," 80.

70. Vivian Sobchack, "The Scene of the Screen: Envisioning Photographic, Cinematic, and Electronic 'Presence,'" in Denson and Leyda, *Post-Cinema*, 120.

71. Saidiya Hartman, quoted in Judith Butler, "Is Kinship Always Already Heterosexual?," *differences: A Journal of Feminist Cultural Studies* 13, no. 1 (Spring 2002): 15; Marriott, *Haunted Life*, 32.

72. See the chapter "Unworlding, or the Involution of Value," in Bradley, *Anteaesthetics*, 281–315.

73. Here I am invoking and modifying Laura Mulvey's classic theorization of the apparatic in "Visual Pleasure and Narrative Cinema," *Screen* 16, no. 3 (Autumn 1975): 6–18.

74. On Topsy as the paradigmatic figure of the pickaninny, see Bernstein, *Racial Innocence*; Patricia A. Turner, *Ceramic Uncles and Celluloid Mammies: Black Images and Their Influence on Culture* (Charlottesville: University of Virginia Press, 2002); Jayna Brown, *Babylon Girls: Black Women Performers and the Shaping of the Modern* (Durham, NC: Duke University Press, 2008); Tavia Nyong'o, "Racial Kitsch and Black Performance," *Yale Journal of Criticism* 15, no. 2 (2002): 371–391.

75. Stowe, *The Annotated Uncle Tom's Cabin*, 249, 260; Bernstein, *Racial Innocence*, 45.

76. Stowe, *The Annotated Uncle Tom's Cabin*, 260; emphasis in original.

77. Stowe, *The Annotated Uncle Tom's Cabin*, 249–250.

78. Christina Sharpe, *Monstrous Intimacies: Making Post-Slavery Subjects* (Durham, NC: Duke University Press, 2010), 214n2.

79. See the chapter "The Corporeal Division of the World, or Aesthetic Ruination," in Bradley, *Anteaesthetics*, 105–146.

80. Hartman, *Scenes of Subjection*, 20.

81. Hartman, *Scenes of Subjection*, 26.

82. Stowe, *The Annotated Uncle Tom's Cabin*, 258.

83. Sianne Ngai, *Ugly Feelings* (Cambridge, MA: Harvard University Press, 2007), 95.

84. Ngai, *Ugly Feelings*, 95.

85. Ngai, *Ugly Feelings*, 97

86. That being said, I believe Hortense Spillers's suggestion that the figure of Uncle Tom serves as a cipher for the simultaneous expression and displacement of a nineteenth-century white feminine desire for the "dyadic taboo— . . . the 'black man' and the 'white woman'" (*Black, White, and in Color*, 191–194)—notwithstanding the fact that, as Robin Bernstein notes, "Eva's physical engagement with Tom is chaste in comparison to the unbridled sensuality between Eva and Mammy" (*Racial Innocence*, 93). For not only is the subsequent aesthetic life of *Uncle Tom's Cabin* across a myriad of mediums and forms at least as significant as, if not more significant than the letter of the novel itself, but as I have argued throughout *Anteaesthetics*, Spillers's analysis of the racially disjunctive economies of touch which are constitutive of the modern world also goes far beyond the reduction of touch to an axiomatic conception of literal, tactile contact.

87. Stowe, *The Annotated Uncle Tom's Cabin*, 259.

88. Bernstein, *Racial Innocence*, 30–68.

89. Fred Moten, *Black and Blur* (Durham, NC: Duke University Press, 2017), 66–85.

90. Moten, *Black and Blur*, 71.

91. Doane, *Emergence of Cinematic Time*, 1; James Brander Matthews, "The Kinetoscope of Time," *Scribner's Magazine* 18 (July–December 1895), 733–744.

92. Cf. Fisher, *The Weird and the Eerie*, 18.

93. Matthews, "Kinetoscope of Time," 734.

94. Matthews, "Kinetoscope of Time," 741, 742.

95. Matthews, "Kinetoscope of Time," 744.

96. Doane, *Emergence of Cinematic Time*, 2.

97. Railton, "Readapting Uncle Tom's Cabin," 67.

98. Doane, *Emergence of Cinematic Time*, 3.

99. Srinivas Aravamudan, *Tropicopolitans: Colonialism and Agency, 1688–1804* (Durham, NC: Duke University Press, 1999), 161.

100. Doane, *Emergence of Cinematic Time*, 3.

101. See, inter alia, Adam Barrows, "Time without Partitions: *Midnight's Children* and Temporal Orientalism," *ariel: A Review of International English Literature* 42, no. 3–4 (2012): 89–101.

102. See, inter alia, Gayatri Chakravorty Spivak, *Death of a Discipline* (New York: Columbia University Press, 2003), 79–81. For a Native Studies critique of the postcolonial interpretation of colonialist historicity, see Jodi A. Byrd, *The Transit of Empire: Indigenous Critiques of Colonialism* (Minneapolis: University of Minnesota Press, 2011).

103. Lindon Barrett, *Racial Blackness and the Discontinuity of Western Modernity* (Urbana: University of Illinois Press, 2014), 76.

104. Calvin L. Warren, *Ontological Terror: Blackness, Nihilism, and Emancipation* (Durham, NC: Duke University Press, 2018), 97; emphases in original.

105. See Michel Foucault, "Of Other Spaces: Utopias and Heterotopias" (1967), trans. Jay Miskowiec, *Architecture/Mouvement/Continuité*, no. 5 (October 1984), 46–49.

106. On the dancing commodity, see Karl Marx, *Capital*, vol. 1 (1867; repr., London: Penguin, 1990), 163–164.

107. Moten, *In the Break*.

108. Sobchack, *Carnal Thoughts*, 147; emphasis added.

109. Kathleen Stewart, "Atmospheric Attunements," *Environment and Planning D: Society and Space* 29, no. 3 (2011): 445–453.

110. See Patricia Saunders, "Defending the Dead, Confronting the Archive: A Conversation with M. NourbeSe Philip," *Small Axe* 12, no. 2 (June 2008): 63–79.

111. On the relation between the minor and the major, see Erin Manning, *The Minor Gesture* (Durham, NC: Duke University Press, 2016).

112. Chude-Sokei, *The Last Darky*, 35.

113. Denise Ferreira da Silva, "Toward a Black Feminist Poethics: The Quest(ion) of Blackness toward the End of the World," *Black Scholar* 44, no. 2 (Summer 2014): 81–97.

114. Stowe, *The Annotated Uncle Tom's Cabin*, 254.

115. For an extended reflection on this "originary displacement," see Nahum Dimitri Chandler, *X—The Problem of the Negro as a Problem for Thought* (New York: Fordham University Press, 2013), 129–170.

116. Saidiya Hartman, "The Belly of the World: A Note on Black Women's Labors," *Souls: A Critical Journal of Black Politics, Culture, and Society* 18 (2016): 166; Chandler, *X—The Problem of the Negro*, 129–170.

117. See, inter alia, Moten, *In the Break*; Fred Moten, *Stolen Life* (Durham, NC: Duke University Press, 2018); Moten, *Universal Machine*; Nathaniel Mackey, *Paracritical Hinge: Essays, Talks, Notes, Interviews* (Iowa City: Iowa University Press, 2018).

118. James Weldon Johnson, ed., *The Book of American Negro Poetry* (1922; repr., Auckland: Floating Press, 2008), 10, 11.

119. For my previous reading of black femininity's lyrical surplus, see Bradley, "Reinventing Capacity: Black Femininity's Lyrical Surplus and the Cinematic Limits of *12 Years a Slave*," *Black Camera* 7, no. 1 (2015): 162; see also Moten, *In the Break*, 38.

12 Our Glenn

Thomas Lax

S Is for Shadows

One of the first moments Glenn Ligon realized he could become an artist occurred in the dark, or to be more precise, among shadows. It was 1979, Ligon tells us in a 2008 abecedaria titled "Untitled." He was at the Heiner Friedrich Gallery in SoHo, New York, and Andy Warhol was showing his *Shadow* paintings—a series of monochromatic canvases onto which photographs of shadows, taken in the artist's studio, have been silkscreened. They were presented edge to edge around the perimeter of the gallery and its adjacent office. "I remember thinking that it was an awfully big room in which to show paintings of nothing," Ligon writes about that encounter. "I realized that if disappearance could be a subject matter, I could be an artist."

As is often the case with Ligon, a read (as in, to tell someone about themself) is condensed into a single word—in this instance, the adverb "awfully." And as is also often the case with Ligon, a read is also just a fact. For Ligon, saying things as they are is typically an occasion for words to resound in multiple ways. While at first the "awfully" in the sentence above seems to anticipate "nothing"—that is, "it was too big a room for all this nothing"—the word's meaning shifts to evoke a sense of awe at just how big an idea nothing could be.

When Ligon's words echo across several registers of meaning, other people are welcomed into the scene. Ligon the artist emerges, both in his own psyche and for the reader, in this shady brush with Warhol. Ligon places himself in Warhol's literal and metaphorical shadow, between the earlier artist's work and his own artistic production. Addition—one panel after another, one artist after another—is thematized as a mode of self-making that also hastens the self's disappearance.

Ligon's encounter with Warhol's work is one of several origin stories set, so to speak, in the dark. He describes a second moment of illumination in the essay "Black Light: David Hammons and the Poetics of Emptiness." It was 2002, and Hammons's *Concerto in Black and Blue* was on at Ace Gallery in New York. The twenty-thousand-square-foot space with twenty-five-foot ceilings was empty except for the visitors, who carried tiny pressure-activated LED flashlights. Ligon writes: "What Hammons has done is to provide the space in which Blackness can be constructed in light, like the famous photo of Picasso drawing a centaur in the air with a flashlight, except this time it's us with our little blue flashlights, signaling one another in the dark." Reflecting on the participatory dimension of the installation, Ligon casts "lightness" not in an antithetical or negative relationship to darkness, but rather as embedded within Blackness. A linguistic trickster, like Hammons before him, Ligon doubles the meaning of "lightness" as luminescence with "lightness" as play to describe the levity, archness, and antigravitational pull of Hammons's dark room.

Acts of Repetition

If shadows—those literal projections of the self in which distended figures are cast from our funny forms—occur in multiples, it is precisely because we can't help but repeat our fantasies and stories about our own formation, ongoingly. These dawning stories recur in Ligon's writing too. For example, in "Warhol's Shadows," which Ligon first gave as a lecture at Dia:Chelsea in 2007, he delves deeper into the origins of Warhol's installation. At one point, he enjoins, "Let us now move from the shadow to the act,"[1] and turns to Warhol's journal entries, which provide a primal scene of the works' construction and a story often left out of their account.

> **Saturday, July 2, 1977**
> Victor called and said he wanted to take me to dinner in the Village. I picked him up (cab $4). We went into porno magazine stores for research materials for the "landscapes" ($36). . . . The Village was so packed with everybody who couldn't afford Fire Island. Victor had a "big black number" coming over to his house that he wanted me to photograph

as a "landscape," so we cabbed back ($3.60). Then the big black number called and said that he wouldn't be there for hours, so Victor and I cabbed to Studio 54 ($3). It was filled with beautiful people.

Tuesday, August 30, 1977
Chrissie said she and Burt Reynolds were talking about me recently, and that's why she wanted to [be photographed]. Victor came in and started dragging out the Shadow paintings of cocks and assholes that I've been doing—the paintings all the "landscapes" have been posing for—and somebody had to tell him not to.[2]

Whether or not these "landscapes" became those "landscapes" is undecidable, Ligon tells us, while nevertheless gifting us some of the social coordinates that might have later led Warhol to describe this body of work as "disco décor."[3] Whether or not these *Shadow* paintings became those *Shadow* paintings is, Ligon also tells us (citing Proust), "intelligible to the . . . 'connoisseur . . . of a pleasure too singular, too hard to place, which is offered him, the confrère with whom our specialist could converse in the strange tongue.'" And whether or not Warhol's paintings are indeed images of "cocks and assholes," his dates and dollar amounts provide a knowable net of his desire, within which the "big black number" sits stolidly. The number might have come later that night or might have had to wait until Ligon and the rest of us showed up. But a late arrival still counts as some kind of presence.

Ligon's essay then shifts from Warhol's journals to his own, speaking in a more personal, diaristic register about his visit to the *Shadow* paintings at Dia:Beacon, New York.

Saturday, October 20, 2007
There are four couches in the room. People come and go, sit down, get up, sit down again. Occasionally, guards walk through. They are young, dressed in black pants and shirts with walkie-talkies hooked to their belts—college students, I imagine. One has potential. Black hair, a little stringy and long, thin and tall. Pale skin, ghostly almost. Piercings. Twenty-three? Twenty-four? Hard to tell. He shuffles his feet a little when he walks, seems shy. Thelma's voice is in my ear: "Never the owner, always the coat-check boy." Still, there is something about this one that keeps me staring.

For many reasons, I love that Ligon, like and also unlike Warhol before him, has turned his inner monologue into a dialogue with us. For one, "I imagine" rhymes with the question marks after "twenty-three" and "twenty-four," as well as with "hard to tell." For seconds, "ghostly almost" flitters in the same descriptive field as Warhol's disappearing figures. Thirdly, has there ever been a sentence as full as "Piercings"? What's more, it's true that someone else's voice, at times, can become so indistinguishable from your own voice that you hear it in your ear, and at the same time you can pay it no mind, no matter how on point the observation.

In a 2019 conversation with curator Hamza Walker, Ligon responded to Walker's extended quotations of his own words by saying, "I always thought the writing was so constrained by what I thought I needed to do. So I'm surprised by how loose the voice is in some of these things." Writing is not unlike love in that both require us to loosen our voice in order to find it. And in writing, as in love, we are often surprised when we see ourselves reflected back.

Reading these essays when they were first published gave me a pathway through the art world as a younger curator. Reading them anew, I sometimes had the feeling of being told a story I had heard before but whose meaning I hadn't fully understood the first or second time around. It was as if their full significance was still emerging, not unlike the way you know the unmistakable feeling of true love the first time you feel it, but nevertheless must practice receiving it, repeatedly over time. Love is a subtext and refrain in Ligon's essays. At least twice, Ligon invokes a phrase from bell hooks: "Love will take you places you might not ordinarily go." De Kooning's "Flesh [is] the reason . . . oil paint was invented" is also reprised across the writings. Who knew hooks and de Kooning had so much in common? If these figures return, it's because their words seem to travel with Ligon; they are other voices in his ear. In a recent conversation with Helga Davis, Ligon tells her, "[The] act of repetition . . . causes a transformation. . . . That's my work, basically."

Repetition of the stories we can't help but tell ourselves about ourselves can inure us to the possibility of being changed by another. But repetition can also break us down, and in doing so, open us to receive what we say we've been waiting for all along. "We all have the powerful fantasy that we'll one day meet someone who will be everything, who will know us as well as we know ourselves. Sometimes that person is a lover. Sometimes that person is a friend," Ligon writes in "My Felix," in which he describes putting two clocks side by side to make a homemade copy of Felix Gonzalez-Torres's *"Untitled" (Perfect Lovers)* (1987–1990). Writing, a mode of careful facsimile, is another way to reproduce and carry those friends and lovers. "Other people's words are my life companion, I guess," Ligon says in his discussion with Helga Davis. Companionship is as sure a bet as it gets.

Love, in the revolutionary traditions Ligon cites, is also ushered in by unlikely forms of racial identification.[4] In the glossary of terms in which he offers us "S is for Shadows," he also gives us the following under "R is for Race": "Childhood crushes: Race Bannon on *Jonny Quest*, and Racer X on *Speed Racer*. Every Saturday morning I would wake up at 6:00 a.m. to wait for my cartoon paramours to appear in black and white on the old console TV we had in the living room of our apartment."

"Race," which we might at first assume will describe a calculus of skewed life chances,[5] instead ushers in desire in propulsive, animated form. Again, Ligon traverses the meanings of the word—from social category to childhood game—to get more from it. Like love, racial identification can be opaque and unknowable, giving one a voice as it threatens to dissolve it. But desire for that zaddy cartoon character and anime twink nevertheless projects outward from Ligon's childlike imagination.

Rather than engage in the race of a winner-take-all competition, Ligon's both-a-read-and-a-fact mode of criticism—in which skepticism can be alchemized into belief—brings more sociality, more desire for an "us." If Ligon's artwork, following Warhol and Hammons, is premised upon the idea that disappearance can usher in form, his writing moves with the shadows of others to engender the emergence of new formations as well.

For the Children

A is for the aphorisms:

"In America, what you can't sell, you kill."

"No need to speak on that."

"Joy works in mysterious ways."

A is also for the "and whatnots":

the "knickknack money"

the "play-play"

the "doowutchyalike"

A is, additionally, for the asides:

"What's so great about being married to a man?"

"Too much information!"

Ligon's literary forms compress as much as they open up. His aphorisms offer a fulsome critique of the American project even as they don't bother to waste more time on said project than is necessary. In "Untitled," for example, he writes, "Nowadays, following white people's behavior is not an option because there is so little of it left to emulate"—an entire dissertation on appropriation in just nineteen words. Elsewhere, the repetitive rhythm of anaphora allows Ligon to hold a contradiction. In a litany of phrases in "Remember the Revolution?," he borrows from and improvises on queer writer Joe Brainard's 1970–1975 experimental memoir, *I Remember*.[6] "I remember 'Say it loud—I'm Black and I'm proud,'" followed immediately by "I remember not being able to say 'Say it loud—I'm Black and I'm proud.'" Time moves forward and backward in his experiment in performance documentation, "Notes on a Performance by Kellie Jones," in which he describes the art historian and curator approaching the podium wearing a beautiful red suit and black hat with a feather: "Went looking for the art and we were the art." Throughout, conjunctive phrases—the "and whatnots," "what have yous," and "somethingsomethings"—also link one time to another. Ligon gives us much feeling with few words. What else is there to do when you read him but exclaim, "Boop!" or audibly exhale?

To the rhetorical figures of aphorism and anaphora, Ligon adds abecedaria, advice column, chronology, diary, glossary, map, travelogue: genres he structures through experimentation. The letters of the alphabet in "Untitled" offer the stage to an unlikely coterie of cultural figures, including CocoRosie, Elmo, and Krazy Kat, signaling the undetermined uses to which we might put the characters on offer. The self-portrait consisting of places he has lived, "Housing in New York: A Brief History, 1960–2007," uses chronology as a way of both narrating and depersonalizing that most intimate of political mythologies: the home. And the travelogue "Walking in Memphis" compresses the highs and lows that accompany traveling as a Black person in the American South into the following scene: "When [the Black Lips] played a laconic version of 'Dixie' as an interlude, I knew it was time to leave. The one consolation was the shirtless guys in the mosh pit, who, after they finished jumping on each other and hurling beer cans at the band, politely said 'Excuse me' as they passed me on their way to the bathroom or to have a smoke. Folks got manners down South."

Feast of Scraps

If some of these quips and stories bear a trace of the unsolicited wisdom you might have received from your worldly-wise uncle or aunt, that is no coincidence, since a few came verbatim to Ligon from his Uncle Tossy. It's Uncle Tossy who tells us, in "Black Light," that "there are two kinds of niggers in the world: niggers and crazy niggers." (It likely won't surprise you that Tossy, Ligon remarks, was one of the latter.) It's from Uncle Tossy that we get the term "a complicated Negro" and the expression "No need to speak on that." And some of Ligon's lyrical storytelling is built on Uncle Tossy's recollections of seeing Billie Holiday and Thelonious Monk perform in nightclubs in the Bronx, where Ligon grew up.

Ligon and Tossy don't have the same voice. But they do share a tendency to state things as they are, especially about those facts that official culture has invented entire classes of fiction to disfigure. In his conversation with Hamza Walker, Ligon recounts someone's comment on the figure of Tossy: "'Oh, that's just your way of saying things you want to say, and you invented this character.'" Tossy is no greater of an invention than Ligon himself. But like the animated superheroes Race Bannon and Racer X, or like a shadow self, Ligon's writing is itself a proxy, offering an occasion for him to throw his voice and say exactly what it is he's thinking but might not have otherwise expressed.

In his paintings and installations, Ligon has made a signature of using other queer and Black thinkers' texts "along the lines of a cover song" (to borrow Hamza Walker's phrase) in "a gesture of love, an homage, a dialogue, a dance." Writing is a related, if particular, "act of substitution," made from the scraps of other works. Postmodern literary theory has taught us that authorship is always a "quasi-collaborative"[7] endeavor between those whom one explicitly or implicitly cites and one's reader. But for Ligon, reading, in all senses of the word, is a particular terrain of self-making, a process analogous to his architectural metaphor about the mysteries of identification: "What we might call 'identity' or the 'self' is a storage room with a busted lock: we go in looking for 'me' and instead find 'we,'" he writes in "My Felix."

If some of Ligon's genres are explicitly directed at younger people, all of his writing implicitly forms a connection between those of us who have been affected by him and those whom he has been affected by in turn. In "Untitled," for example, you can feel Ligon's unvarnished yet exalted pride when he sees Rodney McMillian's canvas in the 2005 exhibition *Frequency*, its strokes of latex paint and charcoal falling across the floor and traveling eight feet up the wall: "I thought, 'The children believe they can fly.'" In "Black Light," you can sense Ligon's surprise and vulnerability when he encounters a 2004 silkscreen painting by Adam Pendleton in which the words "TWOPEOPLETOGETHERISAMIRACLE" are printed on canvas. And you can hear Ligon's biting laughter, in the same essay, when he watches Dave McKenzie's 2004 video *We Shall Overcome*, in which the artist wears an oversize Bill Clinton mask: "Ultimately, McKenzie is not interested in Clinton at all (trifling men are all alike!)." Throughout, you know that, as with the handmade Christmas cards he tells us he made as a child, Ligon is sending notes that document his affection as he simultaneously makes critical and discursive room for others.

Perhaps it is this anticipatory mode of address that orients Ligon's interest in representations of the future, from the retrofuturist cultural markers of his youth to Sun Ra's music, which he describes in koanlike terms as "sound against waiting" in the piece "Sound and Vision." Ligon's writing looks to the past for a prediction of what is to come, filling out the unrealized possibilities of his artistic precursors as he opens the door to those who have not yet been invited in. Like Glenn the child, who attended a private day school on the Upper West Side and was one of the only Black kids in his class, Ligon the artist came up showing his work as one of the only Black makers. But contrary to the only-room-for-one logic of the art world of the 1990s, he knows it's more fun with all of us in the room.

In his conversation with Helga Davis, Ligon reflects on a time before the work of Black Yale art school grads was sold for six figures at auction, acknowledging that reality has changed. But he does so without nostalgia or self-congratulation. Rather, he offers a means of conveying some of the values that attended the before times, teaching a little history for those who might not have known that world. Ligon's account in the same conversation of going for eight or nine years without selling a work of art is an object lesson in cultivating curiosity toward oneself, and a belief in the importance of interiority against the lure of celebrity.

Through the careful attention to others that animates his writing, Ligon pays respect not only to his peers but also to the para-institutions that held—and hold—them. "Every artist needs someplace that loves him or her," he says of the Studio Museum in Harlem in his discussion with Thelma Golden, repeating that word—"love"—and naming the people he associates with that institution: Golden and Kellie Jones. Throughout, Ligon offers us an account of finding a way through an inhospitable art world. "Dealers are not your friends," he counsels in "Advice for Young Artists." "Your friends don't take 50 percent of your money." In so doing, he bears witness to and then enacts the terms of another, simultaneous value system.

Orange Feelings

Writing is a way of bearing witness as much by putting things into words as by bracketing what remains unsaid. Failure also has effects.

In his conversation with Davis, Ligon describes the moment when, before he'd ever encountered Warhol or Hammons, he told his mother that he wanted to be an artist. She responded by asking, "Why do you always have to follow what white people do?" (He adds a note about her own dreams, saying that "she had aspirations to be a singer—I don't know if she would've made it professionally, but she loved it.") His accomplishments are filtered through disappointment and disenchantment. For example, when Ligon's mother came to his first exhibition at the Whitney Independent Study Program, a blackout occurred in the middle of the opening. "She must have thought, 'What the hell are you entering this world for? They can't even keep the lights on.'" Before Hammons and before Warhol, there was Mother.

It was Ligon's mother who encouraged him to follow his curiosity past the point of failure, spurring his identification as an artist. In the same interview, Ligon tells Davis the following story:

> I think I must have been eight or nine years old. My mom got a set of dishes by Corelle, and they were advertised as unbreakable. The curious child that I was, I asked, "Why is this unbreakable?" And my mom—you know, single parent, fighting for that child support from my dad, living in the projects—was like, "I don't know. Let's see."

So she took a plate out and gave it to me, and I dropped it. I dropped it on the floor, and it shattered into a million jagged, dagger-like pieces. We were finding pieces of that plate for weeks afterward. But thinking about that, it's clear that my mom was open enough to my curiosity to do crazy things like let me smash a plate she had just bought. Just because that was the kind of child I was. So that encouragement of "you can try things, you can make your own way, you can figure stuff out"—I think that started with her.

In retelling this story, I risk rehearsing a framing device Ligon describes in "My Felix," when he cites curator Gerardo Mosquera's description of Felix Gonzalez-Torres: "He also set aside a good deal of time for his family and friends. . . . 'There are times,' he would tell me, 'when you need your grandma's black beans.'" Ligon responds by writing "TMI" in the margin of the book he's read this in, but immediately follows up by saying he appreciates Mosquera's insistence on the "Latinoness" of Gonzalez-Torres's project. Sometimes, I hear him saying in his note in the margin, the only way to get out of a stereotype is to speak directly into it, to say too much.

In other words, there are some matters of style that one must just try on, even if it doesn't work out. That's also the lesson I gleaned from the story Ligon tells in "Remember the Revolution?" about his mother's youngest brother, Uncle Donald, and his pair of white vinyl boots. Ligon was thirteen, it was 1974, and, in addition to marking Nixon's resignation and the end of the Vietnam War, it was the year when "I realized that I was not going to be quite like other boys and that I needed a new paradigm for how to be this person I was becoming." He continues: "White vinyl was the frontier of masculinity. It signaled that the wearer was unconcerned with trivialities such as gender and sexuality, that he had reached higher ground. In my adolescent mind those were the boots we would wear when we, as a people, marched into the Promised Land, and I had to have a pair."

Despite his mother's concern about his "Proustian tendencies," Ligon convinces her to buy him a pair. Once he gets them, he tries them on at home: he looks as if he "were wearing galoshes bought in some shrimp fisherman's supply store." He wears them out three times before being convinced by "double takes from adults on the street and ridicule from [his] classmates . . . to retire them to the back of [his] closet." Ligon has given me the gift of trying on white vinyl boots: a representation of both the future and the past. When I write a one-word sentence—"Piercings"!—or talk about a trick and my mother in the same essay, I realize that it was by imitating Ligon that I first found a voice. Even if I too had to retire things that didn't quite work or look as good on me as they did on him, this kind of intergenerational influence makes for queer forms of reproduction, copies and imitations I can't help but want to put on my wall.

Notes

The author would like to thank Shiv Kotecha and Cameron Rowland for reading earlier versions of this essay. All quotations from Ligon are taken from *Distinguishing Piss from Rain: Writings and Interviews by Glenn Ligon*, ed. James Hoff (New York: Hauser & Wirth Publishers, 2024), to which the present essay served as introduction.

1. Ligon's phrasing borrows from Ralph Ellison's essay "The Shadow and the Act." In Ellison's discussion of anti-Black racism in film, he notes the precursors of such racism outside of it: "In the beginning was not the shadow, but the act, and the province of Hollywood is not action, but illusion." Ellison, "The Shadow and the Act," in *Shadow and Act* (New York: Vintage, 1972), 276.

2. Andy Warhol, *The Andy Warhol Diaries*, ed. Pat Hackett (New York: Warner Books, 1989), 70.

3. Andy Warhol, "Painter Hangs Own Paintings," *New York*, February 5, 1979, 9, as quoted in *Andy Warhol: Shadows*, exhibition brochure (New York: Dia, 2018), n.p.

4. Ligon's reference points for this kind of revolutionary love include Jean Genet's *Prisoner of Love*; Malcolm X, or at least Marc Andre Robinson's version of him; Audre Lorde; Adrienne Rich; June Jordan; John Rechy; and Toni Morrison, among others.

5. See Saidiya Hartman, *Lose Your Mother: A Journey along the Atlantic Slave Route* (New York: Farrar, Straus and Giroux, 2008).

6. Joe Brainard, *I Remember* (1970/1975; repr., New York: Granary Books, 2001).

7. In her conversation with Ligon, curator Thelma Golden uses the phrase "quasi-collaborative manner" to describe her solicitation of his opinion in her process of making exhibitions.

Index of Names

Page numbers in italics indicate illustrations.